Marketing and Sales Strategy

Pippa Riley

Viva Books

New Delhi | Mumbai | Chennai | Kolkata | Bengaluru | Hyderabad | Kochi | Guwahati

First Indian Edition 2011

VIVA BOOKS PRIVATE LIMITED

- 4737/23 Ansari Road, Daryaganj, New Delhi 110 002
  E-mail: vivadelhi@vivagroupindia.net, Tel. 42242200
- 76, Service Industries, Shirvane, Sector 1, Nerul, Navi Mumbai 400 706
  E-mail: vivamumbai@vivagroupindia.net, Tel. 27721273, 27721274
- Jamals Fazal Chambers, 26 Greams Road, Chennai 600 006
  E-mail: vivachennai@vivagroupindia.net, Tel. 28290304, 28294241
- B-103, Jindal Towers, 21/1A/3 Darga Road, Kolkata 700 017
  E-mail: vivakolkata@vivagroupindia.net, Tel. 22836381, 22816713
- 7, Sovereign Park Apartments, 56-58, K. R. Road, Basavanagudi, Bengaluru 560 004
  E-mail: vivabangalore@vivagroupindia.net, Tel. 26607409, 26607410
- 101-102 Mughal Marc Aptt., 3-4-637 to 641, Narayanguda, Hyderabad 500 029
  E-mail: vivahyderabad@vivagroupindia.net, Tel. 27564481, 27564482
- First Floor, Beevi Towers, SRM Road, Kaloor, Kochi 682 018, Kerala
  E-mail: vivakochi@vivagroupindia.net, Tel: 0484-2403055, 2403056
- 232, GNB Road, Beside UCO Bank, Silpukhuri, Guwahati 781 003
  E-mail: vivaguwahati@vivagroupindia.net, Tel: 0361-2666386

Published by arrangement with

BPP Learning Media Ltd.
BPP House, Aldine Place
London W12 8AA

ISBN : 978-81-309-1765-8

Published by Vinod Vasishtha for Viva Books Private Limited, 4737/23, Ansari Road, Daryaganj, New Delhi - 110 002.

Printed and bound by Raj Press, R-3, Inderpuri, New Delhi - 110 012.

Contents

Introduction

Viva-BPP Learning Media's Business Essentials range is the ideal learning solution for students studying for business-related qualifications and degrees. The range provides concise and comprehensive coverage of the key areas that are essential to the business student.

Qualifications in business are traditionally very demanding. Students therefore need learning resources which go straight to the core of the topics involved, and which build upon students' pre-existing knowledge and experience. The BPP Learning Media Business Essentials range has been designed to meet exactly that need.

Features include:

- In-depth coverage of essential topics within business-related subjects
- Plenty of activities, quizzes and topics for discussion to help retain the interest of students and ensure progress
- Up-to-date practical illustrations and case studies that really bring the material to life
- A full index, with key terms highlighted in bold

Each chapter contains:

- An introduction and a list of specific study objectives
- Summary diagrams and signposts to guide you through the chapter
- A chapter roundup, quick quiz with answers and answers to activities

Titles in the Series

- Accounts
- Business Decision Making
- Business Environment
- Business Maths
- Business Strategy
- Economics
- Finance: Management Accounting and Financial Reporting
- Human Resource Development and Employee Relations
- Human Resource Management
- Management: Communications and Achieving Results
- Management: Leading People and Professional Development
- Managing Finance
- Marketing and Promotion
- Marketing and Sales Strategy
- Marketing Principles
- Organisations and Behaviour
- Research Project

Study Guide

This Course Book includes features designed specifically to make learning effective and efficient.

- Each chapter begins with a summary diagram which maps out the areas covered by the chapter. There are detailed summary diagrams at the start of each main section of the chapter. You can use the diagrams during revision as a basis for your notes.
- After the main summary diagram there is an introduction, which sets the chapter in context. This is followed by learning objectives, which show you what you will learn as you work through the chapter.
- Throughout the Course Book, there are special aids to learning. These are indicated by symbols in the margin:

Signposts guide you through the book, showing how each section connects with the next.

Definitions give the meanings of key terms. The *glossary* at the end of the book summarises these.

Activities help you to test how much you have learned. An indication of the time you should take on each is given. Answers are given at the end of each chapter.

Topics for discussion are for use in seminars. They give you a chance to share your views with your fellow students. They allow you to highlight holes in your knowledge and to see how others understand concepts. If you have time, try 'teaching' someone the concepts you have learned in a session. This helps you to remember key points and answering their questions will consolidate your knowledge.

Examples relate what you have learned to the outside world. Try to think up your own examples as you work through the Course Book.

Chapter roundups present the key information from the chapter in a concise format. Useful for revision.

- At the end of each chapter, there is a **chapter roundup** and a **quick quiz** with answers. Use these to revise and consolidate your knowledge. The chapter roundup summarises the chapter. The quick quiz tests what you have learned (the answers often refer you back to the chapter so you can look over subjects again).
- At the end of the book, there is an index.

Part A

Advertising and Promotion

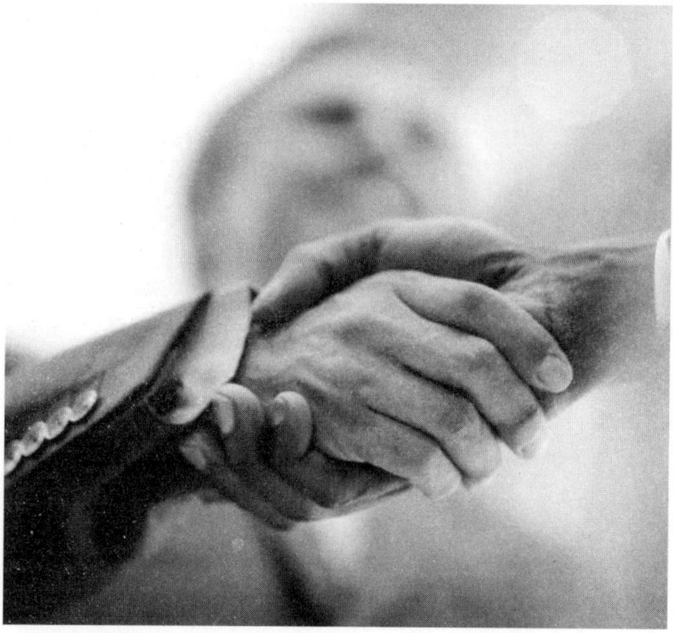

Chapter 1 :
MARKETING COMMUNICATIONS

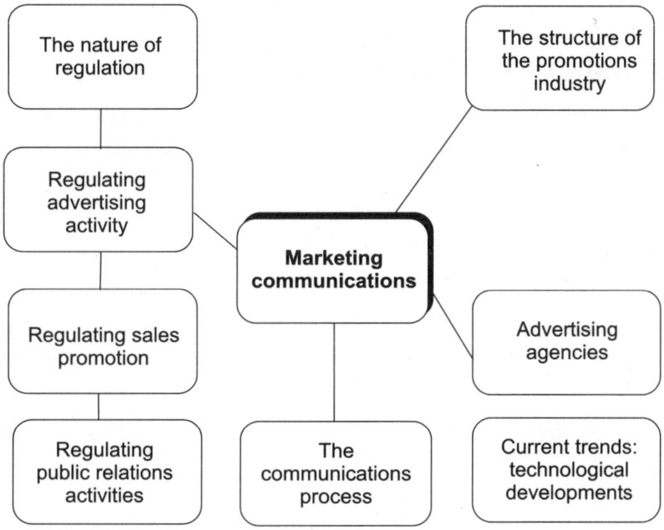

Introduction

This chapter begins our analysis of advertising and promotion. It starts by discussing the basic process of communication, as this is fundamental to an appreciation of how marketing communications function. Communications will be considered from the consumer's perspective and various models will be evaluated.

The structure of the promotions industry is as varied as the range of skills and services which those within the industry can offer. Recent years have seen an increasing degree of specialisation within the field of advertising, although there will inevitably continue to be some degree of overlap between the different agency providers.

The laws and codes of practice regulating the marketing communications industry are constantly being reviewed. The amount of legal control (as opposed to self regulation) varies from country to country, and with the growth of the powers of the European Community, there is concern over the standardisation of these controls. Regulation will be discussed with reference to three key aspects of marketing communications – advertising, sales promotion and public relations.

Finally, contemporary marketing communications issues are considered. These include media developments such as media fragmentation, and the importance of the Internet.

Your objectives

In this chapter you will learn about the following.

(a) The structure of the promotions industry

(b) How advertising agencies operate

(c) The difference between legislation and regulation

(d) What the current developments are in the communications environment

1 THE COMMUNICATIONS PROCESS

The prime aim of marketing communications is to influence consumers' buying behaviour. A framework needs to be established for considering the **communications** process. Models can be used to develop frameworks for the understanding of communication activity.

1.1 Kotler's model

Kotler (2008) has put forward a sender-receiver model of the communication process to provide a framework for answering these questions. This is shown in the diagram below.

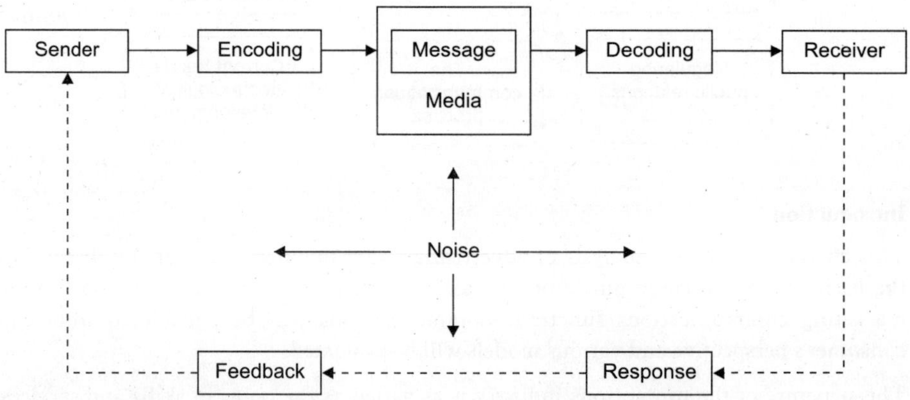

Figure 13.1: The communication process

The elements of the model can be classified in the following way.

(a) **Parties**

(i) Sender
(ii) Receiver

(b) **Communication tools**

(i) Message
(ii) Media

(c) **Communication functions**

(i) Encoding
(ii) Decoding
(iii) Response
(iv) Feedback

1.2 How the model works

- The **sender** is the party sending the message to the other party, and may also be referred to as the communicator or the source. The **receiver** is the party who receives the message, and who may also be known as the audience or the destination.
- The **encoding** process encompasses the means by which a meaning is placed into symbolic form (words, signs, sounds and so on).
- The **media** is the communication channel or channels through which the message moves from sender to receiver.
- The **decoding** process is carried out by the receiver who converts the symbolic forms transmitted by the sender into a form that makes sense to him. In other words, it is how the receiver interprets the message sent.
- When the message has been decoded the receiver will react to it – this is the **response**.
- **Feedback** is the part of the receiver's response that the receiver communicates back to the sender.

As Kotler states, this model underscores many of the factors in effective communication. Senders need to understand the motivation of their audiences in order to structure messages that the audience will interpret correctly through the decoding process. The sender also has to ascertain the most effective communication media through which to reach the audience and also establish effective feedback channels in order to find out the receiver's response to the message.

Activity 1 **(45 minutes)**

Find some adverts – watch TV for half-an-hour or flick through a newspaper or a magazine and analyse each ad in the above terms. Consider who are the parties involved (*you* may not be the intended receiver), what communication tools are used, what sort of codes are used and how they will be decoded (for example by people in different income brackets or with different tastes), what form feedback will take, and so on.

FOR DISCUSSION

The challenge of marketing communications is to communicate the right message, in the right way, to the right people, in the right place, at the right time!

Definition

Noise. Distortions created in the encoding or decoding process that can result in inaccurate interpretation of meaning.

1.3 Noise and selectivity

This communication process is not carried out in isolation. There are many senders competing with their messages for the attention of the receiver. As a result there is considerable noise in the environment and an individual may be bombarded by around 3,500 commercial messages each day, from all kinds of media. In one 45-minute journey, the average London commuter is exposed to more than 130 adverts. The task of the sender is to get his message to the receiver but, as Kotler states, there are a number of reasons why the target audience may not receive the message.

FOR DISCUSSION

What noise factors might prevent a consumer receiving the intended message sent by an orgnisation via a TV adevert shown at 9 pm before a major film?

1.4 Selective attention

A receiver will not notice all the commercial messages that he comes into contact with, so the sender must design the message in such a way so as to win attention in spite of the surrounding noise.

1.5 Selective distortion

In many cases receivers may distort or change the information received if that information does not fit in with their existing attitudes, beliefs and opinions. In other words, people hear what they want to hear. Selective distortion may take a variety of forms:

(a) Amplification (where receivers may add things to the message that are not there); or

(b) Levelling (where receivers do not notice other things that *are* there).

The task of the sender is to produce a message that is clear, simple and interesting.

1.6 Selective recall and message rehearsal

A receiver will retain in his permanent memory only a small fraction of the messages that reach him. The sender's aim, therefore is to get the message into the receiver's long-term memory, because once in the long-term memory the message can modify the receiver's beliefs and attitudes. However, to reach the long-term memory the message has to enter the short-term memory, which has only a limited capacity to process information. Kotler *et al* (2008), state that the factor influencing the passage of the message from the short- or the long-term memory is the amount and type of **message rehearsal** by the receiver.

In message rehearsal the receiver elaborates on the meaning of the message in a way that brings related thoughts from the long-term memory into his short-term memory.

(a) If the receiver's initial attitude to the object of the message is positive and he rehearses support arguments then the message is likely to be accepted and have high recall.

(b) If the receiver's initial attitude is negative and the person rehearses counter arguments against the object of the message then the message is likely to be rejected, but it will remain in the long-term memory.

1.7 The promotion mix

Kotler *et al.* (2008) identify four **categories of promotional activity.**

Promotional	Comment
Advertising	Any **paid** form of non-personal presentation and promotion of ideas, goods or services by an identified sponsor.
Sales promotion	Encourage through incentives, over a short-term period, the purchase of the good or service.
Personal selling	The oral presentation of the goods or services, either to make a sale, or to create goodwill to improve the prospects of sales in the future.
Public relations	Unlike advertising, publicity cannot be bought and it might be thought of as unpaid advertising. Although organisations will spend large sums of money on publicity, they do not formally buy space in a newspaper or time on television or radio. Nor do they usually control the content of the publicity message, and so some publicity can be bad rather than good. However, they often try to manage publicity through the use of public relations.

Marketing communications convey information about the product and the company. Recently, the trend is towards **integrated marketing communications**. In other words, the marketing communications should be integrated with the business strategy, the other elements of the marketing mix, and with each other. Few organisations practise an integrated communications approach in any systematic way. The various tools of marketing communications have traditionally been the exclusive preserve of different groups within the organisation.

Promotion is the element of the mix most under control of the marketing department. Piercy (1987) suggests that, as far as managers are concerned, there are a number of issues which must be considered strategically for each form of communication.

Issue	Comment
Role	**Each form of communication has a different target**. Media advertising is direct to the end user, whereas personal selling may be preferred for distributors.
Objectives	Each form of communication needs specific objectives: • Advertising: raising awareness, repositioning • Public relations: favourable press exposure • Personal selling: sales targets, client relationships • Sales promotion: sample rates
Process management	This covers relationships with external suppliers, budgeting, recruiting and personnel

Integration	**The elements of the mix should be integrated so that all customers get the appropriate message, and the different elements of the mix do not conflict with each other.**

Key strategic developments in promotion

Development	Consequence
Database marketing and data mining	This enables targeting of promotional messages.
Digital TV, many channels	It will be harder to reach a single audience: rather like the trade magazine sector, fragmentation may cut advertising rates.
Internet	Internet advertisements are generally **sought** out by 'surfers', possibility of interactive marketing, concerns about junk e-mail, concerns about low profitability of Internet firms.
Call centres	Telephone call centres are mushrooming over the country and increasingly are located overseas. They provide sales and customer support activity. They tend to be rigid and bureaucratic in style.
Sponsorship	Sports and cultural organisations are seeking sponsors. Like all forms of activity, the sponsor has objectives to fulfil. This can be a difficult relationship. Sponsorship is not intrusive.
Personal advice and loyalty	As service industries develop, there will be greater scope for personal service such as financial services.
Lobbying	Some decisions regarding product standardisation and safety will be taken at EU level. Expertise in this area is necessary.

2 THE STRUCTURE OF THE PROMOTIONS INDUSTRY

2.1 Industry structure

The structure of the promotions industry is a relatively complex one, with many thousands of companies supplying specialist services.

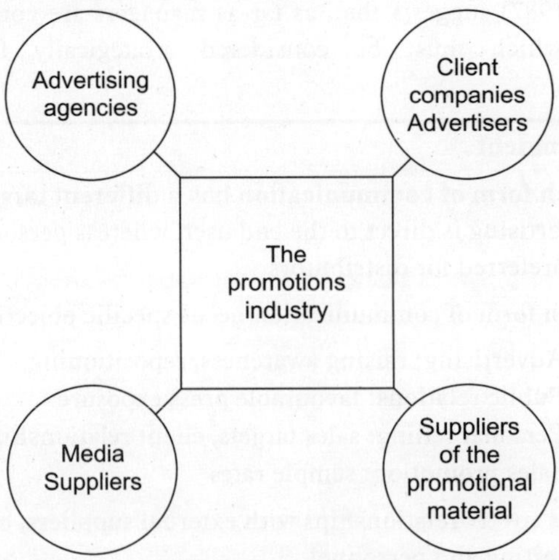

Figure 1.2: Simplified structure of the promotions industry

(a) **Agencies**. Although these still tend to be called advertising agencies they do in fact provide a wide range of promotional and marketing services. The activities of agencies are described in more detail later in this Course Book. The main ones include:

- (i) The planning of campaigns
- (ii) The design of creative components
- (iii) The scheduling and buying of media
- (iv) The buying and integration of other promotional materials
- (v) The administration and accountancy for the process
- (vi) The implementation of campaigns
- (vii) The monitoring and evaluation of the results

In effect an agency acts as an additional resource to the client company's own marketing resources.

(b) **Clients**. These are properly known as the 'advertiser' and are really the lynchpin in the whole structure. Their role is a very obvious one which can be summarised as:

- (i) Providing the original need for the campaign
- (ii) Selecting and briefing the agency
- (iii) Discussing and agreeing campaign plans
- (iv) Integrating the promotional planning into marketing planning
- (v) Evaluating and controlling the campaign
- (vi) Financing the whole process

(c) **Media suppliers**. The media suppliers consist of the commercial television companies, commercial radio companies, newspapers and magazine owners, poster companies and a whole variety of new media owners. For example, a football club which features the branding of a sponsor on its strip can be regarded as a media supplier.

(d) **Suppliers of the other promotional materials**. A vast range of other specialist suppliers exists, from printers to producers of promotional gifts, from exhibition organisers to co-ordinators of corporate hospitality. These specialist services are provided cost effectively and are bought directly by client companies or managed through advertising agencies.

EXAMPLE

The UK will become the first major economy to see advertisers spend more on the internet than on TV ads, according to the latest forecast from a leading media buying agency. Group M predicts that UK internet ad spend will overtake TV, which has been the leading advertising medium for half a century, in 2009.

Group M predicts that UK internet revenue is likely to climb by 30.8% this year, to £3.4bn, compared with just 1% year-on-year growth in TV ad spend to around £3.56bn.

It is said that the UK is a "special case" when it comes to TV and internet advertising. Its TV share [of all media spend] is depressed by the presence of the BBC, there is still a large and healthy print sector, and Britons are among the world's heaviest internet users.

This does not necessarily mean the demise of TV as a major advertising medium, because the internet is not one medium - its growth rate is a blend of three distinct businesses growing at different speeds: search, display and classified. Most of the growth is coming from search advertising, and that is being fuelled either by new budgets or from the direct marketing sector, not so much from TV ad budgets.

http://www.guardian.co.uk

---

3 ADVERTISING AGENCIES

3.1 Types of agency

In-house

The advertising function can be handled in a variety of ways. First, if a potential advertiser has sufficient expertise, they may decide to handle advertising in-house.

Full service agency (or one-stop shop)

Alternatively, an advertiser may decide to use a full service agency. This is an agency which provides a complete advertising service encompassing creative work, production, media planning and buying. The full service agency may also provide or sub-contract research services for a client. Some large advertising agencies will provide other communications services, for example direct marketing, public relations or sales promotion. Doubts are frequently raised within the industry about the wisdom and economy of using these. Often their services do not strictly encompass the full range of activities as typically they are part of a larger group of agencies.

Creative hot shops

The 1980s saw some agency personnel breaking away from their full service employers in order to provide specialist creative services to clients. These smaller operators became known as creative shops or sometimes 'hotshops' or 'boutiques'. These agencies specialise in creative ideas and solutions.

Media independents

Clients may choose to combine the services of a creative hot shop alongside **media planning and buying** services from a media specialist. These media independents specialise in planning and buying media. They buy space and time (eg TV) from media owners, and sell to agencies and advertisers.

À la carte

A client may decide to share out their communication tasks, choosing to cherry pick services *à la carte* from the different providers available. For example, they may decide to use only the creative and account planning services of a full service agency but, although a media department is also available to them from the full service agency, they may choose to use media planning and buying services from a media independent. Likewise, sales promotion, public relations, direct marketing and research services may be commissioned and used on an *ad hoc* basis as required. Responsibility for controlling and co-ordinating the activities of these service providers rests with the client, usually in the form of the Brand or Marketing Manager.

There is also a growth in freelance 'creatives' and designers within the UK who work with a small number of specific clients.

Marketing agencies

Many providers now call themselves **marketing agencies**. An internet search using this term will reveal that such agencies provide a range of services but are principally concerned with sophisticated research and communication techniques relating to Internet-based interactions with the market. Website design is a major activity.

Definition

> **Virtual agencies:** Term used to describe the selection of specialist individuals from different agencies or from within an agency group to work together as though they were members of the same agency.

3.2 Selecting an agency

The pages of the trade magazine *Campaign and Marketing* regularly carry news of client accounts on the move from their incumbent agencies. There are a number of reasons why clients may change agencies. As mentioned above, the client may feel the agency is lacking in new ideas, or that it is overcharging them for services. Alternatively, a new client won by the agency may result in a conflict of interests between new and old clients. Often, a change in personnel on either the client or the agency side can result in an account moving on.

3.3 Search

The process of selecting a new agency is likely to follow a series of fairly well defined stages, the first of which is an initial search for suitable agency candidates. New clients can find out about agencies from a number of sources, such as *Campaign Portfolio* or the Advertising Agency Register (AAR).

When considering agency options it is important to be realistic. A budget of, say, £5 million, will not be of paramount interest to the larger full service agencies who are used to dealing with budgets several times that amount. However a medium-sized full service agency would certainly be interested in doing business with a client with this amount to spend.

When choosing any agency the task is further complicated by the number of variables which need to be considered in the decision-making process.

3.4 Agency selection criteria

(a) **Services offered** – Planning, creative, research, integrated, international?

(b) **Agency size** – How many clients, is it part of a group?

(c) **Quality of work** – Past and present, any creativity or effectiveness awards?

(d) **Relevant experience** – In market sector and promotional discipline?

(e) **Competing accounts** – Are there any current or potential clashes or conflicts of interest?

(f) **Cost** – What is the likely cost and method of remuneration?

(g) **Location** – Is the agency conveniently located for meetings?

(h) **Reputation** – Track record, working relationships and success.

3.5 Credentials short-list and brief

Definition

> **Credentials presentation**: An opportunity for agencies to present their organisational details in order to persuade a potential client to short-list them.

The agencies selected are usually invited to a credentials presentation and then a short-list of three or four agencies is determined. Those agencies will then attend a briefing meeting. The brief will usually include company history, marketing communications objectives, target markets, marketing mix strategies, budget and time considerations.

Definition

> **Client brief**: A presentation, usually accompanied by a brief report, outlining relevant background information and the marketing communications task to be undertaken.

3.6 Pitch

The time allowed between the delivery of the brief and the pitch is usually between four and six weeks and the cost can vary significantly depending on the nature of the brief.

Definition

> **Pitch**: Abbreviated from agency sales pitch, the pitch is an opportunity for the agency to sell itself, its creative ideas and its response to a client's brief. This is usually a competitive process.

3.7 Final selection

The **final selection** will involve a judgement about how well the client believes the agency has responded to the brief in terms of the strategic thinking involved the creative work (if presented) and the agency's all round understanding of the client's industry. Courtesy dictates that the client should inform both the successful agency and the unsuccessful ones in a prompt manner.

Activity 2 **(10 minutes)**

What factors are most likely to cause a breakdown in relationships between an agency and a client?

3.8 Agency remuneration

Historically, agencies have earned their money through commission on media space purchased for their clients. The practice arises from the time when the advertising agent was a media broker who also provided other services. This method of payment also highlights the agency's legal standing. The agency is liable for bills to the media if the client defaults on payment.

Agency commission

The advertising agency earns money from the commission given by the media. This allows the agency to pay media invoices to TV stations, newspapers, magazines and so on, net of commission, but to charge the client the gross cost. Creative and other services are charged to the client at cost plus an equivalent mark up.

15% used to be the standard rate of agency commission. This is now no longer the case. Some large clients, who spend highly on media have argued that they should pay the agency a discounted rate of commission, because of the volume of media throughput that the agency handles. Other clients, themselves under pressure to make advertising money work harder, have argued that 15% is too high, and that the agency should charge a lower rate. Commission rates of 10% or 13% are now not uncommon.

(a) **Agency perspective**

Advantages	Traditional and therefore comfortable
	It encourages media buyers to get good discounts by taking advantage of bulk buying
	Can result in good profits when the media spend is high
	The agency is paid irrespective of performance
Disadvantages	There is no financial recognition for a successful campaign
	May be difficult to calculate if all costs have been covered

(b) **Client perspective**

Advantages	They are used to it and it is simple
	They know that it can encourage the agency to get good deals
Disadvantages	Fees are not known in advance and thus budgeting is made problematic
	Additional fees may have to be paid to cover production costs
	There is no agency accountability built into the pricing structure
	There is concern that agencies may recommend high cost media for maximum commission

Mark-ups

Agencies will contract work out to third parties, eg print, radio and video production and creative artwork. Agencies will then receive part of their remuneration from an agreed mark-up charged on the cost of purchases from third parties. Mark-up between 10% and 15% would not be unusual but can vary significantly depending on the nature of the work undertaken and the degree of agency involvement.

Fee payment

Some advertisers and their agencies prefer to work on a project-by-project fee system. This ensures the agency earns money, whether or not the work is media based. It is usual for agencies to work on an agreed monthly or quarterly fee, known as a retainer.

Performance-related

Performance-related schemes are being used increasingly. The agency is judged on the effect its advertising has on client company sales. Different rates of commission then come into force, depending on performance to target, over-achievement or under-achievement. The major drawback to this method of remuneration is that it pre-supposes a direct correlation between advertising effort and sales.

Performance related can be evaluated in a number of different ways. Criteria include increased sales, consumer measures (such as increased awareness or spontaneous recall) and other qualitative measures such as brand elevation.

(a) **Agency perspective**

Advantages
- Can compete better on price and can breakdown costs accurately
- Allows for individual performance evaluation
- A successful campaign would generate higher returns
- Might motivate the agency and so improve the client relationship

Disadvantages
- External factors may influence results
- It is more difficult to budget income and there is no guarantee that costs will be covered
- The timings of the evaluation and payments are critical, especially to a small agency
- There is the potential to encourage an atmosphere of distrust
- Creativity may be sacrificed for quick results

(b) **Client perspective**

Advantages
- Could reduce bias in media spending
- Will favour smaller clients, who may be cost conscious, and so reduces their risks
- Will encourage the agency to be more accountable and so develop a closer relationship
- Poor performance could be rectified

Disadvantages	Potentially confusing and complicated to administer
	Measurement means additional costings
	Concentrates on the short-term
	Could result in lots of similar campaigns, as agencies discover what gives fast results
	Uncontrollable elements (eg a poor product) are not taken into account
	Could undermine the relationship between the agency and the media sellers

Performance-related effectively isolates advertising from the other marketing activities of the organisation and as such relies on a false divide. The major difficulty for the industry is to come up with a formula that can assess effectiveness of a particular campaign without penalising the agency for factors beyond its control.

FOR DISCUSSION

From a client's perspective, there is a lot to commend performance-related payment by results remuneration.

3.9 Account management

Within the agency, a **variety of personnel** will be involved in handling the client's business. The account executive or account manager is the lynchpin between the numerous agency personnel and their client. Their role is to liaise with client staff and to brief, supervise and co-ordinate the appropriate agency staff at appropriate times.

The account executive and, through him, the agency should be seen as a natural extension of the client's own marketing resources.

Definition

> **Account planners**: Agency people responsible for developing a clear understanding of the market situation in which marketing communications will take place. Involves research and knowledge of the market, relevant buying processes and the client's position.

The internal structure of an agency can best be explained by considering how the agency handles a piece of client work.

Step 1	**The client problem**
	A client and agency who have been together for some time will have built up a good working relationship. The agency will understand the client's business and will have a good knowledge of the dynamics of the market in which the client operates. Equally, the agency will be aware of the motivations and decision-making processes of end consumers. A new product or service, new situation or changing market conditions may provide the starting point for a new role to be performed by advertising. The client needs to brief the account executive on the task in hand.

Step 2 **The internal briefing**

The account executive will brief the members of the account team who work on the client's business. The account group will usually compromise:

(i) An account planner, responsible for using market research to develop advertising strategy for the client

(ii) A creative team duo of art director and copywriter, responsible for conceiving a creative idea which meets the advertising brief and working that idea up into visual form and written copy

(iii) A media planner/buyer, responsible for recommending an appropriate media strategy and ensuring media is bought cost effectively

Step 3 **The client presentation**

Once the account team have worked on the client brief and are happy with their response to it, the account executive will present back to the client. He will show examples of how the finai advertising execution will look, using rough visuals or storyboards and will explain the rationale for the ideas presented. Depending on the client's reaction to the team's interpretation of the brief, the team will either be asked to go ahead in developing the work, or will be asked to rework their ideas.

The go-ahead stage may include a decision to test the advertising in research prior to full production of the advert.

Step 4 **Production of advert(s)**

Some simple advertising executions will be carried out almost entirely in-house by the advertising agency. For more complex executions, the agency will buy in specialist functions on behalf of the client. For instance, a production company would work alongside the agency in the filming of a TV commercial.

Whilst production is ongoing, the media department will be involved in the actual commitment of the media budget. Dates, times and positions will be agreed with media owners.

During this stage, there will be continuous liaison between the account executive and the client. The client is likely to attend some of the key production stages such as filming or photography of the commercial.

If time allows, further research may take place to identify the need for any additional changes.

Step 5 **The campaign appears**

The time span between the briefing of the account executive by the client and the campaign appearing can be as little as six or eight weeks for a simple photographic newspaper execution, to twenty weeks plus for an animated TV commercial. Once the campaign has appeared, it is important that it is properly evaluated against the objectives initially set.

The staff comprising the account team who work directly on the client's business in creating a campaign are those the client is most likely to come into contact with, although the main point of contact will of course be the account executive. There are other behind-the-scenes staff with whom the account executive must liaise but who will not have direct client contact.

Activity 3 **(45 minutes)**

Look through the previous three issues of marketing industry magazines such as *Admap*, *Campaign*, *Marketing Week*, *Revolution* etc and identify agency operations, remuneration, pitches and new accounts. Write a short report on some of the more significant changes taking place and opinions expressed by industry commentators.

4 THE NATURE OF REGULATION

4.1 Overview

All organisations have to engage in promotional activity, utilising the various elements of the marketing communications mix – advertising, sales promotion, public relations and personal selling. As with other areas of business activity the organisation's freedom of action is constrained by the legal and regulatory process. In contrast to other areas of operations, the regulation of promotional activity is far more dependent on self regulatory codes of practice, particularly with regard to advertising and sales promotion, because of the piecemeal nature of the statutory provision in these areas.

In the UK no one Act of Parliament provides a comprehensive framework for the regulation of promotional activity. Over 150 Acts of Parliament and Statutory Instruments (quite apart from case law) form the legal framework within which advertising and sales promotion operate. New rules are likely as the use of technology such as the Internet becomes widespread.

Despite the impression that all these statutes might create, the UK tends to favour a broadly voluntary code of practice because of the advantages this has over legal controls. Many of the Acts affect very specific areas of business and are not necessarily applicable to all.

The rules governing the acceptability of communication can be summed up in a phrase that is widely recognised by advertising practitioners and the general public alike: communication must be 'legal, decent, honest and truthful.' We will look at each aspect in turn.

4.2 Decency

The **Obscene Publications Acts 1959 and 1964** state that it is an offence to publish an obscene article, 'whether to gain or not.' An article is defined as obscene if 'the effect is likely to deprave or corrupt persons who are likely to see, read or hear the matter embodied in it.' Basically promotions should not contain anything likely to cause widespread offence, fear or distress.

4.3 Honesty and truthful presentation

These last two elements can be combined as the legal provision in this area does not make a clear distinction between the two for practical purposes. The main statute covering this area is the **Trade Descriptions Act 1968**, which prohibits any person, in the course of a trade or business, from applying a false description to goods, or from supplying or offering to supply any goods with a false trade description.

Definition

The Act defines a **trade description** as an indication, either direct or indirect, regarding such issues as quantity, size, composition, method of manufacture, fitness for purpose, approval or endorsement by any individual or organisation and the past history of the product. The scope of this legislation applies to all areas of promotion, including packaging, illustrations, advertisements, demonstrations and oral statements.

Local government **trading standards offices** help businesses operating in the UK to comply with legislation by providing advice, guidance and information. They deal with such matters as animal health and welfare; consumers' rights; food hygiene and labelling; product safety; and weights and measures.

4.4 Legality – other legislation

Advertisements should not contain anything which is in breach of the law or omit anything required by law. A range of further legislation and statutory regulation applies here.

(a) **Discrimination.** Advertising should not show discrimination on the grounds of colour, race or ethnic origin (Race Relations Act 1976) or on the grounds of sex and marital status (Sex Discrimination Act 1975), or on the grounds of disability (Disability Discrimination Act 1995).

(b) **Sale of Goods Act 1979.** Anyone supplying goods must ensure that they conform with their description, are fit for their purpose and are of satisfactory quality. These rights cannot be excluded from the contract of sale.

(c) **Supply of Goods and Services Act 1982.** The aim of this act is to protect consumers against bad workmanship and poor provision of services. It covers both work and materials and provides further statutory rights that cannot be excluded from a contract. These are that work will be carried out with reasonable care and skill and, in the absence of specific agreements, in reasonable time and at reasonable cost.

(d) **Consumer Credit Acts 1974 and 2006.** This act makes it a criminal offence to supply goods to consumers on credit or to lend consumers money unless registered with the Office of Fair Trading (OFT). The rights provided by the act include a cooling-off period; shared liability by credit card companies; and access to credit agency records if turned down for credit. The OFT website says 'the Consumer Credit Act and regulations are changing as a result of implementation of the Consumer Credit Directive (CCD). Regulations were laid on 30 March 2010 and are due to come into force on 1 February 2011.' The Department for Business, Innovation and Skills website has this to say.

'The key new elements in the new consumer credit regime are:

- a duty on the lender to provide adequate explanations about the credit on offer to the consumer

- an obligation on the lender to check creditworthiness before offering or increasing credit
- requirements concerning credit reference databases
- a right for consumers to withdraw from a credit agreement within 14 days, without giving any reason
- requirements to inform consumers when debts are sold on
- requirements on credit intermediaries to disclose fees and links to creditors
- a right to make partial early repayments of credit'

(e) **Consumer Protection from Unfair Trading Regulations 2008**. The OFT website says these regulations 'came into force on 26 May 2008. They implement the Unfair Commercial Practices Directive (UCPD) in the UK, and replace several pieces of consumer protection legislation that were in force prior to 26 May 2008. The Regulations introduce a general duty not to trade unfairly and seek to ensure that traders act honestly and fairly towards their customers. They apply primarily to business to consumer practices (but elements of business to business practices are also covered where they affect, or are likely to affect, consumers).'

(f) **Consumer Protection (Distance Selling) Regulations 2000**. The key features of the regulations are that suppliers must give consumers clear information in writing before they buy, including details of the goods or services offered, delivery arrangements and payment, the supplier's details and the consumer's cancellation rights. The consumer has a cooling-off period of seven working days.

4.5 Data Protection Acts 1984 and 1998

The **Data Protection Act 1984** was the first piece of legislation to come into force that addressed growing popular fear that information about individuals which was stored on computer files and processed by computer could be **misused**. In particular, it was felt that an individual could easily be harmed by the existence of computerised data which was **inaccurate** or misleading.

The Act attempted to afford some measure of protection to **the individual** regarding data which is processed mechanically, that is by 'equipment operated automatically in response to the instructions given for that purpose'.

(a) **Personal data** is information about a living individual, including expressions of opinion about him or her.

(b) **Data users** are organisations or individuals who control the contents and use of files of personal data.

(c) A **data subject** is an individual who is the subject of personal data.

(d) A **computer bureau** processes personal data for data users, or allows data users to process personal data on its equipment.

The main features of the Data Protection Act were as follows.

(a) With certain exceptions, all data users and all computer must **register** under the Act with the Data Protection Registrar.

(b) Data subjects are awarded certain legal rights, such as the right of access to information held about them.

(c) Data users and computer bureaux must adhere to data protection principles.

(d) The Act establishes certain civil proceedings and a number of criminal offences.

(e) The office of Data Protection Registrar was set up to establish a register of data users and computer bureaux and to consider complaints about the contravention of the principles or the Acts' provisions.

The terms of the Data Protection Act 1984 have now been extended by the **Data Protection Act 1998**, which implements the EU Data Protection Directive in the UK. It contains familiar elements from the 1984 legislation, but there are additional requirements imposed by the EU Directive.

It is now possible for a data subject to find out not only what data is being held, but what it is being held for. In the case of inaccurate data, an individual can apply to the courts for correction, blocking, erasure or destruction. The Act specifies the following.

(i) **Express consent** is needed when processing sensitive data such as ethnic origin or criminal convictions. Data subjects will have the right not to have certain decisions made about them which are based solely on automated processing, eg psychometric tests for recruitment decisions.

(ii) The 1998 Act is extended to cover data held in any kind of 'relevant filing system' where 'specific information relating to a particular individual is readily accessible.' This may be taken to include **manual filing methods.**

(iii) The Data Protection Registrar is renamed the **Data Protection Commissioner**, whose powers will be strengthened.

(iv) The transfer of personal data **outside the EU** is restricted.

4.6 Self-regulatory codes of practice

These are the main statutory requirements as far as promotion is concerned. However there is another vehicle that regulates activity in this area which is designed to complement the statutory provision – self-regulatory codes of practice, administered by the communication industry itself. Self-regulatory codes of practice are usually issued by the bodies representing the marketing communications industry in order to establish standards for members to follow. Under the provisions of the Fair Trading Act 1973 the Director General of the Office of Fair Trading (OFT) is obliged to encourage the creation and dissemination of such OFT approved codes. Prime examples are the *British Codes of Advertising and Sales Promotion* which are administered by the Advertising Standards Authority (ASA). The current versions came into effect in February 1995 and was the ninth edition of the Advertising Code and the sixth edition of the Sales Promotion Code.

The principal advantages of self-regulation controls over legal controls are that they are significantly more flexible, easy to administer and can be changed relatively easily and quickly to take account of changing circumstances. Adoption of self-regulatory controls show the promotions industry in a favourable light and can encourage public respect.

5 REGULATING ADVERTISING ACTIVITY

Advertising is, in practice, controlled according to the media used, the nature of the product or service advertised and the nature of the business of the advertiser.

5.1 General

The media used

Because of the different characteristics of the various media from which an advertiser can choose, different levels of regulation as to what constitutes acceptable and unacceptable practice exist. Television is the most heavily regulated medium in terms of constraints being placed on advertisers' freedom of action and the products that can be advertised.

The nature of the products or service advertised

Varying levels of regulation may exist, by virtue of the nature of the product advertised. Those products that are potentially harmful, such as alcohol and cigarettes, have a great level of regulation. However, increased levels of regulation also apply where the target audiences could be more easily manipulated because of their credulity (such as children) or their strong desire for the increased social acceptance that use of the products may bring (such as slimmers).

The nature of the business of the advertiser

Some organisations that provide products and/or services of a sensitive nature may face a greater level of regulation. For example, organisations such as matrimonial and dating agencies are not allowed to advertise on television. This regulation also applies to undertakers.

However, as has been stated, there is no one comprehensive Act of Parliament covering advertising activity and this is why the Codes of Practice are so important. The Advertising Standards Authority (ASA), which administers the codes of practice relating to advertising, use the framework articulated in the statement that all advertising must be 'legal, decent, honest and truthful' as the starting point for their provisions. Prior to 1962, when the ASA began, advertisers did not need to consider the concept of 'substantiating claims' as they now do.

5.2 The Advertising Code

In its first year the ASA received 100 complaints.

EXAMPLE

The Advertising Standards Authority (ASA) received a record number of complaints over television adverts in 2008. The ASA's 2008 annual report shows the watchdog received 26,433 complaints about 15,556 adverts, with a 27 per cent increase in the number of formal upheld rulings.

The watchdog said it had placed a greater emphasis on issues that could have a serious affect on consumer's finances, in response to the economic downturn.

The ASA claims misleading comments in adverts accounted for over 45 per cent of the complaints, with issues relating to offensiveness and 'harm' also accounting for large numbers of complaints.

Of the top ten most complained about adverts none were found to have breached advertising codes. An advert by the charity Barnardo's received the most number of complaints last year - 840. The ad was designed to raise awareness of domestic child abuse but viewers complained over the repeated scenes of violence and drug-taking. The ASA admitted that distress and offence may have been caused but ruled the ads were scheduled appropriately and their aim justified the use of strong imagery.

An advert by Volkswagen involving a singing dog received the second largest amount of complaints, with 743 individual objections. Again the complaints were rejected by the watchdog.

Commenting on the report, chairman of the ASA Lord Chris Smith said: "British advertising is known for its creativity and the overwhelming majority of ads we see deliver effective messages in a responsible way.

"It is the ASA's role to respond to public concerns proportionately and with common-sense whilst robustly applying the Codes in areas where people need protecting.

"In 2008, we delivered on this central duty and made it a priority to keep an active check on sensitive sectors such as financial advertising and price comparisons."

http://www.inthenews.co.uk 29 April 2009

The regulatory provisions embodied in the Advertising Code apply to the following forms of advertising.

- Magazine and newspaper advertisements
- Radio and TV commercials (not programmes or programme sponsorship)
- Television Shopping Channels
- Posters on legitimate poster sites (not flyposters)
- Leaflets and brochures
- Cinema commercials
- Direct mail (advertising sent through the post and addressed to you personally)
- Door drops and circulars (advertising posted through the letter box without your name on)
- Advertisements on the Internet, include banner ads and pop-up ads (not claims on companies' own websites)
- Commercial e-mail and SMS text message ads
- Ads on CD ROMs, DVD and video, and faxes

The code imposes two main obligations on the advertiser. The first is that the **primary responsibility** for observance of the code falls upon him, even when delegated, for all 'practical purposes', to an advertising agency or other intermediary. The second obligation is that of **substantiation**, which means that before offering an advertisement for publication, the advertiser should have available all documentary and other evidence necessary to demonstrate the advertisement's conformity to the code. This information should be made available without delay if requested by the regulatory authorities.

There are also provisions regarding safety (adverts should not encourage unsafe practices, especially drinking and driving), violence and anti-social behaviour.

The code also provides specific rules regarding particular categories of advertisement.

- Alcoholic drinks
- Children
- Motoring
- Environmental claims
- Health and beauty products
- Slimming
- Distance selling
- List and database practice
- Employment and business opportunities
- Financial services and products

There is a special set of rules for cigarette and tobacco advertising – the Cigarette Code. In essence, no advertisement should incite people to start smoking or encourage them to increase their cigarette consumption. Various way in which this might be done (sex, cult figures, wholesome images) are discouraged.

EXAMPLE

From July 2007, foods aimed at children which were defined by the Food Standards Authority as being high in fat, sugar or salt (HFSS) were subject to a new set of advertising rules. Due to high degree of change in advertising these products, the rules are to be phased in. The rules specify that HFSS food and drink adverts should not be scheduled around programmes with an appeal to children up to the age of 16. By mid-August 2007 however, the FSA had to override its nutrient profiling system because it would mean that whole milk could not be advertised to children on TV. Asda, who were concerned that their ads would fall foul of Ofcom rules, raised the issue. It was also of interest to the Milk Development Council who were planning a campaign to promote the health benefits of drinking milk. To overcome the problem, the FSA recalculated the fat content of whole milk and used an annual average because the fat content varies throughout the year.

5.3 Implementing the Code

FOR DISCUSSION

The ASA only require one complaint to trigger an investigation. Is this a good policy?

The Advertising Code is administered by the Advertising Standards Authority (which deals with complaints from members of the public) and its sub-committee, the Committee of Advertising Practice (CAP) which deals with complaints from commercially interested parties. Both groups act in response to complaints made in writing about published advertisements.

Complaints received by the ASA are investigated free of charge but they must be in writing or be submitted via their website and be accompanied by a description or copy of the offending promotion. Complaints fall into one of five broad categories.

1 Promotions which conflict with the Code.

2 Complaints where there is a well-founded case for investigation.

3 Promotions where the promoter needs only to make minor modifications.

4 Complaints where the complainant's interpretation of either the promotion or the Codes does not correspond with the ASA's.

5 Promotions which are outside the scope of the Code.

A number of sanctions exist where an advertisement or promotion is in conflict with the Codes.

1 The media can refuse to accept the advertisement.

2 Adverse publicity may result from the ruling.

3 Trading sanctions may be imposed.

4 Financial and other incentives provided by trade, media or professional organisations may be withdrawn.

5 Legal injunction to prevent further appearance.

6 A mandatory two-year pre-vetting.

Definition

Pre-vetting: The process of checking and approving advertisements before they are released.

EXAMPLE

The main principles of the CAP code state that:

2.1 All marketing communications should be legal, decent, honest and truthful.

2.2 All marketing communications should be prepared with a sense of responsibility to consumers and to society.

2.3 All marketing communications should respect the principles of fair competition generally accepted in business.

2.4 No marketing communication should bring advertising into disrepute.

In addition general rules confirm that:

2.5 Marketing communications must conform with the Code. Primary responsibility for observing the Code falls on marketers. Others involved in preparing and publishing marketing communications such as agencies, publishers and other service suppliers also accept an obligation to abide by the Code.

2.6 Any unreasonable delay in responding to the ASA's enquiries may be considered a breach of the Code.

2.7 The ASA and CAP will on request treat in confidence any genuinely private or secret material supplied unless the Courts or officials acting within their statutory powers compel its disclosure.

2.8 The Code is applied in the spirit as well as in the letter.

"ASA's dim view of Bright-Life UK"

Mail order company Bright-Life UK has been rapped for misleading "winners" of their prize draw. The firm's mailing began: "CONGRATULATIONS! GUARANTEED LIVERPOOL BANK GIFT CHEQUE TO WINNERS".

Later, it said: "Congratulations", "GREAT NEWS!", "YOU were officially selected as the LATEST recipient of a special gift cheque award ..." and "REMEMBER, YOU ARE GUARANTEED TO RECEIVE MONEY DUE YOU WHEN YOU TAKE ACTION ...".

The Advertising Standards Authority believed that anyone who got the mailing was "likely to infer .. that they had been awarded a considerable sum".

In fact, in small print clarified that everyone who responded would share a £100,000 jackpot and could get as little as 31 pence. The ASA said: "Respondents were likely to receive a relatively low value cheque and the text .. implied they were luckier than they were likely to be."

Parent company JDM Marketing, in Liverpool, were told to change their mailings in future.

ttp://blogs.mirror.co.uk January 14th 2009

FOR DISCUSSION 

The number of items that receive complaints is only a very tiny percentage of all marketing communications. Of this, still fewer complaints are upheld.

5.4 ASA partner organisations

The ASA is supported by three other organisations.

The **Broadcast Advertising Clearance Centre** pre-checks ads on behalf of TV broadcasters before they go on air, eliminating almost all problems before transmission.

The **Radio Advertising Clearance Centre** pre-checks national radio ads and ads for specific categories before they are aired.

The **Committee of Advertising Practitioners (CAP)** Copy Advice team provides a pre-publication advice service for the ad industry to avoid problems with ads in other media.

5.5 Ofcom

The Office of Communications (Ofcom) was established by statute in 2002 to regulate the TV and radio industries, fixed and mobile telecommunications systems and the frequency spectrum used for wireless devices. Its website, www.ofcom.org.uk, describes its role like this:

'We regulate the TV and radio sectors, fixed line telecoms and mobiles, plus the airwaves over which wireless devices operate.

We make sure that people in the UK get the best from their communications services and are protected from scams and sharp practices, while ensuring that competition can thrive...

Accountable to Parliament, we are involved in advising and setting some of the more technical aspects of regulation, implementing and enforcing the law.

Ofcom is funded by fees from industry for regulating broadcasting and communications networks, and grant-in-aid from the Government.'

FOR DISCUSSION

Many local managers will perceive a central advertising campaign to be dull and disappointing because it is based on the lowest global common denominator – those common cross-cultural characteristics that somehow find commonality across borders that can result in dull ideas.

---

6 REGULATING SALES PROMOTION

6.1 The law

The statutory framework governing sales promotion in the UK is not comprehensive. Like advertising, sales promotion is governed by small sections of a large number of Acts of Parliament, the provisions of which are often somewhat ambiguous.

The British Codes of Advertising and Sales Promotion include the following legislative controls on this area of marketing activity.

- Consumer Credit Act 1974 (and regulations and orders thereunder)
- Consumer Protection Act 1987 and the Code of Practice for Traders on Price Indications, published thereunder
- Consumer Transactions (Restrictions on Statements) Order 1976
- Control of Misleading Advertisements Regulations 1988
- Data Protection Acts 1984 and 1998
- Fair Trading Act 1973
- Financial Services Act 1986 (and regulations and orders, and rules of the Securities and Investments Board, recognised self-regulating organisations and recognised professional bodies made thereunder).
- Income and Corporation Taxes Act 1988
- Lotteries and Amusements Act 1976 (and amendments thereto)
- Mail Order Transactions (Information) Order 1976
- Misrepresentation Act 1976
- National Lottery Act 1993 and National Lottery Regulations 1994

- Sale of Goods Act 1979
- Supply of Goods and Services Act 1982
- Trade Descriptions Act 1968
- Trading Stamps Act 1964
- Unfair Contract Terms Act 1977
- Unsolicited Goods and Services (Amendment) Act 1975.

With such a diverse range of statutory provision the law in this area has an 'individual and often unintended effect' (Circus and Painter, 1989). Given these circumstances it is hardly surprising that the regulatory framework imposed from within the industry by voluntary codes of practice is an important restraining influence. The most important codes include:

(a) the British Codes of Advertising and Sales Promotion
(b) the Institute of Sales Promotion Promotional Handling Code of Practice
(c) the Institute of Sales Promotion Competition Rules
(d) the Institute of Purchasing and Supply Rules for Trade Promotions

Given the complexity of the regulatory framework, restraining the freedom of action of a promoter through a variety of means, it is essential that promoters take expert legal advice in the early stages of planning sales promotion activity.

We will now go on to look at the regulatory framework for sales promotion in more detail, considering the influence of the law in this area and the complexities arising from its ambiguity, and then looking at the relevant codes of practice, both self regulatory and statutory, that try to remove this ambiguity in practical terms and thereby act as a true complement to the statutory provision.

6.2 Sales promotion – the regulatory framework

Contract law

With regard to sales promotion, the offer of goods and/or services with incentives by a promoter, and the acceptance of that offer by the consumer, constitute a contract that is enforceable in law. The basic requirements for the existence of a contract are the **capacity to contract**, the existence of an offer, the acceptance of that offer and consideration.

(a) Both parties to a contract must have the legal *capacity to contract.* In other words they must be fully aware of the formal legal consequences of their actions. This is particularly relevant with regard to young people entering into contracts. The Sales Promotion Code defines a child or young person as someone under 16 years of age and warns that promotions addressed to, or likely to attract, young people should not take advantage of their credulity or lack of experience.

(b) With regard to the **contract obligations** of the promoter, the basic principles of the Sales Promotion Code ensures that the consumer is fully aware of the implications of a specific promotion.

(c) Some general legal principles with regard to the **offer** of contract include the fact that the offer can be made to one person or can be of general applicability. The offer must be communicated before it is capable of being accepted and the terms of the offer must be clear.

(d) As the **acceptance** of an offer of goods with incentives constitutes a legal contract the **terms** of the offer must be clearly stated by the promoter, as stated in the Sales Promotion Code. This is particularly appropriate if any exclusions apply to participation (eg time limits, number of prizes per household) and if any limits on eligibility are imposed by the promoter. If such terms are not clear and easy to understand then any dispute over the contract will most likely go in favour of the consumer.

Acceptance of an offer must be made to the person making the offer and it must be without qualification otherwise it becomes a counter offer. Postal acceptance of an offer is valid from the time of posting and not at the moment of delivery.

The last requirement for a contract to exist is **consideration**. English and law will not enforce a mere promise. Each party to the agreement must provide somthing of value to the other party. Thus, in a coupon-based sales promotion, for example, the company provides the good or service promised, while the customer surrenders the coupon. The fact that the coupon's value is negligible is unimportant: its value is greater than zero.

Product liability

In terms of the quality of goods and incentives offered by promoters all products must comply with the implied conditions of sale stated in the **Sale Of Goods Act 1979** – namely, that the goods are of merchantable quality, fit for the purpose(s) for which they are sold, and that they are as described.

The remedy that a consumer can claim in law for any breach of the implied conditions of sales of the Sale of Goods Act is a refund of the purchase price. A seller may offer to exchange the goods, give a credit note or repair the goods, but the consumer is not obliged to accept any of these, nor the seller to give them.

Trade descriptions

The Trade Descriptions Act 1968 applies to sales promotions just as much as advertising, and implicit in the Sales Promotion Code is the requirement upon the promoter to ensure that all information is presented clearly and is not misleading. Incomplete information or information that is complete but confusing is likely to render a contract unenforceable in law.

Lotteries and amusements

It is in this area that the requirements of statute law create the most problems for promoters, particularly with regard to prize competitions. (Note that separate legislation and regulations apply to the National Lottery.) Section I of the Lotteries and Amusements Act 1976 states that all lotteries which do not constitute gaming (playing games of chance for money) are illegal. The Act provides no definition of a lottery, but this has been largely accomplished by common law, as follows.

> 'A lottery consists of the 'distribution of prizes by chance', that is to say where there is no element of skill whatever on the part of the participant. If there is a degree of skill involved then there is no lottery'
>
> (*Whitbread and Co v Bell* (1970))

Therefore a lottery is a distribution of prizes where those prizes are distributed by chance and no element of **skill** should be required, otherwise the promotion will not be a lottery. The emphasis on the absence of skill is shown by the following ruling.

> Any kind of skill or dexterity, whether bodily or mental, in which persons can compete would prevent a scheme from being a lottery if the result depended partly upon such skill or dexterity.' (*Scott v DPP* (1914))

Such rulings, while clarifying the situation somewhat, still leave much scope for interpretation of the law and it is recommended in the Sales Promotion Code that any promoter intending to implement a competition with prizes seek expert legal advice because of the continuing uncertainty as to what constitutes an appropriate element of genuine skill, which makes the promotion legal.

6.3 Statutory codes of practice

The aim of statutory codes of practice is to facilitate the implementation of particular Acts of Parliament. Of particular relevance to sales promotion is the *Code of Practice for Traders on Price Indication* which deals specifically with pricing and bargain offers. The law in this area was reworked in 1989 with the repeal of Section II of the Trade Descriptions Act 1968 and the Price Marking (Bargain Offers) Orders 1979. These provisions have been replaced by the Consumer Protection Act 1987, Part III which states that a trader will be guilty of an offence:

> 'If, in the course of any business of his, he gives (by any means whatever) to consumers an indication which is misleading as to the price at which any goods, services, accommodation or facilities are available (whether generally or from particular persons).'

It is also an offence to fail to take reasonable steps to correct an indication as to the price of any goods, services, accommodations or facilities given to consumers in the course of a business where the indication has subsequently become misleading.
This legislation has been backed up by the *Code of Practice for Traders on Price Indications*, adherence to which will ensure good trading practices. The code of practice states a variety of general principles relating to price marking and then articulates specific guidelines with regard to the indication of bargain offers that are of particular relevance to promoters.

There are a number of self-regulatory codes of practice relevant to sales promotion, the most important of which is the* Sales Promotion Code, *which remains the most comprehensive framework for the regulation of this area. This section considers its provisions and those of other relevant codes.

6.4 The Sales Promotion Code

The aim and scope of the 1995 Sales Promotion Code is to regulate:

> 'the nature and administration of promotional marketing techniques. These techniques generally involve providing a range of direct or indirect additional benefits, usually on a temporary basis, designed to make goods or services more attractive to purchasers'.

In order to accomplish the aim of the code more specifically, the Code states that all promotions should be, 'legal, decent, honest and truthful', echoing the parallel codes regulating advertising activity. Sales promotions should be prepared with a sense of responsibility to consumers and society, they should be fair, and they should not disappoint unnecessarily.

Many of the provisions are similar to those in the Advertising Code, as described above. Certain others, such as stipulations about participation have also been covered above.

Free offers

If the word 'free' is used in a promotion the code has no objection to making a free offer conditional on the purchase of other items, but regards such a description as inappropriate if there is a cost to the consumer attributable to the offer. The code allows a charge not exceeding current public rates of postage, the actual cost of freight or delivery of the promotional goods, or the cost, including incidental expenses, of any travel involved if the consumer collects the offer.

Promotions with prizes

The code identifies several types of prize promotions – competitions, free draws and instant win offers – and advises that promoters seek expert legal advice in this area before beginning a promotion. However some guidelines are laid down regarding conditions of entry, availability of results, advertising of such promotions and their handling and administration. The code states that instructions for entry should be clearly worded and that supplementary rules should be avoided if at all possible.

6.5 Trade promotions to employees and distributors

Trade incentives and competitions should be designed and implemented so as to take account of the interests of everyone involved and should not compromise the obligation of employees to give honest advice to consumers.

Promoters should secure the prior agreement of employers if they intend to ask for assistance from or offer incentives to any other company's employees.

6.6 Codes of practice relating to trade promotions

Trade promotions are also the subject of regulation by the Institute of Purchasing And Supply (IPS) Ethical Code, The IPS Rules For Trade Promotions and the Incorporated Society of British Advertisers, *Trade Incentives – Good and Bad Practice.*

The IPS *Ethical Code* considers the relationship between promoter and recipient of a trade promotion from the point of view of the recipient.

(a) The code states that business gifts other than items of small intrinsic value should not be accepted and that 'modest hospitality' is allowable.

(b) The ISBA *Trade Incentives – Good And Bad Practice* emphasises the importance of adherence to the relevant statute laws and codes of practice in this area and advises that, in a company using trade incentives, a policy defining the proper use and administration of such incentives should be laid down by the board in writing, making it clear that improper payments will not be sanctioned or condoned in any circumstances. This policy should be broadcast both internally and externally.

6.7 Institute of Sales Promotion regulation

The Institute of Sales Promotion endorse two self-regulatory codes of practice – the ISP *Competition Rules* and the ISP *Promotional Handling Code of Practice.*

ISP Competition Rules

The ISP encourages registration of any promotional competition with themselves. The intention of this is 'to improve on current working practice. In particular, ISP's aim is to secure closer adherence to the Sales Promotion Code, issued by the Committee of Advertising Practice (CAP) Committee, of which the ISP is a member.' Registration of a promotional competition confers the benefit of objective advice from the ISP Secretariat on competition copy, with specific regard to conformity with the Sales Promotion Code. A 'reminder' service is also available from the ISP Secretariat advising promoters, shortly before competitions are due to be judged, of recommended practice regarding the judging and publication of results. The emphasis is to reassure both consumers and promoters that the competition is being conducted in accordance with recognised best industry practice.

7 REGULATING PUBLIC RELATIONS ACTIVITY

7.1 Institute of Public Relations

An important document for the regulation of public relations activity in the UK is the *Code of Professional Conduct* drawn up by the Institute of Public Relations (IPR). The aim of the IPR Code is 'to set down standards, which will, it is hoped, make for good relationships and reputable business dealing by public relations practitioners.' The Code of Professional Conduct is binding on all IPR members.

Complaints about breaches of the code by IPR members can originate from an individual or an organisation. Any complaint is investigated by the Institute's Professional Practices Committee which, if considered appropriate, may refer the complaint to the Disciplinary Committee for further action.

(a) Regarding conduct towards **the public,** the media and other professionals the code states that a PR practitioner should conduct his or her professional activities with proper regard to the public interest, emphasising the importance of responsible behaviour. The code calls for a responsible attitude to all sections of the public, recognising the fact that the public interest is not easy to define as the interests of different public groups may be contradictory.

(b) In relationships with **employers and clients** the code states that the PR practitioner should safeguard the confidences of both present and former employers or clients and should not use these confidences to the disadvantage or prejudice of such employers or clients, or to the financial advantage of the member (unless this information has been released for public use or permission for disclosure has been given). However, the code states that this clause can be overruled by a Court of Law.

7.2 The Public Relations Consultants Association (PRCA)

The Public Relations Consultants Association (PRCA) says that:

> Persuasion in Public Relations is perfectly justified in a democratic society, provided it is handled honestly, openly and professionally. All members of the Public Relations Consultants Association adhere to the Professional Charter in order to ensure that their clients and outside bodies (such as the media) act professionally in all respects.

The PRCA sees it as its objectives (amongst others) to raise and maintain professional and ethical standards in PR consultancy practice, to promote confidence in public relations consultancy and public relations as a whole, and to act as spokesman for consultancy practice and to help members improve their efficiency, understanding, skills, professionalism and ethics. The PRCA publishes a disciplinary code, setting out the procedure that will be followed if a member breaches its professional charter.

FOR DISCUSSION

The complete PRCA charter is set out below. You should skim-read it: there is no need to learn it by heart. It is included to give you the full flavour of self-regulation. Is it strict enough or does it merely encourage self-interest?

PRCA Professional Charter

1 A member firm shall:

1.1 Have a positive duty to observe the highest standards in the practice of public relations. Furthermore a member has the responsibility at all times to deal fairly and honestly with clients, past and present, fellow members and professionals, the public relations profession, other professions, suppliers, intermediaries, the media of communication, employees, and above all else the public.

1.2 Be expected to be aware of, understand and observe this code, any amendment to it, and any other codes which shall be incorporated into this code, and to remain up-to-date with the content and recommendations of any guidance or practice papers issued by the PRCA, and shall have a duty to conform to good practice as expressed in such guidance or practice papers.

1.3 Uphold this code and co-operate with fellow members in so doing by enforcing decisions on any matter arising from its application. A member firm that knowingly causes or permits a member of its staff to act in a manner inconsistent with this code is party to such action and shall itself be deemed to be in breach of it. Any member of staff of a member company who acts in a manner inconsistent with this code must be disciplined by the employer.

A member firm shall not:

1.4 Engage in any practice nor be seen to conduct itself in any manner detrimental to the reputation of the Association or the reputation and interests of the public relations profession.

2 *Conduct towards the public, the media and other professionals*

A member firm shall:

2.1 Conduct its professional activities with proper regard to the public interest.

2.2 Have a positive duty at all times to respect the truth and shall not disseminate false or misleading information knowingly or recklessly, and to use proper care to avoid doing so inadvertently.

2.3 Have a duty to ensure that the actual interest of any organisation with which it may be professionally concerned is adequately declared.

2.4 When working in association with other professionals, identify and respect the codes of these professions and shall not knowingly be party to any breach of such codes.

2.5 Cause the names of all its directors, executives and retained consultants who hold public office, are members of either House of Parliament, are members of Local Authorities or of any statutory organisation or body, to be recorded in the relevant section of the PRCA Register.

2.6 Honour confidences received or given in the course of professional activity.

2.7 Neither propose nor undertake any action which would constitute an improper influence on organs of government, or on legislation, or on the media of communication.

2.8 Neither offer nor give, nor cause a client to offer or give, any inducement to persons holding public office or members of any statutory body or organisation who are not directors, executives or retained consultants, with intent to further the interests of the client if such action is inconsistent with the public interest.

3 *Conduct towards clients*

A member firm shall:

3.1 Safeguard the confidences of both present and former clients and shall not disclose or use these confidences, to the disadvantage or prejudice of such clients or to the financial advantage of the member firm, unless the client has released such information for public use, or has given specific permission for its disclosure; except upon the order of a court of law.

3.2 Inform a client of any shareholding or financial interest held by that firm or any member of that firm in any company, firm or person whose services it recommends.

3.3 Be free to accept fees, commissions or other valuable considerations from persons other than a client, only provided such considerations are disclosed to the client.

3.4 Shall list the names of its clients in the Annual Register of the Association.

3.5 Be free to negotiate with a client terms that take into account factors other than hours worked and seniority of staff involved. These special factors, which are also applied by other professional advisers, shall have regard to all the circumstances of the specific situation and in particular to:

(a) The complexity of the issue, case, problem or assignment, and the difficulties associated with its completion.

(b) The professional or specialised skills and the seniority levels of staff engaged, the time spent and the degree of responsibility involved.

(c) The amount of documentation necessary to be perused or prepared, and its importance

(d) The place and circumstances where the assignment is carried out in whole or in part.

(e) The scope, scale and value of the task, and its importance as an issue or project to the client.

A member firm shall not:

3.6 Misuse information regarding its client's business for financial or other gain.

3.7 Use inside information for gain. Nor may a consultancy, its members or staff directly invest in their clients' securities without the prior written permission of the client and of the member's chief executive or chief financial officer or compliance officer.

3.8 Serve a client under terms or conditions which might impair its independence, objectivity or integrity. Represent conflicting or competing interests without the express consent of clients concerned.

3.9 Represent conflicting or competing interests without the express consent of the clients concerned

3.10 Guarantee the achievement of results which are beyond the member's direct capacity to achieve or prevent.

3.11 Invite any employee of a client advised by the member to consider alternative employment; (an advertisement in the press is not considered to be an invitation to any particular person).

4 *Conduct towards colleagues*

A member firm shall:

4.1 Adhere to the highest standards of accuracy and truth, avoiding extravagant claims or unfair comparisons and giving credit for ideas and words borrowed from others.

4.2 Be free to represent its capabilities and services to any potential client, either on its own initiative or at the behest of the client, provided in so doing it does not seek to break any existing contract or detract from the reputation or capabilities of any member consultancy already serving that client. A member firm shall not:

4.3 Injure the professional reputation or practice of another member.

5 *Discriminatory conduct*

A member is required to take all reasonable care that professional duties are conducted without causing offence on the grounds of gender, race, religion, disability or any other form of discrimination or unacceptable reference.

Activity 4 **(1 hour)**

Identify current examples of marketing communications you suspect might contravene the regulations. Using these as examples, prepare a presentation giving a balanced case for regulatory control while maintaining freedom of speech and information.

Having given a broad overview of the industry and regulatory environment we now cover some technological issues.

8 CURRENT TRENDS: TECHNOLOGICAL DEVELOPMENTS

Developments in telecommunications, electronics and computing have opened up new opportunities for marketing communications. The term 'new media' has been used to reflect these new opportunities and is associated almost exclusively with such high tech developments as digital and interactive TV, teletext and videotext, the World Wide Web and the Internet, CD-ROM, DVD, video and multimedia.

Significantly and increasingly, the technology associated with new media permits:

- Interactivity
- More direct and sophisticated communications
- Shorter response times

8.1 The Internet

Definition

The **Internet** is the name given to the technology that allows any computer with a telecommunications link to send and receive information from any other suitably equipped computer. Terms such as 'the net', 'the information superhighway', 'cyberspace', and the 'World Wide Web (www)' are used fairly interchangeably, although technically the 'web' is what makes the 'net' user-friendly (rather as Windows did for MS-DOS).

In 2009, 18.31 million UK households had Internet access, representing 70% of the population. This is an increase of 1.85 million households since 2008. It is worth noting that Internet access varies widely across the world. See the following for more details:

http://www.internetworldstats.com/stats.htm

Certainly in the developed world, access to the Internet has become easier and cheaper: most new PCs now come pre-loaded with the necessary software, and developments in telecommunications networks will eventually render modems unnecessary. Wireless application protocol (WAP) ensures that the Internet can be reached from mobile phones. In reality, the majority of organisations see huge opportunities from use of the Internet: it can be used by organisations for business-to-consumer and/or business-to-business purposes. In the UK a large proportion of Internet activity is still **business-to-business related,** although as more members of the public get on-line and telephone and access costs reduce so this divide should narrow. Internet usage in the workplace has become a source of concern for employers as it has been cited as one of the biggest distractions and is one of the key factors in lost productivity amongst office workers.

8.2 Websites

Most companies of any size now have an Internet website. This is a collection of pages providing information in text and graphic form, any of which can be viewed simply by clicking the appropriate button, word or image on the screen. The user generally starts at the site's 'home page', which sets out the contents of the site.

FOR DISCUSSION

Go on to a corporate website you are familiar with. What are the key elements of the homepage? Discuss with a colleague any differences or similarities bewteen the sites.

8.3 Business to business (B2B) Internet activity

Much of the growth in B2B Internet activity is driven by companies recognising such advantages as convenience, cost saving, customer and competitive pressure, as well as opportunities to generate new revenue.

Online procurement, pioneered by large, global organisations represents a large part of B2B online commerce. A US survey showed that 73% of organisations use the Internet for indirect purchases and 54% for purchases of direct material, with organisations with big purchasing budgets reporting the greatest involvement (Faloon, 2001). IBM spent over $43 billion via e-procurement during 2000, and Boeing processes more that 20,000 daily transactions via its websites (Pastore, 2001).

8.4 Internet Service Providers (ISPs)

Connection (if not available through a user's organisation) is made via an Internet Service Provider (ISP). The user is registered as an Internet subscriber and pays a monthly fee together with *local* telephone call charges, even if contacting other users on the other side of the world. This model is changing as some ISPs offer free access for a monthly fee.

ISPs such as America Online (AOL) and MSN provide their own services, in addition to Internet access and e-mail capability. For instance, AOL also offers a main menu with options such as Life, Travel, Entertainment, Sport, Kids. It is rather like a quality Sunday newspaper, except that the sections are updated at least daily, and it provides much larger information resources (one option in the travel section, for instance, is to find out about train and plane timetables throughout the UK or worldwide).

There are many ISPs offering a combination of cost and performance and change is swift. At present, internet users in the US are only charged by their service providers. There are no telephone costs. This has undoubtedly contributed to the growth in internet usage in the US. Telephone charges have tended to limit the use of the internet in Europe and elsewhere in the world. It is highly likely that this situation will not continue.

8.5 Browsers, search engines and promotion

Most people use the Net through interface programs called **browsers** that make it more user-friendly and accessible. The most popular and best known ones are Internet Explorer and Firefox. Surfing the Net is done using a **search engine** such as Yahoo! or Google. These guide users to destinations throughout the world: the user simply types in a word or phrase such as 'beer' to find a list of thousands of websites that contain something connected with beer.

Google now dominates the search engine market and has generated a huge revenue stream by displaying targeted advertising alongside its search results. Thus, our search for 'beer' would produce not only a list of websites linked to beer, but also a display of advertisements for beer and places to buy it.

Definition

> **Search engine**: Website that maintains an index of other web pages and sites that may be searched using key words. Access to other sites is facilitated by hypertext links – links that may be simply clicked on to move from one site or page to another.

Companies such as Google make money by selling advertising space. Microsoft is currently trying to challenge Google's dominance of this area by teaming up with Yahoo!

Another form of web advertising is the 'popup'. Popups appear on top of the current web page and have to be deliberately closed, since they prevent the webpage from being seen.

> **Activity 5** **(1 hour)**
>
> Spend an hour surfing the Internet. Contrast the websites of different organisations and assess their communications impact – what features work best, how is advertising managed, what about the quality of content and graphics?

Before we look at some of the strategic issues associated with marketing communications and the Internet, it is important to establish what is meant by some key terms, namely, eCommerce and Internet marketing.

8.6 Social networking

Social networking has become a key influence for online advertisers. The phenomenon began with sites such as Friends Reunited, which aims to put old school friends back in contact, and was launched in 2000. The latest generation of social networking sites such as YouTube, MySpace, Facebook and Twitter have wide appeal for those who wish to host their own web page. Interest groups, celebrities and the general public (especially a young demographic) have taken to the idea of publicising themselves using this media. Those who do not publish personal information use the sites to find out more about people or issues they are interested in. Ad spend is increasing dramatically for these sites.

EXAMPLE

UK Social Network Ad Spend to Grow 148% 2008-2012

Social networking sites are on the rise in the UK and ad spending on such sites is expected to reach £285 million by 2012, according to eMarketer's recently released "UK Social Network Marketing: Ad Spending and Usage" report.

Some 11 million people, or 30 percent of UK Internet users, spent time at sites like Bebo, MySpace and Facebook, eMarketer estimates.

Though social sites account for only a tiny portion of UK online ad spending (3.4 percent in 2008), social-network ad spend is expected to rise 77 percent this year to £115 million. Spending in 2012 will have increased 148 percent over 2008 levels

Social networks have been part of the UK Internet landscape for several years, and the UK dominates social-network spending in Western Europe with 68 percent of the market.

http://www.marketingvox.com

Definition

A **blog** is a private webpage published by an individual or group. Usually blogs take the form of a diary or journal and are regularly updated.

Blogs usually relate to a specialist subject or interest. Sometimes blogs are written from an academic or consultant perspective, with the aim of sharing knowledge, while others provide a more personal aspect to providing information. Amazon and Dell for example write blogs to speak to consumers while The Tescopoly Alliance have a blog called 'Every little hurts' to challenge Tesco.

Review sites provide the opportunity to rate products and services while forums enable consumers to ask to advice and comment. Both are highly useful to companies and consumers as they enable companies to identify consumer problems and raise ideas for product development. For consumers, by reading others' reviews they can reduce the perceived risk associated with making a purchase.

EXAMPLE

The travel industry is one of the most reviewed sectors online with consumers able to select hotels based on previous travellers opinions. The organisation Holiday Which? Magazine studied these sites in 2007 and found that a significant proportion of these reviews were bogus with hotels encouraging staff to write positive reviews for their own hotel and dreadful ones for their competitors.

UK companies that post bogus reviews now face criminal prosecution.

New legislation will see local Trading Standards officers and the Office of Fair Trading given powers under the Unfair Commercial Practices Directive (UCPD) to prosecute those who falsely represent themselves as a consumer.

8.7 Marketing and eCommerce

Definition

Ecommerce (also known as ebusiness) is about transactions involving the **exchange of goods and services, for payment**, using the Internet and related digital facilities.

Internet marketing is about the application of the Internet and related digital facilities to help determine and **satisfy marketing objectives**.

Although Internet marketing is not concerned with the mechanics associated with payments and security, the boundaries between ecommerce and Internet marketing are becoming blurred. As a result of this these phrases will be used interchangeably.

Activity 6 **(15 minutes)**

Look at the Iceland and Tesco websites – what advantages do they offer the customer who does not want to shop in store? What are the potential disadvantages from the retailers' perspectives?

How does online grocery retailing compare with a specialist party goods site?

8.8 Ecommerce and website management

Management need to attend to three main decisions concerning their Internet and digital related facilities. These are their **development, maintenance and promotion**. All of these use resources and management need to be clear about the level of support that is appropriate. One of the key concerns is the web site itself. To be successful the web site should

- **Attract visitors** – with online and off line methods
- **Enable participation** – interactive content, and suitable facilities to allow for transactions
- **Encourage return visits** – design targeted at needs of particular segments, free services and added value facilities
- **Allow for two-way information sharing** – personalisation reflecting visitor preferences, direct marketing and information retrieval provide visitors with the information they are seeking
- **Create 'sidelines'** – encourage visitors to look at the site for extended periods.

8.9 Potential pitfalls of Internet marketing

The Internet offers exciting prospects for marketers to assist in many aspects of marketing, from communications and research to relationship marketing with customers and other stakeholder groups. Here is a list of potential disadvantages, many of which can be overcome with effective management.

(a) **Poor targeting** – as more websites are developed it becomes more difficult to differentiate. The fact that the user is proactively surfing means that effective search engine registration is vital.

(b) **Cost** – development and maintenance of the site and any customer database connectivity can be high.

(c) **Lack of synergy** – websites need to be developed with input from the marketing department to ensure integration.

(d) **Medium immaturity** – at present the internet is surfed by a large number of early adopters/early majority but until the speed, cost and reliability issues are improved, then the medium is unlikely to be adopted by the mass market.

(e) **Security** – research indicates that concerns over security and in particular credit card transactions are still a major barrier.

(f) **Search difficulties** – casual users may find searching for sites frustrating and time consuming.

FOR DISCUSSION

The Internet offers tremendous new opportunities to all businesses – this is set to continue.

8.10 Digital TV

Digital TV is available via terrestrial networks , satellite and cable.

(a) Transmitting programmes by digital signal rather than by conventional means **dramatically increases the number of services which can be delivered to audiences**: as many as ten digital services will be able to occupy the frequency previously occupied by one conventional 'analogue' service.

(b) Digital broadcasting allows viewers greater choice over how and when they watch, eventually allowing them to interact with programmes and select their own programme content.

(c) At the touch of a button, viewers are able to get supplementary information on the programmes they are watching.

(d) Broadcasters are also able to make use of the improved sound quality available on digital television to offer alternative soundtracks, for example the original language version of foreign films.

8.11 Multimedia and home shopping

Multimedia can be defined as the combination of different formats, including text, pictures, animation, narrative, video and music into a single medium. Applications are increasingly likely to be interactive allowing viewers to control where they want to go. Viewers are attracted to multimedia as it is more interactive and multi-sensory. They can explore at their own pace, experiment and receive immediate feedback.

Some examples of the use of multimedia for marketing communications are:

(a) Promotional material – products can be demonstrated, annual reports made more interesting, can be viewed on home PCs

(b) Customer interaction – eg in car showrooms to avoid feeling pressured by sales people, multimedia kiosks can be accessed directly by customers who can view models from different angles, design their own cars and have their questions answered

(c) Staff training – advantages include ease of use, cost savings and effectiveness

8.12 CD-ROM/DVD

CD-ROM stands for compact disk – read only memory. DVD stands for digital versatile disk. Both are thin plastic disks covered with a coating onto which digital data has been encoded. The read only aspect refers to the fact that once the information is recorded on a disk it cannot be overwritten and the disk can only be used to retrieve information.

A single CD-ROM can hold around 200,000 pages of text, making it a very size and cost efficient means of storing data. DVDs are able to store and retrieve significantly more data so that it is possible to view an entire feature-length film from disk.

FOR DISCUSSION

The interactive nature of the Internet creates opportunities for data gathering. Is it acceptable for this data to be used for further promotional and marketing activities?

8.13 Micromarketing

Segmentation, as part of target marketing, looks certain to play an even more crucial role in the marketing strategies of consumer organisations in the years ahead. The move from traditional mass marketing to **micromarketing** is rapidly gaining ground as marketers explore more cost-effective ways to recruit new customers. Micromarketing, or niche marketing, means marketing to a very small number of people. This has been brought about by a number of trends.

(a) The ability to create large numbers of product variants without the need for corresponding increases in resources is causing markets to become overcrowded.

(b) The growth in 'minority' lifestyles is creating opportunities for niche brands aimed at consumers with very distinct purchasing habits.

(c) The fragmentation of the media to service ever more specialist and local audiences is denying mass media the ability to assure market dominance for major brand advertisers.

(d) The advance in information technology is enabling information about individual customers to be organised in ways that enable highly selective and personal communications, for example database marketing and the internet.

Such trends have promoted the developments in benefit, lifestyle and geodemographic segmentation techniques outlined. Consumer market segmentation has developed so much in the last few years that the vision of multinational marketers accessing a PC to plan retail distribution and supporting promotional activity in cities as far apart as Naples, Nottingham and Nice is now a practical reality.

Micro-marketing is made possible by **mass customisation**. Mass customisation enables the combination of:

(a) The huge economies of scale of mass production
(b) The tailoring of products precisely to the customer's requirements

New manufacturing technology makes this possible. There is less need for a 'standard' or 'average' product if people's individual preferences can be catered for.

Chapter roundup

- The prime aim of marketing communications is to influence consumers' buying behaviour.
- Selective attention, distortion and recall can contribute to a message not being received.
- The structure of the promotions industry is a relatively complex one, with many thousands of companies.
- Types of agency include in-house, one-stop shop, creative hot shops, media independents and a la carte and virtual agencies.
- The agency selection process involves a credentials shortlist followed by a pitch.
- Agency remuneration can be by commission, mark ups, fee payment or performance related.
- All marketing communications should be legal, decent, honest and truthful.
- Self regulatory codes of practice are issued by the bodies representing the marketing communications industry in order to establish standards for members to follow.
- The Advertising Standards Authority deals with complaints from the public and commercially interested parties.
- Developments in telecommunications, electronics and computing are combining to form a new era of marketing communications opportunities.
- Successful websites should attract visitors, facilitate participation, encourage return visits and allow for two-way information sharing.
- Digital TV is likely to have a significant impact on video-on-demand, home shopping and home banking services.
- Micro-marketing is made possible by mass customisation.

Quick quiz

1 What are the key elements of the communications model?

2 Define what is meant by the term noise when referring to communications.

3 What are the main activities of agencies?

4 In the UK what medium accounts for the greatest advertising expenditure?

5 What is a virtual agency?

6 When selecting an agency, what criteria can be considered?

7 What are the agency advantages of performance related remuneration schemes?

8 What does ASA stand for?

9 What is the basic remit of the 1968 Trade Descriptions Act?

10 Who are the PRCA?

11 What is the Internet?

12 What is an ISP?

13 What can multimedia communications be used for?

14 What does micromarketing mean?

Answers to quick quiz

1 Parties (sender and receiver), communication tools (message and media) functions (encoding, decoding, response, feedback).

2 Those distortions created in the encoding or decoding process that can result in inaccurate interpretation of meaning.

3 Planning, creative work, scheduling and buying media, promotional integration, administration, implementation, monitoring and evaluation of campaigns.

4 Press.

5 A term used to describe a selection of specialist individuals from different agencies or from within an agency who work together. (para 3.1)

6 Services offered, agency size, quality of work, relevant experience, competing accounts, cost, location and reputation.

7 Can compete better on price and breakdown costs accurately; allows for individual performance evaluation; a successful campaign would generate higher returns; might motivate the agency and so improve the client relationship. (para 4.7)

8 Advertising Standards Authority.

9 This Act prohibits any person, in the course of trade or business, from applying a false description to goods, or from supplying or offering to supply any goods with a false trade description.

10 The Public Relations Consultants Association.

11 The Internet is the name given to the technology that allows any computer with a telecommunications link to send and receive information from any other suitably equipped computer.

12 Internet Service Provider.

13 Promotional material, customer interaction and staff training.

14 Marketing to a very small number of people.

Answers to activities

1 The answer will depend on the advertisements you have identified.

2 Answers could include:

- Lack of personal chemistry
- Overpriced production
- Going over budget
- Inability to learn from experience
- Poor business results
- Lack of strategic insights
- Poor communication
- Lack of pro-active thinking
- Poor creative performance
- Unreliable delivery

3 The answer will depend on what you have uncovered in the relevant magazines.

4 There is no specific answer to this activity.

5 There is no specific answer to this activity.

6 You would expect that Tesco has a wide range of products on offer compared to Iceland. Tesco has a significant non-food aspect to its retail strategy. A party goods site may be able to offer a more personal level of service and harder-to-find products.

Chapter 2 :
ADVERTISING

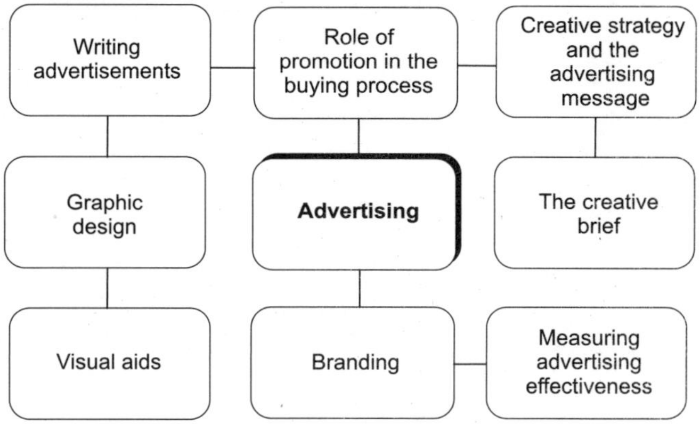

Introduction

This chapter will provide an understanding of advertising as just one element of the marketing communications mix. It is important to recognise this as many individuals use the word advertising when referring to all forms of promotional activity.

Branding will be discussed, as branding is not just a case of placing a symbol or name onto products to identify the manufacturer. A brand is a set of attributes that have a meaning, an image and produce associations when being considered by a consumer.

The creative aspects of advertising will be considered in terms of strategy and the advertising message and the importance of the development of a clear creative brief.

The last part of this chapter will introduce the operational aspects of advertising, some guidelines for writing advertisements, principles of graphic design, the use of visual aids and finally the challenges of measuring advertising effectiveness.

Your objectives

In this chapter you will learn about the following.

(a) The role of advertising

(b) The aspects of brand management

(c) The importance of creative strategies

(d) The function of the creative brief

(e) Guidelines for writing advertisements

(f) The principles of graphic design

(g) The main issues in using visual aids in advertising communications

(h) The methods of measuring advertising effectiveness

1 ROLE OF PROMOTION IN THE BUYING PROCESS

The simple model below shows clearly the four flows that occur in an exchange process between the marketing company and the customer.

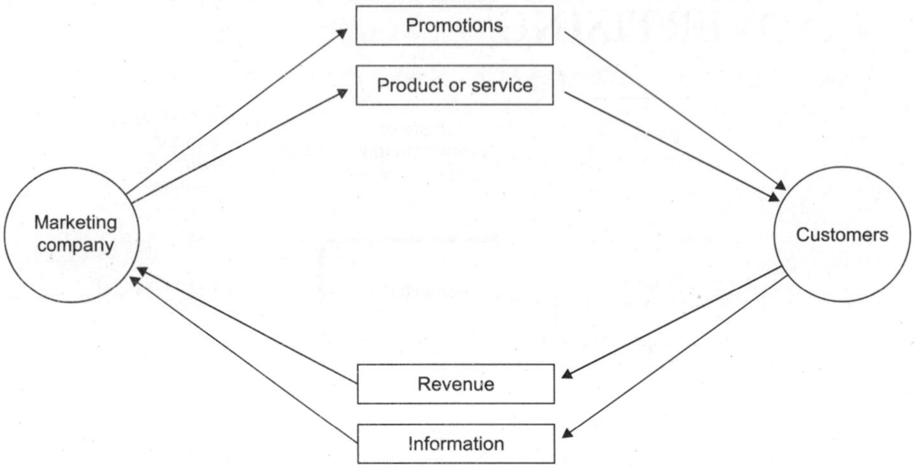

Figure 2.1: *Model of the exchange between the marketing company and customers*

This model shows the importance of promotion in influencing the customer to buy a product or service.

1.1 The role of advertising

Definition

> **Advertising** can be defined as any paid form of non-personal promotion transmitted through a mass medium. The sponsor should be clearly identified and the advertisement may relate to an organisation, a product or a service.
>
> *Brassington and Pettitt* (*2006*)

It is an impersonal communications tool. Advertising is a means of reaching large audiences in a cost-effective manner. Personalised feedback from an advertising message is not usually obtained.

The purpose of advertising is to achieve set objectives. These objectives will vary depending on the product or service to be advertised; the stage it has reached in its life cycle; the marketplace in which it operates and the role advertising is to play.

It is *not* the purpose of advertising to win awards for creativity (though winning any sort of award is good publicity). In this chapter we are concerned with the practicalities of arranging for advertising to be used as a promotional tool.

1.2 The advertising process

The starting point for developing an advertising strategy is a clear definition of marketing strategy. Advertising is one element of the marketing mix and decisions regarding advertising expenditure should not be taken in isolation. In particular, a product's competitive positioning needs to be taken into account.

The following diagram shows the major decisions that need to be taken when developing advertising strategy.

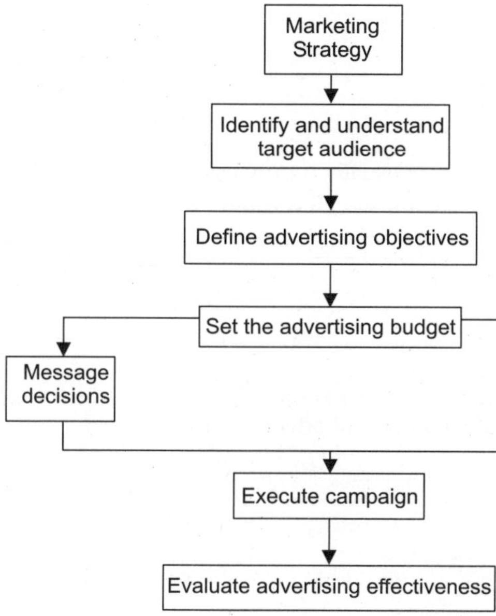

Figure 2.2: *Developing advertising strategy*
Source: *Jobber (2007)*

1.3 Advertising objectives

The following are examples of advertising objectives, couched in broad terms.

- To support sales increases
- To encourage trial
- To create awareness
- To inform about a feature or benefit
- To remind
- To reassure
- To create an image
- To modify attitudes
- To gain trade and sales staff support

Advertisers will be expected to express objectives in 'SMART' terms. The broad objectives given above should always be worked up into Specific, Measurable, Achievable, Relevant, Timed terms. Here are some examples.

(a) To support a sales increase on product X from 400,000 units to 500,000 units over the next 12 months.

(b) To raise awareness of service A amongst its target audience from its current level of 30% to 50% by the end of 2010

(c) To reinforce retailer Z's image as a company who offer a good range of basic food products at value for money prices.

Advertising is targeted at specific audiences segmented by demographic, geographic, behavioural or lifestyle variables.

FOR DISCUSSION

Classified advertisement columns are usually tightly packed with limited opportunity for individual advertisements to create impact. How can they be effective?

Activity 1

Over the next week, note down one example of a print advertising campaign from each of the following categories of advertising.

- Consumer goods
- Durables
- Retail
- Business to business
- Services
- Charity or not for profit

Try to analyse the advert, working backwards from the creative execution. Answer these questions:

(a) Who were the target market(s)?

(b) What were the advertising objectives?

(c) In your judgement, did the campaign succeed in meeting its objectives? Give reasons for your answer.

1.4 Principal benefits of advertising

- Reach mass audiences quickly
- Effective targeting
- Low unit cost
- Economical, efficient and effective at reaching large audiences
- Repetition means that a brand positioning concept can be communicated effectively

1.5 Response hierarchy models

Response hierarchy (or hierarchy of effects) models attempt to predict the sequence of mental stages that the consumer passes through on the way to a purchase. Some of the major response hierarchy models are:

(a) The AIDA model

(b) The adoption model

(c) DAGMAR (Defining Advertising Goals for Measured Advertising Response) (*Colley* 1961)

(d) Lavidge and Steiner's model

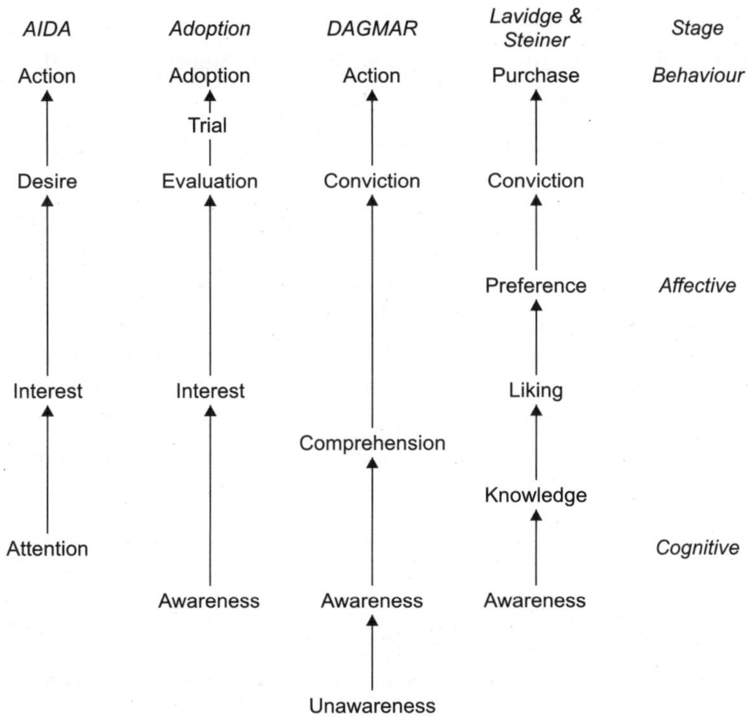

Figure 2.3: *Response hierarchy model*
Source: *Smith and Taylor (2004)*

These models are useful in the sense that they attempt to **prioritise the communication objectives at various stages of the buying process.**

(a) These objectives can be classified into three main areas – cognitive, affective or behavioural. **Cognitive objectives** are concerned with creating knowledge or awareness in the mind of the consumer.

(b) **Affective objectives** are concerned with changing the consumer's attitude to the product as a whole or a specific aspect of the product.

(c) Behavioural objectives are concerned with getting the consumer to act in some way (buy the product).

These models have some drawbacks, as identified by Smith and Taylor (2003). As has been said, the core model of buying behaviour is most applicable to complex buying behaviour. In other situations the consumer may not go through the staged process of information search and evaluation of objectives before the purchase decision. Indeed, some of the stages might occur simultaneously, as in the case of an impulse purchase. Buyers may also bypass the hierarchy of stages. For example, during the evaluation stage a buyer may go back to the information search stage in order to obtain more information before making the decision to buy.

However, AIDA and similar **'Hierarchy of Effects' models** are now considered to be **too rigid, inflexible** and an **inappropriate explanation** of the communication process.

1.6 Sales, persuasion, involvement and saliency

The **Sales, Persuasion, Involvement** and **Saliency** frameworks (Hall, 1992) are considered by some to be more acceptable.

Sales	Advertising works on the basis that affects sales directly, and nothing else is worth considering.
Persuasion	Advertising works by persuading people to act (to buy products and services) in ways that they might not have acted had they not seen/heard the advertising message. For example, Ronseal (wood staining and preservatives), Pantene.
Involvement	Advertising works by drawing people into an advertisement and making associations between the advertisement and the product/brand. For example, Nescafe Gold Blend, Yellow Pages.
Saliency	Advertising works by standing out and being different from other advertisements, especially those in the same category. For example, Pot Noodle or Tango.

Activity 2 **(10 minutes)**

Identify two further examples for each of the persuasion, involvement and saliency interpretations of advertising.

Underpinning many of these views is the notion that advertising can persuade people to purchase products.

1.7 The ATRN model

Definition

Ehrenberg (1992) counters this view with an **ATRN (Awareness, Trial, Reinforcement and Nudge)** model, which interprets advertising as a 'Weak Force'. This says that advertising reinforces previous purchase decisions and serves to defend them and maintain market share.

Awareness

Trial

Reinforcement

Nudge

Figure 2.4: *The ATRN model of advertising awareness* after *Ehrenberg (1992)*

Both models accept that **awareness is a necessary prerequisite** for purchase, although it may not always be through advertising. Ehrenberg argues that there is no evidence that consumers feel anything like desire when they buy toilet cleaning products or coffee or tinned tomatoes. If a potential purchaser shows some interest in a product, perhaps because it is new or significant to them at that particular time, then they might try or **experiment** with the product. If this is successful then a repeat purchase may be made. With reinforcement, the purchaser might be encouraged to add the product to their repertoire or evoked set (a small cluster of brands in each product category from which purchase decisions are made, as loyalty to a single brand is rare).

Advertising can assist any of these stages and can nudge people into buying one particular brand from their repertoire.

There is no fixed model of advertising. However, research suggests that advertising might be more effective when combined with brands, so that potential purchasers are enabled to develop links or associations between a brand and its advertising and related communications. IMC has a significant role to play in assisting the development of co-ordinated messages in order to help develop this brand/advertising association.

1.8 Advertising media

Traditional advertising media may be said to include poster sites, the press, TV, radio and in-store methods. Of these media, TV, radio and the press are regarded as communication primarily within the consumer's home, while posters and in-store methods are known as ambient, outdoor or out-of-home methods.

1.9 Trends in advertising media

There has been considerable **fragmentation** of the media traditionally used to communicate within the home. In the past, there were large audiences for a small number of TV and radio channels and for a relatively limited range of local and national newspapers and magazines. The growth of satellite and cable TV, the expansion of radio and terrestrial TV channels and the introduction of podcasts mean that the broadcast audience is now fragmented into relatively small groups. In the print media there has been a steady growth in the number of general and special interest periodicals. This means that traditional mass-marketing advertising has become less effective. Since advertising using these media can no longer reach mass audiences, it must be carefully targeted for clearly defined, narrow market segments. The corollary of this is that funds for individual advertisements are now much reduced and they must be produced more cheaply.

At the same time, there has been an expansion of ambient methods. Traditional poster sites are now supplemented by a wide range of new advertising locations: these are often very small and exploit occasions of close interaction between consumer and advertiser. Here are some examples.

- Fuel pump nozzles
- Till receipts
- Car park tickets
- Shopping trolley handles
- Commercial vehicle livery (especially taxis)

At the same time, there has been a growth in product placement and brand placement. Typically these methods are based on the insertion of real brand and product names into cinema, music, literature and broadcast media. The placement may be paid for, in which case it is clearly a form of advertising, or it may be more the result of effective PR, using such methods as press releases.

New media – email and text messages

Both emails and mobile phone text messages can be used in essentially advertising applications. Junk email is now as ubiquitous as junk mail. Unsolicited e-mail is probably more intrusive than traditional 'junk mail', though less so than the telephone. However, bad use of e-mail can have the habit of upsetting large numbers of people, to the extent that in Europe regulation is felt to be needed.

Text messages, because of the limitations of the medium can give an air of urgency and are frequently used for announcements and updates intended to prompt rapid action, such as those relating to popular cultural events.

We might summarise the marketing uses of email and text messages like this:

- To advertise a product or service, usually with a link to a website
- To update a subscriber to a product or service with useful information
- To confirm an order
- To invite users to write in or to respond to a helpline

Viral marketing

Many users of email and text messaging aim to achieve a 'viral' effect; they hope that the content of their messages will be sufficiently interesting that the recipients will forward them to their own contacts. Clearly, this is unlikely to happen with any ordinary advertisement: viral marketing, therefore, relies on some form of inducement. Typical inducements are humour and offers of value of some kind. A person who receives an email that contains a good joke is likely to pass it on; similarly, a plausible offer of a free drink or a competition entry may well be passed on.

2 BRANDING

As the choices available to the consumer becomes ever wider and products themselves become ever more similar in terms of the benefits and quality they offer, organisations are realising that they will only be able to compete effectively if their product has a distinctive 'voice', that helps consumers to single out their product above the noise made by competitors. In marketing this voice is called the **brand.**

Activity 3 **(15 minutes)**

What beliefs and expectations do you have about the following brands? How far are these due to promotion as opposed to personal experience?

(a) Fairy Liquid

(b) Persil washing powder

(c) Barclays bank

(d) Your own company's or college's brand

(e) Land Rover

(f) Aldi

You might find it easier to focus if you compare the brands listed with other brands of the same product.

Definition

Branding is the process by which companies distinguish their offerings from the competition. By developing a distinctive name, packaging and design, a brand is created. (*Jobber* (*2007*)

2.1 Branding strategy

Not long ago most products were sold unbranded from barrels and bins. Today in developed countries hardly anything goes unbranded. Even salt, oranges, nuts and screws are branded. There has however been a limited return recently to generics. These are cheap, unbranded products, packaged plainly and not heavily advertised.

EXAMPLE: COMPANY NAMES

In suburban Philadelphia is a retail establishment called Ed's Beer Store. It's a wonderfully prosaic name. Customers know what they can buy there, and if they have a complaint they know whom to talk to.

But what about companies with names like Agere, Agilent or Altria? Or Diageo, Monday and Verizon? Or Accenture, Cingular and Protiviti?

Except for Monday, which may be a strange thing to call a company but it is nonetheless a real word, all these names are fabricated. What's more, none of them, even Monday, tells potential customers anything about the businesses they are in. Plus, they sound so contrived that you might conclude they will do nothing but elicit snickering and confusion in the market place.

According to marketing professors at the University of Pennsylvania's Wharton School, however, that is not necessarily the case. They say peculiar names, by themselves, may mean nothing to begin with. But if backed by a successful branding campaign, they will come to signify whatever the companies want them to mean.

Branding is a very general term covering brand names, designs, trademarks, symbols, jingles and the like. A **brand name** refers strictly to letters, words or groups of words which can be spoken. Branding and a firm's reputation are linked. The important thing to remember is that a brand is something that **customers** value: it exists in the customer's mind. A brand is the link between a company's marketing activities and the customer's perception.

(a) **Brand identity** conveys a lot of information very quickly and concisely. This helps customers readily to identify and select the goods or services and so helps to create a **customer loyalty** to the brand. It is, therefore, a means of increasing or maintaining sales.

(b) Advertising needs a brand name to sell to customers, and advertising and branding are very closely related aspects of promotion; the more similar a product (whether an industrial good or consumer good) is to competing goods, the more branding is necessary to **create a separate product identity**.

(c) Branding leads to a readier acceptance of a manufacturer's goods by **wholesalers and retailers.**

(d) It **facilitates self-selection** of goods in self-service stores and also makes it easier for a manufacturer to obtain display space in shops and stores.

(e) It reduces the importance of **price differentials** between goods.

(f) Brand loyalty in customers gives a manufacturer more **control over marketing strategy** and his choice of channels of distribution.

(g) Other products can be introduced into a brand range to 'piggy back' on the articles already known to the customer (but ill-will as well as goodwill for one product in a branded range will be transferred to all other products in the range). Adding products to an existing brand range is known as **brand extension strategy**.

(h) It eases the task of **personal selling.**

(i) **Branding makes market segmentation easier**. Different brands of similar products may be developed to meet specific needs of categories of users.

The relevance of branding does not apply equally to all products. The cost of intensive brand advertising to project a brand image nationally may be prohibitively high. Goods which are sold in large numbers, on the other hand, promote a brand name by their existence and circulation.

There are three main brand name strategies (Jobber, 2007)

(a) **Family**. A single brand name is used for all products as, for example, in the case of Microsoft. The power of the family name to assist all products is being used more and more by large companies. In part, this is a response to retailers own-label goods. It is also an attempt to consolidate highly expensive television advertising behind just one message rather than fragmenting it across the promotion of numerous individual items. Individual lines can be promoted more cheaply and effectively by other means such as direct marketing and sales promotions. This approach also has the advantage of enabling the global organisation to introduce new products quickly and successfully. The cost of introducing the new product in terms of name research and awareness advertising will be reduced.

(b) **Individual branding.** Each product is branded separately as in the case of Procter & Gamble, for example, who have a wide range of different products, each requiring a different brand image. Examples from the Proctor & Gamble stable of brands are Daz washing powder and Pampers disposable nappies. Individual branding can be appropriate when the firm wishes to move into a different market segment: a good example is Toyota's up-market Lexus brand.

(c) **Combination brand names.** Combination brand names use both the family brand and the individual product name. This exploits the family brand while allowing the individual product to be identified. An example is VW Golf.

Within these basic approaches, a range of tactics may be employed.

(a) **Brand extension** is the use of an established brand name for a new product in the same general category, as when the Lucozade name was used for the sports drink Lucozade Sport. This approach has two advantages.

- They require a **lower level of marketing investment**, since the brand already exists.
- Consumers are reassured by the brand name and encouraged to try the new product.

(b) **Brand stretching** goes beyond brand extension by using the brand name for a new product of a different type (though probably sold in the same market segment). An example is the stretching of the Bic brand name from ball-point pens to disposable cigarette lighters.

(c) **Brand proliferation** is the opposite of brand extension and occurs when new products are given new brand names. This is essentially the basic individual branding strategy already discussed. Brand proliferation can help to expand both the market and the firm's market share by increasing the variety offered to the customer. This can be used where little or no brand loyalty is noted, the rationale being to run a large number of brands and so pick up buyers who are constantly changing brands. This is called **multi-branding**. However, if the products are insufficiently differentiated, it can lead to their competing with one another, an effect known as brand cannibalization.

The terminology of brand management.

A wide and confusing range of terms is used in brand management. Here are some explanations adapted from Jobber (2007).

The strength of a brand in the marketplace is reflected in the tangible value it adds to the company in terms of sales and profits. This strength is called **brand equity** and it derives from two sources.

(a) **Proprietary-based brand equity** consists of discernible assets belonging to the company, such as intellectual property and established distribution channel relationships.

(b) **Customer-based brand equity** exists when customers react more favourably to a product when the brand is identified than when it is not. This kind of brand equity produces a differential effect on customer reaction and leads to strong brand loyalty.

The value of brand equity can be assessed by the processes of **brand valuation**: this is an essentially numerical process involving financial and statistical techniques and you should not confuse it with **brand values,** which are described below.

A brand's position in the market is built on six elements.

(a) **Brand domain** is the brand's target market segment.

(b) **Brand heritage** is the brand's background history and culture.

(c) **Brand values** are the core characteristics that describe the brand.

(d) **Brand assets** distinguish the brand from competing brands; they include symbols, images and relationships.

(e) **Brand personality** is the character of the brand in terms of other entities, such as people, animals or objects.

(f) **Brand reflection** is the way customers perceive themselves as a result of purchasing the brand.

Definition

> **Own-label brand** – product that carries the name of the resellers – wholesalers or retailers rather than the manufacturer's, and is sold exclusively through the resellers' outlets.

Euromonitor defines five main types of own-label branding.

1. Using a different name, eg Marks and Spencer's Per Una
2. Using the reseller's own name
3. 'Exclusive' own label, eg Tesco's Finest range
4. Generics, eg Tesco's Value range
5. Surrogates which are manufacturers' brands that are exclusive to a chain of stores, eg Argos Cooksworks

The term 'own label' is increasingly being replaced with 'retailer brands'.

2.2 Consumer and brand owner brand benefits

	Key benefit	Component
Consumer	Identification	Simplifies improved
	Risk assessment	Guarantees consistent quality
	Representation	Embodies values, eg luxury VFM
Brand owner	Price premium	Increased profits
	Brand loyalty	Reduced threat of price war
	Growth	NPD
	Barriers to entry	Competitors find less attractive
	Legal advise	Protect from counterfeiting and look-a-likes

2.3 Valuing brands

Creating a successful brand can be very expensive in money and effort. When a company makes a significant investment in creating and enhancing a brand, it is appropriate to measure the degree of success that it achieves. This is the process of **brand valuation.**

The valuation of brands is an important aspect of the application of shareholder value analysis (SVA) to marketing management. Shareholders rightly expect to see a return on their investment. The greater the value achieved from a given cash investment, the better the performance of the company and its management is assessed to be. This applies as much to investment in intangible assets, such as brands, as to investment in tangible ones such as machinery or premises. The problem is that intangible assets are much more difficult to value than tangible ones.

It is also necessary to value brands if they are to be sold or licensed.

Should brands be valued at all?

When considering the valuation of brands (or any other intangible asset) you should be aware of the differences in **philosophy** that exist, particularly between financial and marketing staff. Accountants are cautious and even pessimistic as a matter of professional habit. It is their job to be **realistic**. Marketing people, on the other hand, tend to be **optimistic** and not averse to risk. And they want their brand-building efforts to be recognised. As a result of these two orientations, there will often be a problem with brand valuation, with marketers talking about *investment* and attempting to justify high values to accountants, who talk in terms of *cost* and would rather write it all off against profit.

An important consideration is that the rules of financial accounting produce an overall value for the company that tends to be very different from its **real market value**. The difference is made up of **intangible value** residing in such things as brands and the expertise of the employees. This is accepted as a problem, but accounting rules have not moved very far towards acceptance of brands as balance sheet assets since they are so difficult to value.

Currently, a brand may be shown as an asset on the balance sheet only if it has been **purchased,** since only then is it possible to state an unequivocal value, which is based on its cost. Then, like all assets, it must be **amortised**, that is, written down in value each year to recognise its diminishing value.

Methods of valuing brands

(a) **Cost**. The past costs incurred in building the brand are indexed to current values and summed. The problem with using historical cost is that its relevance to current value can be extremely limited; this applies to all assets, tangible and intangible.

(b) **Royalties**. Attempting to estimate what the brand would cost to license is quite a sensible approach and allows for the use of experience in current market conditions. Notional future charges are discounted to give a present value for the brand. Unfortunately, in the absence of plentiful hard data on actual current royalty rates, this technique is no more than guesswork.

(c) **Market value**. Recent sales of comparable brands or businesses may be used as a guide to value. When a branded business is sold, part of the sale price is related to tangible assets and part to intangibles. It will probably be quite difficult to arrive at a value for the tangible assets, and even if this can be done, there remains the problem of analysing out the values of the individual intangible assets: there may be several brands as well as other intangibles such as established dealer relationships.

(d) Economic use value. Extra profits attributable to the ownership of the brand are averaged over, say, the last three years and multiplied by, say, 10. This is a popular method and can be used to compare brands, but the choice of multiple is highly subjective and past performance is a poor guide to the future.

The SVA approach to brand valuation

Doyle proposes that brands should be valued by the standard shareholder value approach; that is, on the basis of the **extra value they will create**. To do this it is necessary to forecast the *extra* future cash flows they are expected to bring over and above what an unbranded product would provide. These sums are then **discounted** to a present value, which is the value represented by ownership of the brand. This approach is subject to the difficulty of establishing a suitable **discount rate** and estimating future **earnings**.

EXAMPLE

Nestlé paid £2.5 billion for Rowntree, a UK confectionery manufacturer, a sum that was six times the balance sheet value. Nestlé was not so much interested in Rowntree's manufacturing base as its brands – such as KitKat, Quality Street, After Eight and Polo – which were major brands with brand-building potential

Activity 4 **(5 minutes)**

Tata Motors own Jaguar, but why are you unlikely to be able to buy a product called a Tata Jaguar'?

2.4 Brand loyalty

Brand loyalty refers to the extent to which consumers will remain with your brand and keep purchasing it. Some companies such as Heinz have previously felt that for a consumer to be loyal then they will not buy competitor brands. This view has been criticised in favour of the concept of brand repertoires where consumers are more likely to purchase a handful of brands depending on the buying and usage scenario. Think about the crisps and snacks sector for example. A consumer may be happy to eat retailer brand multi-pack crisps at home, but prefer to offer branded premium crisps such as Kettle when sharing with friends. Clearly the consumer is not disloyal to Kettle, but buys the brand when it is relevant to them.

2.5 Promotion and branding

Promotion cannot create a brand on its own. Obviously, a brand needs an appropriate price. A Rolex watch needs to be a product made of real gold. You might not want to be seen in an Armani suit if you could buy one in Asda. The whole of the marketing mix plays a part in establishing the personality of the brand.

The term brand 'personality' (or brand 'image') is revealing, though. What a product says to you, what is said about it, how it looks and where it is seen are all aspects of communication. A name and a symbol are key constituents in many definitions of the brand.

People use brand personalities in different ways. Brand personalities act as a form of self-expression, reassurance, a communicator of the brand function and an indicator of trustworthiness. The value of the brand personality to consumers will differ by product category and this will depend on what they use brand imagery for. In self-expressive product categories such as perfume, cigarettes, alcoholic drinks and clothing, brands act as badges for making public an aspect of personality.

Brand personality can also act as a reassurance. For example, the personality of Ferrero Rocher chocolates is sophistication and 'classiness', which does not necessarily correspond with the type of people who buy this mass-market brand.

A third use of brand personality is to communicate the functional characteristics of the brand. Johnson's baby shampoo advertising is an emotional representation of its functional characteristics: gentle, safe, pure and effective.

We shall be looking at the contribution that promotional tools such as advertising, sales promotion, public relations and so on make in communicating the brand image in Chapter 13. The key concept to take with you as you proceed is consistency: all of the tools must be integrated and work together to communicate a single consistent message.

FOR DISCUSSION

The major world advertisers each spend millions of pounds worldwide. Their products are already widely known so that there can be little need to raise awareness levels. If this is so, what is the main purpose of advertising for such advertisers?

2.6 Globalisation

Gradual globalisation of markets is taking place because of the interplay of a number of forces. It is impossible to isolate a simple chain of causation here.

(a) Consumer tastes are becoming more homogeneous in such matters as clothes and entertainment.

(b) As markets globalise, firms supplying them become global customers for their own inputs and seek global suppliers.

(c) Improvements in global communications and logistics reduce costs, make globalisation easier and allow the creation of global brands. The latter feeds back to the homogenisation of taste.

(d) High costs of product development can be spread over longer production runs if products are standardised and sold globally.

Globalisation of markets naturally leads to globalisation of marketing. Under this concept, national boundaries no longer form marketing boundaries and transnational corporations pursue border-crossing marketing strategies that influence the complete marketing mix. Transnational standardisation of mix elements has the obvious potential advantage of scale economy, but decisions must take account of the extent to which standardisation is both possible and profitable. Companies must conform with local legislation and give due consideration to local culture and practice. The usual mantra is 'think globally, act locally', but discerning the implications of this slogan in specific circumstances can be very difficult.

In marketing communications, the emergence of **global media** has led to the development of **global brands.**

Global media

Global media have been developing for over a century. The earliest such media were press agencies, silent film and HF radio. Today, cinema continues to have global reach and has been joined by books, magazines, satellite TV, syndicated TV news channels and recorded music, among others. The growth of global media has been matched and driven by the growth of global media companies, such as Bertelsmann, Time Warner and News Corporation.

In global media, language differences continue to form a barrier, but the emerging dominance of English among educated classes is undermining this. Visuals and music are, to a great extent free of this problem, though consideration of cultural differences is important in achieving acceptability. Perhaps it would be more realistic to speak of transnational rather than global media.

This is particularly true when marketing communications are considered. Product placement in cinema is a technique that has truly global potential, as has advertising promoting brand personality. A good example of the former is the placement of BMW products in the James Bond movie Tomorrow Never Dies. More information-heavy messages, however, are dependent on language.

Global brands

There have been global – or, at least, transnational – brands for many years. Many UK brands, such as Raleigh cycles, became international during the period of their privileged access to imperial possessions. Large US brands, such as Heinz and Ford became widely known simply because of the vigorous expansion and consequent economic power of their owners. Recent years have seen the emergence of what might be called **lifestyle brands** onto the global stage. These are associated with such products as clothing, consumer electronics, alcoholic drinks, fast food and entertainment: examples are Adidas, Sony, Grolsch, Starbucks and MTV.

3 CREATIVE STRATEGY AND THE ADVERTISING MESSAGE

One of the crucial elements in the communication process is the creative stance taken by the advertising agency when designing commercials for television and the artwork for posters and press. The creative aspects may well be the vital ingredient for success. They may equally be the undoing of a carefully planned marketing strategy.

(a) A **generic strategy** is one which is based upon straight facts and does not attempt to make any distinguishing claims between one product and the next.

(b) **Pre-emptive strategy** is used where there are only limited differences between the products within a given product class. A pre-emptive strike attempts to say something about the product, which other competitors would be reluctant to adopt, in case they were labelled as blatant imitators. The constant battle between Procter & Gamble and Unilever in the soap detergent war is a good example of this kind of strategy.

(c) A **unique selling proposition** (USP) relates to the ability of a company to establish and communicate a distinct product benefit which competitors cannot make or refuse to make.

(d) **Brand image** is concerned more with psychological rather than physical differences between products. The aim is to associate the product with symbols and characters who relate to the potential target audience.

(e) **Positioning** attempts to define in the consumer's mind the comparisons between one product and the next. The task is to identify weaknesses in competing products and strengths in your own which can be reinforced so as to gain a competitive edge. (Stella Artois beer is 'reassuringly expensive'.)

(f) A **resonance strategy** is one which 'strikes a chord' with the consumer. The intention is to portray a life style orientation which is synonymous with the target group and one which is easily recognisable. The type of advertisements with which this is associated are typically the 'Is this you' scenario.

(g) **Affective strategy** is currently widely adopted by companies wishing to play on, as much as play to, the emotions of the consumer; it is most frequently used by organisations involved in financial services and fundraising

(h) **Informational strategy** is based on the view that an important element of the creative theme is to convey information, eg drug awareness campaigns.

Some of the more successful advertising strategies will integrate two or more of the above, so as to create maximum impact.

FOR DISCUSSION

Since 2000, grocery retailer Sainsbury's has very successfully used an aspirational celebrity life in its advertising. Jamie Oliver, TV chef, is popular due to his down to earth, cheeky, young Essex man media persona. The series of TV advertisements show him living a hectic lifestyle while apparently effortlessly creating meals together from Sainsbury's ingredients. Research has shown that this character appeals to the target audience of female thirty-something shoppers and his first two years with Sainsbury's were so successful in increasing sales that he was given an extension to his contract. Though the relationship has not been without controversy due to his outspoken comments on food issues, he continues to make advertisements for the supermarket.

3.1 Balance of the message and audience involvement

Our understanding of the **level of involvement** that may exist in the target audience can be used to determine the **overall balance of the message.**

(a) If there is **high involvement** then interested members of the target audience will **actively seek information**. Messages therefore tend to be rational, proclaiming product benefits and the key attributes.

(b) Where there is **low involvement** the audience are not really interested and **need to be drawn to the communication message**. In these cases, image-based appeals tend to be more successful and the use of emotion rather than logic predominates.

HIGH INVOLVEMENT	RATIONAL APPEALS BASED ON PRODUCT ATTRIBUTES INFORMATION PROVISION + BENEFIT CLAIMS
LOW INVOLVEMENT	EMOTIONAL APPEALS BASED ON IMAGERY SOCIAL, EGO AND HEDONIC ORIENTATION

If integration and consistency is to be achieved then adherence to an emotional or rational approach has to be maintained throughout all the promotional tools.

There are a number of ways in which the rational and image based messages can be presented to audiences. These are referred to as message appeals and some of the more common approaches are rational-based appeals and image-based appeals.

3.2 Rational-based appeals

Issue	Comment
Factual	The benefits are presented using reasoned, factual arguments (eg nicotine patches).
Slice of Life	Allow the target customer to identify with the characters and a common problem. Brand X is then perceived as a suitable solution (eg washing powders).
Demonstration	Show the audience how the product solves a problem (eg floor cleaners, before and after use).
Comparative	Through comparison it is possible to achieved enhanced status and superiority (eg credit and charge cards).

3.3 Image-based appeals

Issue	Comment
Fear	The suggestion of physical danger or social rejection might be alleviated through use of the brand (eg car safety; acne cream).
Humour	Attention and mood can be maintained by relaxing the target audience (eg Boddingtons).
Animation	For low interest products/services, animation can attract attention and convey complex products/issues in a novel manner (eg Clover, Tetley Tea Bags).
Sex	Used primarily to attract attention and to be salient (eg Diet Coke, Wonderbra, Citroen Xsara).
Music	Provides campaign continuity and a degree of differentiation through recognition (eg Ford Cougar, Peugeot 406).
Fantasy	Used to engage an audience and to encourage the question 'what is going on here?' (eg Silk Cut, Ericsson).

4 THE CREATIVE BRIEF

Agencies must be briefed on the client's plans and requirements. Intentions for product and brand positioning; target segment details; and outline communications messages must be specified. Much of this basic planning may be done in collaboration with the chosen agency.

4.1 Instructions

Briefs are 'informative' in the sense that they equip people with information that they can use to perform various tasks – but this is a different function from the brief which acts as an **instruction**: guidance and specification for performance.

The main points about a communications brief is that it should be:

(a) Clear
(b) Sufficient

for the agency to proceed to fulfil the instructions to your satisfaction.

4.2 Advertising agency brief

Purpose: To instruct agency/copy writer on which products the client wishes to push, and when and how

To analyse/interpret the market of the product for the agency

To give relevant information about the features and benefits of the product

Audience: May not have technical knowledge/awareness of product

May not know the market for the product as you do
Need something to go on: 'shots in the dark' are expensive

4.3 Suggested structure

	Notes
Purpose/objectives of task (i) What it sets out to achieve. (ii) Where ad will be placed (if known). (iii) Deadlines. (iv) Budget (if known).	(i) eg to counter competitor demand, or launch new products. Be as specific as possible. eg a main launch ad plus three follow-up ads at around half the price of the launch ad. (ii) Media choice may be part of the task.
Information about the market (i) Who are the audience/potential buyers? (ii) Constraints and opportunities. (iii) Buying habits and patterns. (iv) Important features of the market.	(i) Audience tastes, habits, age/sex etc. (ii) Restrictive legislation, competitor activity, new technology etc. (iii) Seasonal demand, tendency to buy through main/retail outlets etc. (iv) Any features of the market that you (and your competitors) take into account: price sensitivity, technology etc.
Information about the product (i) USP (unique selling proposition). (ii) Benefits to consumers. (iii) Price. (iv) Nearest competition. (v) Other features that might inspire the agency.	(i) Any 'edge' your product has over competition. (ii) Why would the consumer *want* to buy?
Information about the client (i) Corporate history and culture. (ii) Customer relations.	Ads should reflect what the organisation feels about itself: the client is in any case unlikely to accept a proposal which is uncongenial to its culture and image.

The 'background' information may, as you can see, be extensive. It may be helpful to provide product brochures and so on. However, a specifically-targeted brief such as the above will highlight the most usable factors, from the agency's point of view: audience characteristics, USP, benefits and so on. A simple **briefing digest** or aid may be prepared by the copywriter from a less helpfully structured brief: or may be provided by the briefing organisation. Here is an example.

(a) **The brief**

The task is to launch a new portable printer for a firm producing small-size office electronics for the home-user and small business. The ad is to appear in national press in February. The printer (the X40) is the first cordless portable on the market. It offers a choice of typestyles, a colour option, and various paper sizes. It costs £210.

The target audience is people who work from home, and people who travel in the course of their work and need printing facilities.

(b) **Briefing aid**

Task: Press advertisement

Media: National press

Deadline: February

Product: X40

Price: £210

USPs:			*Benefits:*	
1	First ever cordless	→	1	Will operate anywhere
2	Compact, lightweight	→	2	Easy to carry
3	Choice of typefaces	→	3	Professional presentation
4	Colour option	→	4	Good for graphics
5	Various paper sizes	→	5	Versatile

Market: Freelance writers/journalists
Small businesses
Home use
Sales executives

The creative brief

Definition

> **Creative brief** – document that provides an outline of the creative task and the basis for creatives to develop their solutions.

A complete and detailed brief may include the following elements.

(a) Desired outcomes or results, including:

(i) The standard to which they should be achieved

(ii) The criteria on which successful performance will be judged

(iii) The time-scale within which the task or project must be completed

(iv) Resources available; financial targets and budgets set; payments agreed and so on

(b) Definition of all relevant terms, to minimise misunderstanding.

(c) A breakdown of the task or project into logical components, and their:

(i) Context
(ii) Requirements
(iii) Resource budgets (if relevant)
(vi) Methods (if required) – don't try to teach the experts their job
(v) Relevant background.

(d) Information required to understand and carry out the task ('briefing' in the other sense).

Much the same structure will be usable for other briefing situations, such as:

(a) Briefing an artist or designer to prepare artwork for ads or sales literature

(b) Briefing a research agency (or staff) to design a questionnaire and research programme to find defined market/customer information

(c) Briefing an employee to:

(i) Prepare a report
(ii) Conduct an interview

EXAMPLE: ARTIST/DESIGNER BRIEF

	Notes
Purpose/objectives of task (i) What task needs to achieve (ii) Media with size/colour requirements (iii) Deadlines (iv) Budget	(i) Purpose, method of campaign. Place of task in campaign (if only one element) (ii) eg A5 6 pp brochure in 4 colour, or A4 mono ad (iv) Including artist's fee + printing costs: a constraint on the artist's imagination
Information about the market and medium (i) Audience composition and tastes (ii) Media style and constraints	(i) Verbally/visually inclined? What images? etc (ii) Glossy magazine, or tabloid. Paper quality, colours, space size etc.

Information about the product and message (i) Priorities (ii) Features (iii) Content	(i) Which are the important items that need emphasising in the design. (ii) What features should be reflected in the design style? (iii) Are there photographs/ drawings/text to be incorporated: if so, of what type, how big? etc.
Information about the client (i) House 'style' (ii) Culture	(i) Logotypes, house style for design or layout etc. Does this task need to match other output? (ii) Is the organisation design-oriented? Modern or old-fashioned? etc.

Activity 5 **(30 minutes)**

Undertake an analysis of marketing communications materials – packaging, press advertisements, posters, direct mailings, exhibition stands etc – to assess the creative treatments used.

Identify the creative themes adopted and compare competitor approaches. Try to place the strategies adopted into one of the earlier listed categories.

5 WRITING ADVERTISEMENTS

Advertisements may, of course, be oral and visual as well as written. The advantage of a **written** advertisement is that it can increase the length and frequency of the recipient's exposure to the advertising message: it can be perused slowly and carefully, and more than once – unlike a radio or television advertisement, which 'goes by'. This enables the advertiser to put **more content** into the advertisement, if he wishes or needs to. Indeed in some contexts, such as advertising in railway stations, trains and newspapers, the length and complexity of the content may add to the audience's motivation and attention: they are attracted to text they can read while waiting for a train.

Written advertisements can be placed in a wide variety of media.

Media can be classified and appraised according to:

(a) **Editorial contents** (news, general interest, special interest, trade/profession)

(b) **Circulation** size (net sales), area (local, national, regional) and type (subscription, bought or free)

(c) **Type of reader**, or 'quality' (socio-economic class, background, special interests, age, profession etc which imply motivation and ability to spend money on the advertised product)

(d) **Frequency** of publication (daily, weekly, monthly, annual)

(e) **Production** (colour or black and white, 'glossy' or newsprint, loose-leaf or bound, size etc)

(f) **Cost of advertising space**, usually calculated as cost **per** page, **per** thousand readers (including extra expenses of colour, special positions etc)

5.1 Selecting the 'right' medium

(a) Identify the target group of people you wish to reach and influence.

(b) Identify media which they read frequently and dependably.

(c) Select, from these media, those which give you:

  (i) **The widest coverage of your target group** (ie wide circulation **and** relevant readership profile)

  (ii) **With the greatest frequency** (not just frequency of publication, eg daily newspapers, but frequency of reference: weeklies like the **Radio Times** are referred to several times)

  (iii) **With the greatest credibility** (where the editorial content is congenial, authoritative and relevant to the target group's motives and interests)

  (iv) **At the lowest cost**

Activity 6 **(20 minutes)**

(a) What media do *you* read regularly? List them.

(b) Classify them according to each of the factors mentioned in Paragraph 5, (a) – (f).

(c) If you wanted to advertise to people like yourself, which would you choose?

FOR DISCUSSION

Advertising is used extensively in industrial and business-to-business settings and not just for consumer promotions. Gulfstream sells its executive jets to companies, not on sexiness or status, but on usage benefits. Its advertisements in trade and business publications emphasise comfort, quality, performance and reliability as well as customer service and after-sales product support.

www.gulfstream.com

5.2 The advertising message

The general purposes of all advertisements are as follows.

(a) **Attract the attention.** You cannot expect – or instruct – people to read your message: you have to gain their attention, in competition with other messages and distractions.

(b) **Hold the attention.** In the words of H C Carter *(Effective Advertising)* you have to 'entice reluctant, busy eyes to scan your message and decide to read on. If, after that, the reader is disturbed by [various distractions], he or she must be sufficiently interested in your advertisement to make a point of returning to it.'

(c) **Persuade the reader,** so that:

(i) Desire (in some form) is aroused, so the reader is 'motivated'.

(ii) An **action or decision** is taken in your favour: whether proactively (the reader calls, sends a coupon, goes out to purchase) or reactively (the reader sees the product in the shop, or is offered the product by a salesman, and – recollecting the positive response to the ad – accepts it).

5.3 The selling theme or 'angle'

An effective advertisement will have a main theme or angle, within which selling points can be conveyed. The selling points will support and build the persuasive argument, but the main theme will hold them together in a single, more powerful message.

Step 1 Start with a list of the product's features.

Step 2 Highlight those features which are new and particularly those which differentiate your product from its competitors in the market. These are your main selling points.

Step 3 Identify those features which are relevant to the purpose and audience (their motives/attributes etc) of the ad: discard those that are negative, or irrelevant, and cannot be 'turned around' in order to be made positive.

Step 4 Now consider what exactly is 'in it' for the customer: how can each selling point or feature be seen as a **benefit** by the customer? Express each selling point and feature as a benefit.

Step 5 Select the selling point/feature/benefit(s) that will **most effectively** persuade the customer to buy the product. Price? Quality? Convenience? Reliability? Prestige? Effectiveness? Environment-friendliness? This will be your **selling proposition,** or **main selling theme.**

Example

Product: BPP HND Coursebooks

Audience: HND students and tutors

Audience motives: Desire for assessment success
Need for confidence
(guideline changes etc)
Fear of risk

Features: (*possible selling points)	→ *Benefits:*
Comprehensive coverage*	Little wasted effort in studying (ease)
Relevant coverage	Reduces uncertainty
Activities	(confidence: success)
Regularly updated*	Reduced risk of outdated knowledge (success)
Easy to use style and features	Makes studying easier (ease)

Main selling themes

You can be confident of assessment success	– combining two major benefits, meeting needs
– comprehensively prepared	– utilising selling point 1
– this year and regularly updated	– utilising selling point 2
(And though it won't be easy, we'll make it as painless as possible.)	– adding third relevant benefit

5.4 The 'copy'

Having already listed all the product's features, expressed them as benefits, selected those most relevant to the prospective buyer, and thereby decided on the main selling theme, you have all the ammunition you require to write your text or **copy**.

(a) Draft a few simple statements to outline your selected propositions and benefits.

(b) Discard any 'extra' benefits – however interesting in themselves – that only dilute your argument, or do not fit into your primary theme.

(c) Find the words which will express your remaining statements most powerfully.

(d) Discard unnecessary words and ideas and use their 'space' to repeat, enliven and highlight the main ideas.

Activity 7 **(30 minutes)**

Adwatch is a UK television archive, highlighting some of television's latest advertising campaigns. Browse its archive of adverts.

Visit: *www.adwatch.tv*

(a) What are the possible objectives of an advertising campaign for a firm?

(b) Discuss what you believe to be essential characteristics of effective advertising, giving examples from the website archive.

Definition

Knocking copy: Text that offers negative or disparaging comments about someone or something else.

5.5 Ten commandments for advertising copy

Carter (1986) puts forward a number of rules which he believes are essential to success in all forms of advertising. We have adapted them as ten Commandments, as follows.

1 **Be simple**

Avoid technical and exclusive vocabulary.

Use short, easy sentences where possible.

Avoid complex reasoning: keep logical progression and links obvious and simple, so an averagely intelligent person can follow you.

2 **Be interesting**

Attract attention: make the reader look – then engage.

Use vivid words, enthusiastic tone, congenial images ('cosy home' for 'comfortable house', say).

Arouse curiosity, where possible: use questions and surprises.

Focus on benefits to the consumer; he will rarely be interested in the product features as such.

3 **Be brief**

Get to the point quickly: be direct.

Small areas of text are easily scanned and so attract the reader.

Leave out unnecessary 'padding' (sentences **and** words).

Prune ruthlessly: retain only what is necessary for sense, style and rhythm.

4 **Be positive**

Convert warnings and negatives ('Don't miss out on') to positive encouragement ('Take advantage of').

Use positive motivations, generally, rather than negative (eg: desire for success, not fear of failure).

5 **Be factual**

Keep to the 'real world' of the product and consumer, unless the need for colourful presentation really requires imaginative fantasy.

6 **Be honest**

The Advertising Standards Authority Code of Practice bans extravagant or misleading claims, indecent copy or illustration, and illegal statements. Besides, dishonest claims get found out (causing disappointment and loss of credibility) and titillating images are generally 'seen through' as the last resort they often are.

7 **Be original**

Original 'angles' and unusual use of design or words create impact.

Don't be too clever: you may lose the sense or credibility of the message.

8 **Be emphatic**

Reduce the number of points or themes to a minimum. Then you can repeat, emphasise and illustrate those points, for impact and recall. Use variation, vividness and humour to disguise repetition and avoid boredom.

9 **Be instructive**

State strongly, frequently and clearly: why, where, when and how to order/ purchase/enquire etc (eg: 'Call us now for details'. 'In all good bookshops now'. 'Send the coupon today: no stamp required'.) Reinforce with incentive if necessary (eg discount for early order, free gift for first order).

10 **Be self-contained**

Avoid direct comparison with competitors by name; it merely gives them free publicity and implies that you are worried by their product/performance: the reader may investigate.

Activity 8 **(30 minutes)**

Get hold of a convenient newspaper journal or magazine. Pick an advertisement that you find interesting.

(a) Why did that particular ad attract your eye?

(b) Evaluate its adherence to each of the 'rules' give above. (If it did not obey them, did that make the ad less effective, in your opinion – or did the copy writer achieve the desired effect in an original way?)

(c) Repeat the exercise with a number of other ads: develop your awareness of advertisers' techniques (good and bad).

5.6 Advertising style

As you can see from the above, advertising style is brief, simple, and 'intense' – packing emphasis, repetition and interest into the small number of chosen points. Applying what we have already said about persuasive style, you should consider the following.

(a) **Emphasis** – by repetition, graphic design (emboldening, underlining, isolation in space, size etc), and sentence/paragraph structure.

(b) **Pace and fluency** – by varying sentence/paragraph lengths, and connecting sentences using logical links. (In advertising, it is considered acceptable to start sentences – actually clauses – with 'and', 'but', 'because' and so on).

(c) **Informality** – by using colloquial language and the kind of style you would use to explain the proposition or describe the product to a friend.

(d) **Appeal to audience motivations.** Words like 'now', 'free', 'new', 'save', 'value', 'quality', 'care' or 'family' – trite though they may seem – have powerful associations with consumers' needs for security, success, and belonging (and related fears) and perceptions of what they want from a product or organisation.

(e) **Credibility and congeniality**. Especially if the product is expensive, the reader will need to trust and relate to the ad before being persuaded – just as in face-to-face selling. So do not exaggerate, bully or patronise. Make sure that the ad is as well-presented, error-free and as helpful as possible.

(f) **Presentation**. We will be looking at graphic design later in this chapter. You should be aware of the use of:

   (i) **Space** – to attract attention, and make reading easy.

   (ii) **Typestyle** – and variation of it: to attract attention and convey impressions.

   (iii) **Illustration** – line drawings, photographs, colour illustrations, symbols etc: to attract attention, add information, or add interest. Consider whether the effect is clear, relevant, in tune with the style of the whole ad, and worthwhile enough to justify the use of space.

   (iv) **Colour** – for visibility, and to convey impressions or moods.

   (v) **Shape and texture** – to attract attention and enhance credibility.

(g) **Headlines and slogans**. Your aim is to attract attention by use of curiosity, or interesting language, or relevance to the audience's needs/wants/interests/ attitudes, or (ideally) all three. A headline should be a statement of the advertisement's main theme or proposition, put as pithily and attention-grabbingly as possible. Use:

(i) Puns, verbal or visual (referring to an illustration). Use carefully – they need to be subtle, yet easy to 'get'.

(ii) Questions.

(iii) Adaptations of well-known phrases or sayings.

(iv) Balanced phrases or word patterns.

(v) Controversial statements.

(vi) Appeals to powerful motivators like greed/loyalty/security/ambition/ friendship.

(vii) Curiosity. ('Teaser' headlines do not sum up the selling proposition, but draw the reader into the copy – where the selling proposition should be immediately introduced).

(viii) Humour. The words need not be humorous in themselves, but may interact in a witty way with a picture.

Activity 9

Study magazines, newspapers and posters to see all of these points in action.

The same advice applies even if you are writing and laying out a simple advertisement for the notice board at your college or workplace. The function of such an advertisement will be primarily to inform. Originality, creativity and competitive attention-grabbing will not be required to the same extent as in a press advertisement, especially if the topic of the ad is relevant to your fairly small, fairly familiar target audience.

5.7 Gaining attention

Here are 35 ways of gaining attention in advertisement.

1 Humour
2 Real life dramatisations
3 Slices of life
4 Testimonials
5 Guarantees
6 Comparisons
7 Problem solving
8 Characters
9 Talking heads
10 Recommendations
11 Reasons why
12 Facts
13 News
14 Emotion
15 Cartoons
16 Animation
17 Charts
18 Computer graphics
19 Claymation
20 Music
21 Symbols
22 Animals
23 Contests
24 Offers
25 Exaggeration
26 Glamour
27 Personalities
28 Spokespersons
29 Freephone numbers
30 The product alone
31 The product in use
32 Different uses of the product
33 Effects of not using the product
34 Before and after
35 The package as the star

6 GRAPHIC DESIGN

6.1 Principles of graphic design

There are no hard and fast rules in graphic design. It is best to be flexible, since appropriateness to the specific context is the most important thing – and the unexpected and unusual can be very effective, too.

6.2 Qualities of good design

(a) **Suitability**

As ever, consider your purpose and your audience. Graphic elements should be appropriately related:

(i) To your message
(ii) To their surroundings

(b) **Consistency**

Allowing for variety and contrast, you should be consistent within each page and within the communication as a whole. Design elements such as margins, headlines, borders, straight or ragged line ends, indentation of new paragraphs and so on should be consistently handled. Even typestyle and size should not be changed unless there is a positive effect to be gained.

(c) **Tension**

Balance – equally sized elements, symmetrically arranged – can be satisfying to the eye as a whole picture. However, it can lead to boredom, indecision and interrupted eye movement when it comes to reading. Tension – created by unequal left/right or top/bottom balance – provides visual interest and 'movement' on the page, and is helpful in pulling the reader onwards through the text. The balance of a page can be altered by focusing interest off-centre: having a larger illustration towards one side, or towards the top or bottom, or using white space to unbalance text (eg by having columns of unequal length.)

Balance

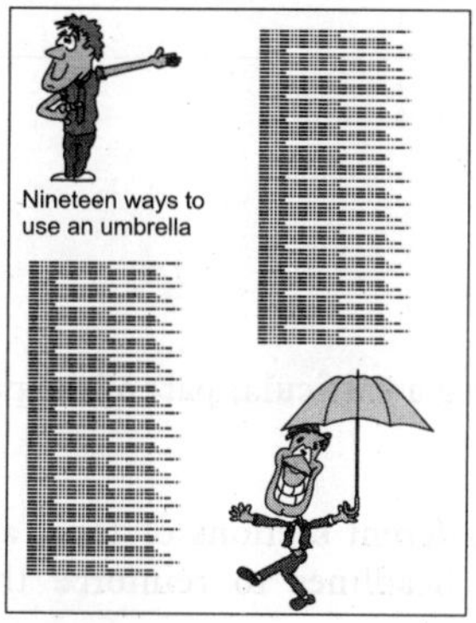

Tension

(d) **Continuity**

Balance on the page can create interrupted eye movement, as the eye attempts to see the whole picture, rather than following the line of meaning through the text. In a more obvious way, if your text is broken up with lots of devices and illustrations, the sense will be interrupted at each one: you risk losing the reader at each point.

(e) **Unity**

Just as a short message should have one dominant idea, and not more than three or four main points, so a page should be kept simple in order not to confuse the reader. There may be a rich variety of visual detail, but the design should give one dominant impression, and ideally have one dominant visual feature: a focal point to which the reader's eyes can be drawn, and on which they can rest, before beginning to move over the page. The dominant element may be:

- A headline
- A large photo or illustration
- A headline and illustration together
- A block of text, surrounded by white space

and so on.

Unifying headline

Unifying illustration

6.3 Colour

(a) **Impact and interest.**

(b) **Emphasis.**

Colour may be a means of highlighting a particular part of the page.

(c) **Organisation**

Different colours can be used for different sections or topic areas. Colour can be used on borders, rules or headlines to reinforce the message's structure for ease of reading.

(d) **Meaning**

Colour can reflect or reinforce the message, especially where there are cultural norms about particular colours.

(e) **Mood**

Again, this tends to be a matter of cultural norms. In general, bright colours convey excitement, while subdued colours add dignity.

(f) **Realism**

Black and white pictures can be highly contrasted and textured, and so make a strong impression, but colour photographs offer a more accurate image of reality as we see it.

6.4 Typestyle

A huge selection of typestyles is now available in word processing packages, and 'typefaces' or 'fonts', as they are called, vary widely in several areas.

(a) **Ease of reading**

(i) **Serif** type, like the text typeface used here, is characterised by small 'feet' or cross-lines at the ends of the main letter strokes. These draw the eye through letters and from one letter to another and make the face very easy to read: serif faces are often used for the body of text.

(ii) **Sans-serif** (without-serif) type, such as the face used in our activities and definitions, is more simple in appearance. It has great clarity, in small doses, and is ideal for headers, sub-headers, captions and writing for children.

(b) **'Personality'** or mood.

(c) **Emphasis and impact**.

Different typefaces have different 'weights'. They may be **thick** (or 'bold') or thin ('light'). Bold typefaces in a small area highlight that area, altering the balance of the page, while light typefaces have an 'airier' appearance, especially where lines of text are also fairly widely spread.

In general, type size should be chosen according to:

(a) **Readability**. Consider your audience. Type size for an outdoor poster size will obviously be different to that in a letter or report: either way, the words should be legible without strain, particularly if the message is lengthy; and

(b) **Emphasis**. Consider balance, tension and unity and choose the relative proportions of your type elements accordingly. By and large your main header will be larger than your secondary headers, which will be larger than your sub-headers and so on.

7 VISUAL AIDS

Visuals can certainly be:

(a) Clearer
(b) More impactful
(c) More memorable

than blocks of figures or text, because they are simplified, patterned and concrete (allowing lengthy or repeated perusal).

On the other hand, visual images are symbols – like language. They only communicate precisely and effectively if they are **shared** by the viewer and the communicator.

(a) **Visuals may be given a common meaning by consensus** – like the road signs used in the Highway Code, safety symbols, scientific and mathematical symbols.

(b) **Visuals may be given a meaning by the communicator**. In this case, he needs to inform the viewer of the meaning he attaches to the symbols he uses, unless it is extremely obvious.

(c) **Visuals may be given a wide range of meanings through association or resonance**. The associations evoked by a given image will be different according to the knowledge, experience, education, perceptions and expectations of the viewer. Symbols such as a cross or a heart have emotional and imaginative resonances beyond the simplicity of the image, because of the powerful associations built up in them over history.

7.1 The need for visual support

Visual aids should not be regarded as decoration or planned as features for their own sake. Visual aids are graphical symbols used to aid or support the main message. The type of visual support required should be clear, if you have properly defined your **purpose** in communicating, and the potential and problems offered by your **audience**.

If you are trying to persuade your audience that your washing powder washes whiter, for example, you might consider the following.

(a) If you are trying to persuade an audience of **chemists,** your aim will be information, explanation and evidence. You might choose to use diagrams of the chemical structure of whatever special ingredient your powder contains, or a graph showing that lower water temperatures do not significantly reduce the powder's ability to kill bacteria.

(b) If you are trying to persuade an audience of **consumers**, your aim may be more to do with attitude change. You might use images of clothes before and after using the powder, to emphasise the after-wash whiteness. Or you may choose to show happy, active people in sparkling white clothes to accompany a verbal assertion that the powder washes whiter.

7.2 Diagrams

A diagram is basically a drawing or plan demonstrating the form or workings of something.

Diagrams have the following advantages for explaining and clarifying information.

(a) They show complex relationships and processes in a single image which can be perused at the reader's own pace, **unlike**:

  (i) A demonstration, which must be 'followed' as the events occur, with a danger of losing track or falling behind.

  (ii) A narrative description, which requires the reader/listener to remember and visualise each stage.

(b) They simplify and stylise the elements of the process or object, removing complicating or irrelevant factors.

In general, drawings are used to support **description**, since they convey appearance and to add visual **interest**, where a photograph would be difficult to obtain or reproduce. Photographs are generally more impactful, but drawings have the advantages of simplification, clarity and cleaner reproduction (where print quality or the surface of the paper may distort subtleties of shading in a photo). Compared to diagrams, illustration is less effective at conveying relationships and processes, but if you wished to show how each stage of a process **looked,** or to encourage reader identification by showing people **doing** whatever-it-was, an illustration would be more helpful: descriptive and 'human'.

7.3 Cartoons and animation

Cartoons are a variant on illustration: they are typically line drawings achieved with the greatest possible simplicity. They are generally associated with the use of humour, either in the images themselves, or in the juxtaposition of images and accompanying words. If you are fairly sure that the joke – or the style of humour generally – will be accessible to your audience, humour is an attention-grabbing and congenial method of emphasising a point, or encouraging the audience to look at something in a new way – to gain an insight into the topic. If humour is not shared by the audience, or is inappropriate to the situation, it may be confusing and /or damaging to the user's credibility as a source.

EXAMPLE

Many TV ads use animated cartoons to tell a story or capture the attention, or provide a readily recognisable symbol. An example is Felix the cat or Tony the tiger.

7.4 Photographs

Photographs, whether black and white or colour, can be very impactful if well reproduced, and have a major advantage when it comes to implying realism, if required to 'prove' an event or situation. Photographic images may contain elements irrelevant to the main feature and message, but this can be avoided, or the viewer's attention can be suitably directed.

The main disadvantages to using photography are if the photographs are poor in quality (clarity, colour, exposure, composition and so on) or cannot be reproduced cleanly (if printing or paper quality is poor). In addition, you should consider whether the meaning and effect are worth the extra costs involved.

7.5 Balancing illustration and text

It is easy to get carried away with visual aids, especially if they seem more interesting, impactful or understandable than the accompanying text. However, visuals cannot contain and convey the same amount of information, with the same precision, as words can. A visual needs to be extremely impactful or significant to justify occupying space on a page that could be used for a number (often a large number) of words.

7.6 Digital imaging

Many graphic projects begin with analogue images such as 35mm slides, transparencies or reflective art. To produce a digital image, these elements are converted to digital files which can be manipulated on a computer system. This step is usually accomplished by scanning the analogue image. The scanner measures reflected or transmitted light from the analogue image, assigning numerical values to the colours or tones in the image to create a digital copy.

With the image translated into a series of numbers, the information can be stored on a computer hard disk or other electronic media such as a removable drive, photo CD or magnetic tape. Once the image has been converted to numbers, it can be transferred from one computer to another or sent electronically.

Definitions

Analogue – data stored in a continuous form.

Digital – data processed using binary numbers via a scanner.

Scanner – an input device that digitises images, creating bit-mapped copies that can be manipulated electronically.

FOR DISCUSSION

World Books, a book club, was concerned about falling response rates to its door-to-door and direct mail campaigns. In certain television regions, therefore, an advertising campaign was developed to tell people that a mailshot or door drop was on its way, and encouraging them to respond to it. Analysis showed that response rates increased by over 25% in areas where advertising was shown and that the 6,000 extra responses generated virtually paid for the television advertising. *(http://www.mediacomuk.com)*

Chapter roundup

- Advertising is a means of reaching large audiences in a cost-effective manner.
- The purpose of advertising is to achieve set objectives.
- Response hierarchy models attempt to predict the sequence of mental stages that the consumer passes on the way to a purchase.
- The promotional mix can be defined as advertising, sales promotion, personal selling and public relations.
- A brand comprises intangible values created by a badge of reassurance.
- Own-label brands have been used by retailers since the mid-1980s as strategic weapons against competitors.
- Brand equity can be viewed from a financial perspective in terms of an asset or from a marketing perspective in terms of the customer perspective.
- Components of brand equity include perceived quality, salience, association, customer satisfaction, repeat purchase and price premium potential.
- Creative strategies will vary depending on the client, the product and the target market.
- A creative brief is used to equip an agency with the information needed to create communications.
- Media selection criteria include coverage, frequency, credibility and cost.
- Guidelines for advertising copy include being simple, interesting, brief, positive, factual, honest, original, emphatic, instructive and self-contained.
- Graphic design, use of colour and typestyle all make an important contribution to effective advertising.
- Visuals are used in advertising as they can be clearer, more memorable than text and create more impact.
- Many images are converted to digital format to facilitate computer manipulation.

Quick quiz

1 How can advertising be defined?
2 Give some examples of advertising objectives.
3 What are the principal benefits of advertising?
4 Name four response hierarchy models.
5 What does Ehrenberg's ATRN model stand for?
6 What is a brand?
7 What are the four main branding strategies?
8 What is meant by the term own-label brand?
9 What are the main brand owner's benefits of branding?
10 What is brand equity?
11 What is meant by the term salience?
12 List eight creative strategy options.
13 What is a creative brief?
14 What is meant by the term knocking copy?
15 What are the five key qualities of good design?
16 Why might analogue images be converted to digital?

Answers to quick quiz

1 Any paid form of non-personal presentation and promotion of ideas, goods or services by an identified sponsor.

2 Increase sales, encourage trial, create awareness, inform, remind, reassure, create an image, modify attitudes, gain trade and sales staff support.

3 Reach mass audience, effective targeting, low unit cost, economical, efficient and effective at reaching large audiences, successful at brand maintenance.

4 AIDA, Adoption, DAGMAR, Lavidge and Steiner.

5 Awareness, Trial, Reinforcement and Nudge.

6 A brand is the totality of what the consumer takes into consideration before making a purchase decision.

7 Corporate umbrella, family umbrella, range branding and individual branding.

8 An own-label brand refers to a product that carries the name of the reseller, wholesaler or retailer – rather than the manufacturer.

9 Price premium opportunities, increased brand loyalty, growth and increased barriers to entry.

10 Brand equity refers to the strength, currency and value of the brand.

11 Salience is the term given to represent the degree of relevance a brand may have to a consumer.

12 Generic, pre-emptive, USP, brand image, positioning, resonance, affective and informational.

13 A creative brief is a document that provides an outline of the creative task and is the basis for creatives to develop their solutions.

14 Knocking copy is text that offers a negative or disparaging comment about someone or something.

15 Suitability, consistency, tension, continuity and unity.

16 So they can be manipulated by a computer system.

Answers to activities

1 Here is the sort of thing that is required. Question (c) is a matter for you to judge.

Example: Full-page Disneyland Paris advert from Sunday magazine supplement

The advert features a full colour drawing of families enjoying Disneyland Paris train and boat rides through Storybook Land, 'a miniature land on a grand scale, where everyone's favourite fairy tales come to life.'

(a) Target markets

(i) ABC1 adults with children or grandchildren under twelve years.

(ii) Families with children living within a 150-mile radius of the Channel ports

(iii) Existing UK theme park users

(iv) Short-break holidaymakers

(b) Advertising objectives

(i) To inform about a new feature attraction within Disneyland Paris

(ii) To create an image of Disneyland Paris as a theme park which takes the visitor away from reality to an exciting fairytale world.

(iii) To remind the holidaymaker about the potential on Disneyland Paris as a holiday venue

(iv) To reassure travel agents and potential visitors of Disneyland Paris's continuing presence in the packaged event holiday market, following adverse publicity during re-financing deals.

2 There is no specific answer to this activity.

3 The answer to this activity hinges on your own tastes and perceptions.

4 The two names represent very different sectors of the car market; Jaguar are at the luxury end and Ford produce mass-market cars. The Jaguar marque would arguably be compromised by association with the Ford name.

5 There is no specific answer to this activity.

6 There is no specific answer to this activity

7 There is no specific answer to this activity.

8 There is no specific answer to this activity.

9 There is no specific answer to this activity.

Chapter 3 :
OTHER TOOLS OF THE PROMOTIONAL MIX

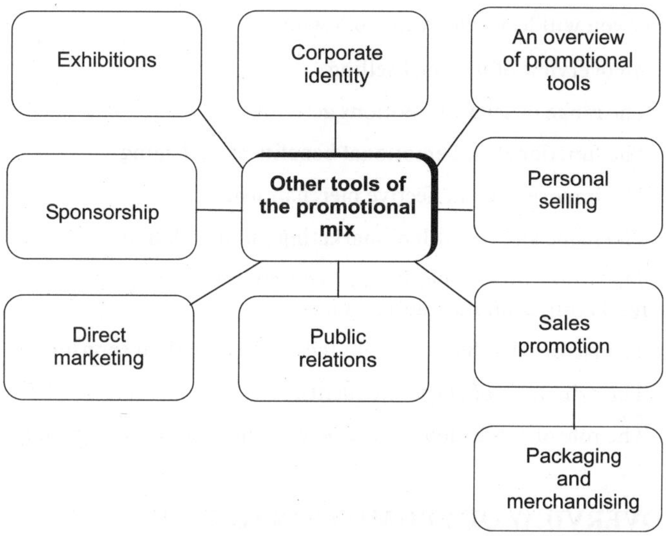

Introduction

This chapter will begin by providing an overview of promotional tools and stressing the importance of personal selling as an integral part of marketing communication. Personal selling is one of the principal areas identified in most descriptions of the promotional mix. Not only is the salesforce an important part of external marketing communications, the salesforce is also an important target group for internal marketing communications to ensure that its members are fully briefed to undertake the marketing communications and selling task they do.

The next section will discuss developments in sales promotions, which is a growth area in the marketing communications mix. Sales promotion's importance to the marketing communications mix should not be underestimated as it adds an extensive range of effective tools to the marketing communications armoury. Packaging will be discussed next as it is widely thought of as the visual identity of the brand and so embodies brand values and differentiates one brand from others.

Merchandising has been included in this section as it incorporates a range of sales promotions activities intended to ensure that products are easily available and prominently and attractively displayed at point of sale.

Public relations follows next and this can be defined as the planned and sustained effort to establish and maintain goodwill and mutual understanding between an organisation and its public. Direct marketing is a marketing system based on individual customer records held on a database, and new developments in database technology have revolutionised the effectiveness of this sector.

Sponsorship is one of the most rapidly growing elements of the marketing mix and yet, while it is one of the most widely used, it is also one of the least well understood. Corporate identity is the means by which corporate personality is projected and this will be evaluated alongside the role of exhibitions.

Your objectives

In this chapter you will learn about the following.

(a) An overview of personal selling

(b) The range of sales promotions activities

(c) The functional and emotional benefits of packaging

(d) The importance of effective merchandising

(e) The scope and breadth of marketing public relations

(f) The role direct marketing communications plays in the integrated marketing communications mix

(g) The factors that have contributed to the growth of sponsorship

(h) The principles of corporate identity

(i) The role of exhibitions in the marketing communications mix

1 AN OVERVIEW OF PROMOTIONAL TOOLS

In this part of the course book, the aim is to make you more familiar with the very broad range of promotional tools and to provide some guidelines for choosing the most appropriate promotional mix. Like any other set of tools the skill of the user is to select and apply the right tool for the particular task in hand. With promotional tools this is not an easy job because usually it is not just one tool that is required but a combination. Indeed, several different combinations could probably achieve the same result.

Having chosen a suite of promotional tools and even allocated them as either primary or supporting, it is important to be able to integrate them into a comprehensive and effective whole. As we shall see, this area of *integrated marketing communications* is becoming more important because of the need to achieve the desired end result cost-effectively.

1.1 The range of promotional tools

The range of promotional tools continues to grow. The variety of media that can be used for above the line campaigns has expanded, both in the printed advertising field and in the broadcast field. There are literally thousands of publications aimed at different target groups. In the personal computer field alone there are hundreds of magazines. In the broadcast field the number of television stations steadily increases through satellite, cable and digital television and the number of commercial radio stations has also grown considerably.

The diagram below shows the range of tools that can be used to influence a customer or potential customer.

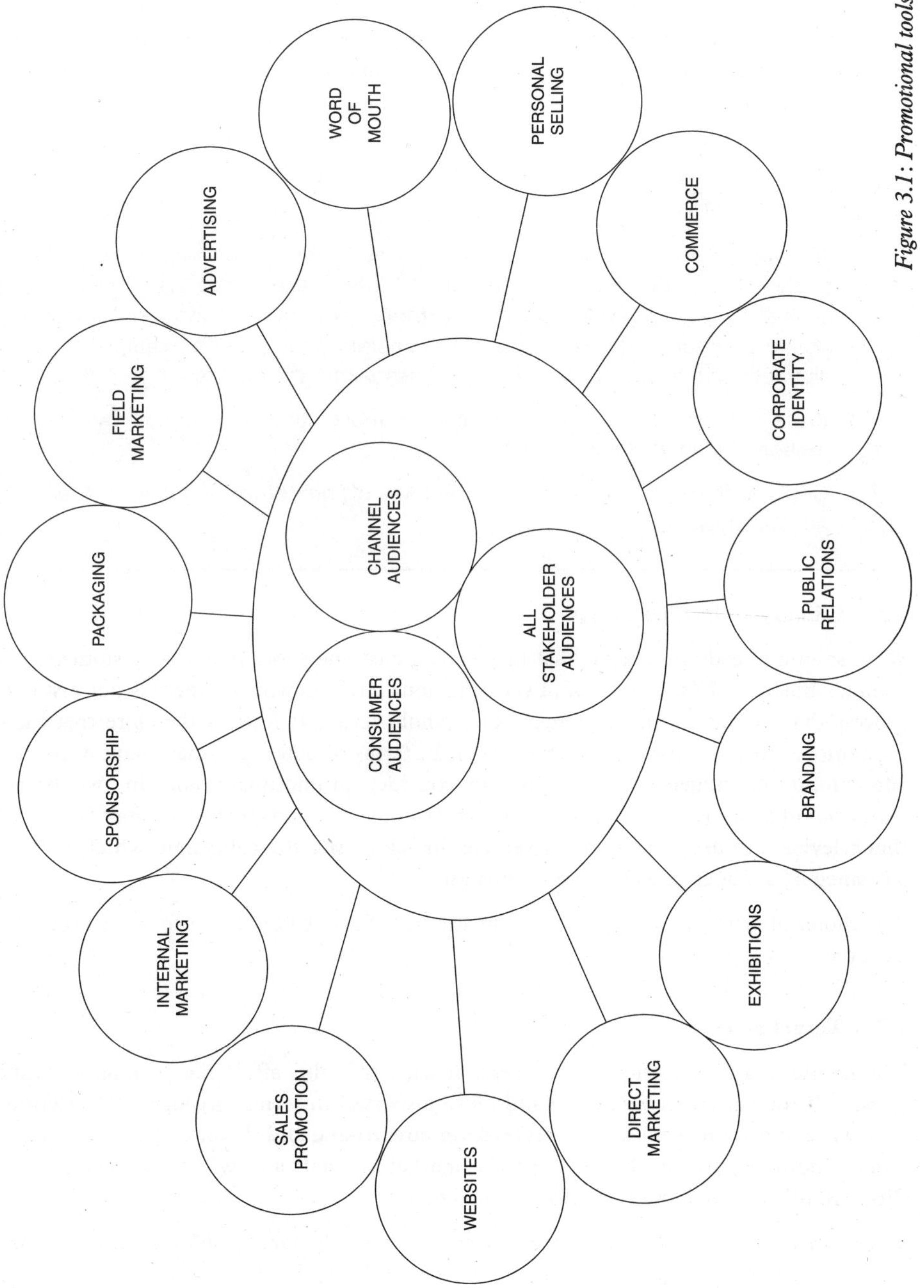

Figure 3.1: Promotional tools

These tools represent the deployment of deliberate and intentional methods calculated to bring about a favourable response in the customer's behaviour. The diagram represents the most obvious promotion methods, though other parts of the marketing mix, including the product itself, pricing, policy and distribution channels, will also have decisive effects.

Activity 1 **(2 hours)**

(a) Actually read your junk mail, wander around the supermarket, read the paper, watch TV, and start collecting those leaflets that are constantly posted through your letterbox. How many examples of the tools shown above can you find? Be on the alert constantly for real-life examples and illustrations that you could use in your assessment answers.

(b) Were you influenced by any of the examples that you found? Did you respond? Can you work out why?

(c) Can you think of (or better, find examples of) any other promotional tools, not shown above?

1.2 Primary and support roles

What should already be clear is that influencing customers and potential customers is a complex business. Discussions of buyer behaviour have shown that there is not just one process that influences the customer but a whole series. It follows therefore that each promotional tool will have a variety of roles. In terms of making management decisions and allocating budgets it is possible to consider promotional tools in two broad categories of **primary** and **support** roles. For example in a consumer campaign it may be that television is used as the main vehicle for launching the campaign, which is then sustained by a longer-lasting poster campaign.

The choice of primary promotion tool can also be influenced by the stage of the product life cycle.

1.3 Target markets

The nature and constitution of the target market will also affect the promotional mix chosen. If the market is very large and quite dispersed in terms of geographic location, then the company may wish to use **television advertising** and national press in order to communicate effectively. However, if the market is small and widely dispersed, then **direct mail** will be a more cost effective method.

In industrial markets, where customers are more easily identifiable but utilise more concentrated distribution channels, personal selling tends to be the preferred communication method. A greater reliance is also placed upon trade press and exhibitions as a means of making contact with the widest possible audience. From time to time however, companies may utilise television as a means of communicating to the target audience.

EXAMPLE

Hewlett Packard has utilised television advertising as a means of communicating in the business-to-business markets. In an attempt to promote their office systems to corporate clients, they realised that the majority of the users of such systems would be office staff and junior managers who could be reached by television. The objective was to build awareness in the minds of this target audience who would then demand these systems within their own companies. Simultaneously, Hewlett Packard were utilising sales personnel, exhibitions and on site demonstrations to target the main influencers of the buying decision-making process within companies.

1.4 Product characteristics

The **attributes** of the product will determine the type of promotional strategy which is employed. If the product is highly technical in nature, then it will require a high degree of personal selling, where potential customers have the opportunity to ask detailed questions about the product. Personal selling will also be utilised to the full when introducing a new product to the market, in attempting to gain adequate distribution and dealer support.

The **price** of the product and its associated image will affect the choice of promotion used. Rolex watches for example, as well as using specified dealers (an example of exclusive distribution), concentrate upon high quality magazines and direct mail to communicate with their existing and potential target groups. There is also an emphasis upon personal service, since the expenditure on such an item is considerable, together with the necessary after sales back-up

Activity 2 **(15 minutes)**

What types of promotional activity will be employed for a product at each stage of the product life cycle? Compare and contrast the differing methods for a consumer product and an industrial product.

2 PERSONAL SELLING

According to Fill (2002), personal selling can be defined as 'An interpersonal communication tool which involved face to face activities undertaken by individuals, often representing an organisation, in order to inform, persuade or remind an individual or group to take appropriate action, as required by the sponsor's representative.'

All organisations have employees with responsibility for contacting and dealing directly with customers and potential customers with a view to selling the company's products. These employees, known as the sales force, provide a vital function to the organisation as they form a direct link to the buyers.

An organisation has a choice as to how it organises itself for selling.

(a) Employ a direct (or company) sales force, consisting of full or part-time paid employees who work exclusively for the company. This type of sales force may, in turn, consist of two groups: inside sales personnel who conduct their business from the company premises via the telephone, or field sales personnel who travel and visit customers.

(b) In contrast, an organisation could employ a contractual sales force, which could comprise sales agents, dealers or brokers who are paid a commission on the sales they generate.

Irrespective of the type of sales force a company may use, the sales force needs the support of other groups within the organisation if it is to operate efficiently and effectively. Kotler (2008) identifies the following groups whose activities impact upon the effectiveness of the sales force.

(a) **Top management** who can be increasingly involved in the selling process, particularly with big orders or key accounts.

(b) **Technical sales personnel** who supply technical information and service to the customer before, during or after the sale of the product.

(c) **Customer service representatives** who provide installation, maintenance and other services to the customer.

(d) **Office staff** including sales analysts, administrators and secretarial staff.

Indeed, Kotler maintains that selling should increasingly be regarded as a team effort involving all these groups.

FOR DISCUSSION

Many selling situations are not one-off situation-specific encounters but long term. This is particularly true in organisational markets where supplier and trade, government or industrial customers work together to create, develop and maintain a network within which both parties thrive.
Gummesson (1987)

2.1 The tasks in the selling process

Personal selling is probably the area of the promotional mix that has the most stereotypes attached to it. The image of the 'travelling salesman' is an enduring one. However, this masks the reality that the term sales representative covers a broad range of positions, which vary tremendously in terms of tasks and responsibilities.

Role	Comment
Order collector	The salesperson's job is predominantly to deal with routine orders normally through telemarketing.
Order taker	The salesperson passively takes orders from the customer. This can be further divided into *inside* order takers, such as shop assistants, or *outside* order takers, such as those salespeople who call on regular customers to take an order periodically. The customer has already been persuaded to use the product, or has been using the product in the past.
Pre-Order caller	The salesperson is not expected or permitted to take an order but is expected to build goodwill or educate the customer in the use of the product. Medical representatives from pharmaceutical companies may fall into this category.
Order supporter	The salesperson's main skill is the application of his technical knowledge relating to the product.
Order getter	The salesperson has to stimulate demand and creatively sell tangible or intangible products.

The 'degree of difficulty' of the salesperson's tasks increases the nearer the person gets to being an Order Getter. However, the art of 'selling' in its narrowest sense is only one of a number of tasks that the salesperson could perform. A salesperson could perform as many as seven different activities.

Activity	Comment
Prospecting	Gathering additional prospective customers in addition to sales leads generated by the company on his behalf.
Communicating	Communicating information to existing and potential customers about the company's products and services can take up a major proportion of the salesperson's time.
Selling	'The art of salesmanship', encompasses approaching the customer, presenting, answering objections and closing the sale.
Servicing	A salesperson may provide various services to the customer, such as consulting about their problems, rendering technical assistance, arranging finance and expediting delivery.
Information gathering	The salesperson can be a very useful source of marketing intelligence because of their links with the end customer. Many salespeople are responsible for supplying regular reports on competitive activity within their particular sales area.
Allocating	The salesperson may assist in evaluating customer profitability and creditworthiness, and may also have to control the allocation of products to customers in times of product shortages.
Shaping	An increasingly important role is to help build and sustain relationships with major customers.

While a salesperson may engage in all these tasks from time to time, the mix of tasks will vary according to the purchase decision process, company marketing strategy and the overall economic conditions of the time. For example, with regard to the influence that the buying decision process may have on the salesperson's mix of tasks, the skills needed for a straight rebuy situation (where the customer has bought the same product under the same conditions of sale in the past) will be totally different from those required to develop a new account.

Salesforce activity must also be undertaken within the context of the organisation's overall marketing strategy.

(a) For example, if the organisation pursues a 'pull' strategy, relying on massive consumer advertising to draw customers into the premises of marketing intermediaries to ask for the brands, then the role of the sales force may primarily be a servicing one, ensuring that retailers carry sufficient stock, allocate adequate shelf space for display and co-operate in sales promotion programmes.

(b) Conversely, with a 'push' strategy, the organisation will rely primarily on the sales force to sell the brands to the marketing intermediaries who will then assume the main responsibility for selling on the brands to the end customer.

The mix of a salesperson's tasks may vary with the prevailing economic conditions. For example, in times of product shortage the art of selling may not be as important and one could argue that the sales force are redundant. However, such a view neglects the other roles of the salesperson that will be of greater importance in such circumstances, such as allocating, counselling customers, communicating company policy to customers and perhaps selling other products that are not in short supply.

FOR DISCUSSION

The prime responsibility of an account manager at Colgate-Palmolive is to maintain and develop business partnerships with major multiple retailer accounts. These relationships in some cases go back over many years. In order to achieve this, the emphasis is on co-operation and customer development through working together in such areas as category management, logistics and merchandising. The account manager must be able to analyse brand and category information in order to develop plans that will help sales of Colgate's personal and household care products. Any account manager who sought short-term sales at the expense of customer trust and goodwill would not benefit Colgate-Palmolive's long-term plans for the account.

---

3 SALES PROMOTION

Definition

> The Institute of Sales Promotion (ISP) defines **sales promotion** as 'a range of tactical marketing techniques, designed within a strategic marketing framework, to add value to a product or service, in order to achieve a specific sales and marketing objective.'

(a) Sales promotion encompasses a range of techniques appropriate for targeting consumers, for instance via price reductions, competitions or gifts with purchases. However, trade and sales force incentives are also implied under the general heading of sales promotion. It typifies what is generally thought of as below-the-line.

(b) Sales promotion is viewed by the ISP as a tactical promotional tool. The majority of companies will use sales promotion as a means of achieving a short-term objective, for instance to gain short-term sales volume or to encourage trial and brand switching by a rival manufacturer's consumers.

(c) Although it is used as a tactical tool, sales promotion works within a strategic marketing framework. Sales promotion should not start with a good idea that came to the Sales Director while in the bath, but with due regard to the strategic objectives for the brand, and the synergies that can brought about through a carefully designed promotional activity.

(d) Sales promotion always seeks to add value to a product or service. Thus consumers are offered something extra for their purchase, or the chance to obtain something extra.

Sales promotion includes the notion of both sales pull and sales push techniques. As we have seen, sales pull techniques incentivise the consumer to buy, thus pulling sales through the chain of distribution via consumer demand. Sales push techniques either encourage the salesforce to sell products, or prompt the trade intermediary to buy, ensuring the distribution pipeline is well loaded, and sales are pushed through the distribution chain.

A vast amount if money is spent on sales promotion. Peattie and Peattie (1993) explain the growth in sales promotion as follows.

(a) Increased impulse purchasing
(b) Sales promotions are becoming respectable
(c) The rising cost of advertising and advertising clutter
(d) Shortening time horizons
(e) Competitor activities
(f) Relative ease of measurability

Definition

> **Below-the-line communications:** Marketing communications that make use of the non-commission paying media.

Be aware of the potential for confusion between the terms promotion (used as a synonym for communication techniques in general) and sales promotion (which is a specialist term reserved for the specific techniques described in this chapter).

FOR DISCUSSION

The advertising to sales promotion ratio (30:70) suggests that more money is spent on sales promotion activities than on all forms of advertising.

3.1 Sales promotion objectives

Examples of consumer sales promotion objectives.

(a) Increase awareness and interest amongst target audiences.

(b) Achieve a switch in buying behaviour from competitor brands to your company's brand.

(c) Incentivise consumers to make a forward purchase of your brand, thus shutting out competitor purchase opportunities.

(d) Increase display space allocated to your brand in store.

(e) Smooth seasonal dips in demand for your product.

(f) Generate a consumer database from mail-in applications.

Sales promotion objectives will link into overarching marketing and marketing communications objectives.

Marketing objective	To increase brand X market share by 2 percentage points in the period January to December 2010
Marketing communications objective	To contribute to brand share gain of 2% in 2010 by increasing awareness of X from 50% to 70% among target consumers.
Sales promotion objective	To encourage trial of brand X among target consumers by offering a guaranteed incentive to purchase.

FOR DISCUSSION

As an incentive to persuade parents to enquire about children's savings plans, Aberdeen Asset Management offered a free Thomas The Tank Engine video. The company was somewhat taken aback, however, when it received over 40,000 enquiries in one month. Things got even worse when the company then offered a second video to customers who actually invested in the plans. Staff found that the warehouse, which normally deals with fund managers' reports, was suddenly crammed with thousands of videos. The number of warehouse staff had to be doubled. *Dow (2001)*

3.2 Sales promotion activities

There is a vast array of possible activities that can be classified as sales promotion. These include:

Consumer

- Sampling
- Couponing
- Premiums
- Money off
- Bonus packs
- Loyalty schemes
- Branded packs
- Contests
- Cause-related
- Merchandising
- Point of sale
- Information

Trade

- Consumer promotions
- Allowances
- Contests and incentives
- Point of sale material and merchandising
- Sampling
- Gifts and free merchandise
- Information

Loyalty schemes

Loyalty in customers is highly prized: loyalty schemes are intended to promote it, usually by providing a benefit in return for further purchases. This may be directly cash-related, such as a discount on a supermarket bill, as provided by Sainsbury's on Nectar points, or something less tangible, such as a frequent flyer lounge.

Loyalty schemes' longer-term effectiveness has been questioned because they are easy to imitate; when each firm competing for a given segment has a scheme, none has an advantage, but everyone's costs have been increased. Costs can be very high indeed. Shell spent £20 million on hardware and software to support its Smart card (Jobber, 2007).

Also, competing schemes can actually encourage disloyalty, with customers shopping around for the one that offers the best benefits.

Jobber (2007) suggests that marketing managers should examine loyalty schemes carefully.

(a) How much loyalty can actually be expected in the market as it exists?

(b) What are the true costs?

(c) Does focussing on a select group of customers encourage neglect of the rest?

Activity 3 **(30 minutes)**

Tesco issues a type of loyalty card which shoppers present when they reach the check-out. Points are awarded for sums spent over a minimum amount and these are added up each quarter. Money-off vouchers to be used against future grocery bills and discounts worth four times the cash value for a further range of benefits are sent to the shopper's home. Other companies, such as Sainsbury, participate in a scheme involving a group of companies, called the Nectar card, whereby shoppers gain Nectar points from transactions in different shops. Compare and contrast these schemes.

4 PACKAGING AND MERCHANDISING

Packaging is a marketing tool that combines graphic design with marketing concepts to create an identity for the brand. An ideal package is one which brings to the customer's mind the essence of what the brand is all about whenever and wherever it is seen. It can be effectively used to influence customer choice at the point of sale in terms of reducing the uncertainty and risk inherent in product choice and it acts as a tangible reminder at the point of sale.

4.1 The benefits of packaging

Packaging comprises a number of physical or functional benefits including the storage of the product, the extension of the product's shelf life, the facilitation of physical storage, the protection of the product during distribution, the communication of usage information and the assurance of consistent quality.

Emotional and psychological benefits of packaging include:

(a) a communication tool to express brand values
(b) aesthetically pleasing
(c) strong visual impact
(d) a living expression of what the brand represents
(e) adds value from a consumer's perspective
(f) a reminder
(g) provides cues to express loyalty
(h) creates an emotional link with the target audience

4.2 Packaging features

To achieve visual impact, packaging should attract the eye through colour and design. Listed below are the most important features of packaging:

Feature	Description
Colour	Powerful emotional signals, symbolic, eg Cadbury's purple is associated with luxury
Typography	Communicates the product image, eg ornate script implies tradition and sophistication
Logo	Signifies the brand's individuality and unique image, eg Coca-Cola and Kelloggs
Type/material	Recyclable, biodegradable, eg boxes, cartons, bags, bottles, tubes, cans, jars etc
Shape and structure	Used to attract attention, eg Jif's yellow lemon and character children's yoghurt
Label or mark	Varies with types and materials of packages, can be printed on the package or other materials
Size	Encourage product usage

EXAMPLE

For many years green packaging would never have been used for meat products because of connotations associated with mould. Nowadays the colour has been accepted as more environmentally friendly and as a result it has been used to package organic and free-range meats.

FOR DISCUSSION

How can packaging impact on a consumer's perceptual process?

4.3 Sales promotion and packaging

Packaging is normally used with sales promotion, in the special or non-routine events when a brand is needing a boost, eg seasonal, sale. Six types of promotional packages are described below.

Package	Characteristic
Money-off pack	Announced on-pack
Bonus size pack	Standard price but additional content
Coupon pack	Packed into the container itself
Pack-on premium	New outer case or shrink wrapping to include for example a smaller version
Pack-in premium	Eg, a free mug with coffee
Self-liquidator	Buying the product at a reduced price by sending in labels, tokens or receipts

Activity 4 **(10 minutes)**

Select a fast moving consumer goods package and associated press advertisement. Do the packaging components reflect/enhance the brand's image? If so, how?

FOR DISCUSSION

McVitie's *(www.unitedbiscuts.co.uk)* has managed to differentiate its Jaffa Cakes *(www.jaffacakes.co.uk)* brand from supermarket brands by producing innovative packaging for mini-jaffa cakes. The pack consists of six individually sealed plastic segments, joined by perforations which can be easily separated. The pack is bright orange, with the texture of orange peel to emphasise the nature of the product. Each segment provides a portion of Jaffa Cake and can be packed into a lunch box or just used as a convenient snack. Meanwhile the other five segments remain sealed and therefore stay fresh until required.

4.4 Merchandising

Merchandising can be defined as the range of sales promotions activities intended to ensure that products are easily available, and prominently and attractively displayed at point of sale. It is also used to describe the activity of making promotional products available, such as those associated with new film releases, eg calendars, figurines, novelty items etc.

Many organisations employ merchandisers whose task it is to develop displays and ensure that products are appropriately displayed. Most retailers use planograms to assist in shelf display and layout. They are especially important if retailers wish to ensure consistency of display in all stores.

Definition

> **Planogram**: Diagrams or plans showing store and shelf layout.

EXAMPLE

As was mentioned earlier, a phenomenal growth area in merchandising has been that associated with new film releases. This is especially so for Disney , who have extensive merchandising experience. Examples of films which have developed merchandise include Star Wars, The Lion King, Titanic and, of course, the Harry Potter phenomenon. Topshop used film releases to great effect by providing clothing for use in films such as Bridget Jones' Diary and then merchandising the range in-store at the time of release.

---

5 PUBLIC RELATIONS

Definition

> The Institute of Public Relations has defined **PR** as 'the planned and sustained effort to establish and maintain goodwill and mutual understanding between an organisation and its publics'.

The Public Relations Consultants Association (PRCA) says that:

> 'Public relations is the name given to the managed process of communication between one group and another. In its purest form it has nothing to do with marketing, advertising or 'commercialism'. It will, however, often promote one group's endeavours to persuade another group to its point of view and it will use a number of different methods, other than (although often alongside) advertising to achieve this aim.'

5.1 Public relations

The problem faced is invariably one of definition in terms of the aims and activities that PR encompasses. These embrace many groups of people known as publics and extend from:

- Advice and counselling
- Relations with employees during redundancy and closure
- Relations with the local community and interest groups
- Lobbying
- Developing goodwill among all publics
- Monitoring public opinion

to:

- Publicity
- Sponsorship and donations
- Dealing with negative publicity and crises

- The preparation of press releases and publications
- Helping to develop and maintain corporate image
- Arranging events

Definition

> **Publics**: Refers to the many target audiences that communications may be focused towards, eg customers, influencers, media, employees, pressure groups etc.

EXAMPLE

Before being placed into administration by the UK government, Railtrack struggled unsuccessfully to regain its reputation and the trust of the rail regulator, investors, train operators, the travelling public and the government. The Paddington rail accident followed by the derailment at Hatfield were significant blows to the confidence placed in Railtrack and the barrage of press coverage following these accidents helped to undermine any recovery. The company became embroiled in crisis PR from which it could not recover. Saying 'Sorry' was not enough to regain confidence against claims of complacency and ineffective management. Its reputation sank so low that the government was faced with little choice but to intervene.

From the list of activities above it can be seen that the scope of **public relations activity,** if implemented effectively, should **embrace the whole organisation.** A number of criteria have been put forward in an attempt to define what constitutes 'excellent' public relations within an organisation, many of which relate to the role and position of the public relations department within the organisation.

(a) Programmes should be managed strategically.

(b) There should be a single integrated public relations department.

(c) Public relations managers should report directly to senior management.

(d) Public relations should be a separate function from marketing.

(e) The senior public relations person should be a member of the organisation's dominant coalition.

(f) Communication should adhere to the 'two-way symmetrical model'.

5.2 Four models of PR

This last factor relates to the way in which public relations is practised. Given the diversity of the role of PR as emphasised above, it is logical to consider different ways in which PR could be practised. A framework for considering this has been propounded by Grunig and Hunt, *Managing Public Relations* (1984), who suggest that there are four models of public relations practice. Each model will be considered in turn.

5.3 Press agency/publicity

The role of PR is primarily one of **propaganda,** spreading the faith of the organisation, often through incomplete, half-true or distorted information. Communication is one-way, from the organisation to its publics: essentially telling the publics the information the organisation wants them to hear.

5.4 Public information

In this model the role of PR is the dissemination of **information,** not necessarily with a persuasive intent. As Grunig and Hunt state, 'the public relations person functions essentially as a journalist in residence, whose job it is to report objectively information about his organisation to the public'. Like the first model, this type of communication is one-way, but it does differ in the fact that public information specialists feel obliged to present a complete picture of the organisation they represent, whereas the press agency specialists do not. The public information model of PR is typified by government information promotions for such issues as health, crime prevention and education.

5.5 Two-way asymmetric

Grunig and Hunt describe the main function of the two-way asymmetric model as scientific persuasion, using social science theory and research about attitudes and behaviour to persuade publics to accept the organisation's point of view and to behave in a way that supports the organisation. The aim is to achieve the maximum change in attitudes and behaviour. However, while the **communication is two-way** in that there is a flow of information back to the organisation from the publics, this flow is asymmetric because the response to this feedback from the publics is to improve the effectiveness of the outgoing communication rather than to stimulate a change in the message *content*, reflecting change within the organisation.

Definition

> **Two-way asymmetric communications** – communications from a sender to a receiver with little or delayed feedback, producing a non-direct dialogue.

5.6 Two-way symmetric

In the two-way symmetric model the **PR practitioner serves as a mediator between the organisation and its publics** with the aim of facilitating mutual understanding between the two. The communication is therefore more of a dialogue than a monologue. If persuasion occurs it is as likely to persuade the organisation's management to change its attitude as it is to persuade the publics to change theirs. In an ideal situation, both management and publics will change their attitudes or behaviour, but if the PR function has brought the two sides together, and as long as both sides communicate well enough to understand the position of the other, then the PR effort will have been successful.

The two-way symmetric model is seen as the ideal that should be aspired to, but Grunig and Hunt recognise that only a minority of companies will achieve it.

Public relations is, therefore, the **management of an organisation's reputation with its publics** and this management involves a close consideration of the relationships involved. The organisation can be either reactive or proactive in its management of these relationships.

(a) **Reactive PR** is primarily concerned with the communication of what has happened and responding to factors affecting the organisation. It is primarily defensive, with little or no responsibility for influencing policies that may change the perceptions of the organisation among its publics. The publics with which the PR function communicates are largely those with whom it is in direct contact and the scope of PR activities is relatively narrow, with the emphasis on media relations and publications.

(b) In contrast, **proactive public relations practitioners** have a much wider role and thus have a far greater influence on overall organisational strategy. They will communicate with a broad range of publics, not only those with whom they are in direct contact but also those who have the potential to influence the future plans of the organisation. The scope of the activities of the PR function is much wider, encompassing communications activities in their entirety, counselling and strategic planning.

FOR DISCUSSION

Publicity can create greater credibility than other forms of promotion. Publicity happens when the media voluntarily decide to talk about an organisation and its commercial activities.

5.7 Classification of techniques

Inevitably some techniques will be more appropriate in certain circumstances with certain types of publics than others. It is possible, therefore, to classify the different types of techniques or media according to the type of project areas in which they appear to be most effective. The most frequently used techniques are as follows.

(a) **Consumer marketing support area techniques**

(i) Consumer and trade press releases
(ii) Product/service literature
(iii) Promotional videos
(iv) Special events (in-store competitions, celebrity store openings)
(v) Consumer exhibitions
(vi) In-house magazines for sales staff, customers and/or trade
(vii) Salesforce/distributor incentive schemes
(viii) Sport, and to a lesser extent, arts sponsorships
(ix) Advertorials

(b) **Business-to-Business communication area techniques**

(i) Corporate identity design
(ii) Corporate literature
(iii) Corporate advertising
(iv) Trade and general press relations, possibly on a national or international basis
(v) Corporate and product videos
(vi) Direct mailings
(vii) Sports and arts sponsorships
(viii) Trade exhibitions

(c) **Internal/employee communications area techniques**

- (i) In-house magazines and employee newsletters
- (ii) Employee relations videos
- (iii) Formal employee communications networks and channels for feedback
- (iv) Recruitment exhibitions/conferences
- (v) Speech writing for executives
- (vi) Company notice boards
- (vii) Briefing meetings

(d) **Corporate, external and public affairs area techniques**

- (i) Corporate literature
- (ii) Corporate social responsibility programmes, community involvement
- (iii) Trade, local, national and possibly international media relations
- (iv) Issues tracking
- (v) Management counselling
- (vi) Local or central government lobbying
- (vii) Industrial lobbying
- (viii) Facility visits
- (ix) Local/national sponsorships

(e) **Financial public relations area techniques**

- (i) Financial media relations on both a national and international basis
- (ii) Design of annual and interim reports
- (iii) Facility visits for analysts, brokers, fund managers, etc
- (iv) Organising shareholder meetings
- (v) Shareholder tracking research

While this is not a comprehensive list it does give an indication of the many types of PR techniques that can be used in various circumstances and how certain techniques will re-occur in various settings. Media relations, for example, is used in virtually all areas of activity.

FOR DISCUSSION

Public relations should not only be thought of in the context of corporate promotions, it has a role in product promotions too.

EXAMPLES

The following cases are found on the website of a leading PR consultancy.

'Companies often come to Charles Barker for political intelligence to enable them to stay one step ahead of the game. Others require a comprehensive strategy in order to amend or oppose a proposed government initiative. Yet others wish to promote a policy or business initiative. In all cases, we work closely with our clients to ensure that their viewpoint is expressed at all appropriate occasions during consultative periods and to all relevant political and official audiences.

Facility visits

Sellafield Nuclear Plant run by British Nuclear Fuels Limited has a visitors' information centre. This plays an important role as part of its promotional and PR activity.

Media conferences

When painkiller, Tylenol was deliberately contaminated with a poison by an extortionist, Johnson & Johnson, the manufacturer, held a media conference as a means of maintaining confidence and quickly and effectively conveying how it was handling the situation. Despite potentially catastrophic consequences, the company was praised for its actions.

---

6 DIRECT MARKETING

Peter Drucker said 'There is only one valid definition of business purpose: *to create a customer*.' (*Drucker* (*1955*). In brief, the aims of direct marketing are to acquire and retain customers. Here are two further definitions.

Definition

The Institute of Direct Marketing in the UK defines **direct marketing** as 'The planned recording, analysis and tracking of customer behaviour to develop relational marketing strategies'.

The Direct Marketing Association in the US define direct marketing as 'An interactive system of marketing which uses one or more advertising media to effect a measurable response and/or transaction at any location'.

Definition

Database: Collection of data, usually on computer, stored to provide useful, convenient and interactive access to information.

It is worth studying these definitions and noting some key words and phrases.

Response	Direct marketing is about getting people to send in coupons, or make telephone calls in response to invitations and offers.
Interactive	It is a two-way process, involving the supplier and the customer.
Relationship	It is in many instances an on-going process of selling again and again to the same customer.

Recording and analysis	Response data are collected and analysed so that the most cost-effective procedures may be arrived at. Direct marketing has been called 'marketing with numbers'. It aims to take the waste out of marketing.
Strategy	Direct marketing should not be seen merely as a 'quick fix', a 'one-off mailing', a promotional device. It should be seen as a part of a comprehensive plan stemming from clearly formulated objectives.

Direct marketing helps create and develop direct relationships between you and each of your prospects, between the consumer and the company on an individual basis. It is a form of direct supply, embracing both a variety of alternative **media channels** (like direct mail), and a choice of **distribution channels** (like mail order). Because direct marketing removes all channel intermediaries apart from the advertising medium and the delivery medium, there are no resellers, therefore avoiding loss of control and loss of revenue.

Definition

> **Relationship marketing** concerns the shifting from activities of attracting customers to activities concerned with current customers and how to retain them. Customer retention is critical since small changes in retention rates have significant effects on future revenues. (*Jobber*, 2004)

EXAMPLE

The Direct Marketing Association holds an awards evening each year. A number of winning categories exist but the Grand Prix selects the winner amongst all gold medallists. The 2007 Grand Prix winner was financial services provider First Direct who created a mail pack described by the judges as 'strong and insightful'. The bank's target audience is mostly in their thirties and forties and so First Direct aimed to create a campaign which reminded them of their childhood. The mail which generated a 6.3 per cent response rate included the children's toy Fuzzy Felt with the line: 'Does your bank give you that warm and fuzzy feeling?' in order to encourage customers to switch from other banks. Fifty-seven per cent of those responding to the mail were converted – meaning that they opened a First Direct account.

FOR DISCUSSION

Direct marketing communications is not restricted to direct mail. Potentially all media can utilise a direct function, eg direct response TV advertising, direct response radio advertising, Internet communications, direct response billboards.

6.1 Components of direct marketing

Direct marketing encompasses a wide range of media and distribution opportunities.

- Television
- Radio
- Direct mail
- Direct response advertising
- Telemarketing
- Statement stuffers
- Inserts
- Take-ones
- Electronic media
- Door to door
- Mail order
- Computerised home shopping
- Home shopping networks

In developing a comprehensive direct marketing strategy, organisations will often utilise a range of different yet complementary techniques.

Direct mail tends to be the main medium of direct response advertising. It has become the synonym for it. The reasons for this is that other major media, newspapers and magazines, are familiar to people in advertising in other contexts. Newspaper ads can include coupons to fill out and return, and radio and TV can give a phone number to ring (DRTV is now very common). However, direct mail has a number of strengths as a direct response medium.

(a) The advertiser can target down to **individual level.**

(b) The communication can **be personalised**. Known data about the individual can be used, while modern printing techniques mean that parts of a letter can be altered to accommodate this.

(c) The medium is good **for reinforcing interest stimulated by other media** such as TV. It can supply the response mechanism (a coupon) which is not yet available in that medium.

(d) The opportunity to use **different creative formats** is almost unlimited.

(e) **Testing potential is sophisticated**: a limited number of items can be sent out to a 'test' cell and the results can be evaluated. As success is achieved, so the mailing campaign can be rolled out.

The cornerstone upon which the direct mailing is based, however, is **the mailing list**. It is far and away the most important element in the list of variables, which also include the offer, timing and creative content.

FOR DISCUSSION

Be wary of 'average response rates'. Response rates vary widely by industry sector, mailing list, creative and offer. The Direct Mail Information Service suggest that response rates overall average 10%. They range from 3.5% for credit cards to over 22% for brown goods such as TVs and hi-fis.

EXAMPLE: DATABASE APPLICATIONS

Computers now have the capacity to operate in three new ways which will enable businesses to operate in a totally different dimension.

'Customers can be tracked individually. Thousands of pieces of information about each of millions of customers can be stored and accessed economically.

Companies and customers can interact through, for example, phones, mail, E-mail and interactive kiosks. ... for the first time since the invention of mass marketing, 'companies will be hearing from individual customers in a cost-efficient manner'.

Computers allow companies to match their production processes to what they learn from their individual customers – a process known as 'mass customisation' which Peppers explains as 'the cost-efficient mass production of products and services in lot sizes of one'.

There are many examples of companies which are already employing or experimenting with these ideas. In the US Levi Strauss, the jeans company, is taking measurements and preferences from female customers to produce exact-fitting garments. The customisation is currently limited to one line of jeans but ... the approach 'offers the company tremendous opportunities for building learning relationships'.

The Ritz-Carlton hotel chain has trained staff throughout the organisation to jot down customer details at every opportunity on a 'guest preference pad'.

The result, he says, could be the following: 'You stay at the Ritz-Carlton in Cancun, Mexico, call room service for dinner, and request an ice cube in your glass of white wine. Months later, when you stay at the Ritz-Carlton in Naples, Florida, and order a glass of white wine from room service, you will almost certainly be asked if you would like an ice cube in it.'

Financial Times

FOR DISCUSSION

In direct marketing communications, the creative approach, although important, has less effect on response rates than the targeting, the offer and incentive and the media utilised. Do you agree?

6.2 Telemarketing as an integrated marketing activity

Role of telemarketing

(a) **Building, maintaining, cleaning and updating databases.** The telephone allows for accurate data-gathering by compiling relevant information on customers and prospects, and selecting appropriate target groups for specific product offerings.

(b) **Market evaluation and test marketing**. Almost any feature of a market can be measured and tested by telephone. Feedback is immediate so response can be targeted quickly to exploit market knowledge.

(c) **Dealer support.** Leads can be passed on to the nearest dealer who is provided with full details.

(d) **Traffic generation**. The telephone, combined with postal invitations, is the most cost effective way of screening leads and encouraging attendance at promotional events.

(e) **Direct sales and account servicing**. The telephone can be used at all stages of the relationship with the prospects and customers. This includes lead generation, establishing buying potential for appropriate follow-up and defining the decision-making process.

(f) **Customer care and loyalty building**. Every telephone contact opportunity can demonstrate to customers that they are valued.

(g) **Crisis management**. If, for example, there is a consumer scare, immediate action is essential to minimise commercial damage. A dedicated hotline number can be advertised to provide information and advice.

Product placement

Product placement is defined as the inclusion of, or reference to, a product or service within the programme in return for payment or other valuable consideration to the programme maker. Both the ITC and BBC are finding it increasingly difficult to control and hard to prove. It is believed that it began in 1951; in the film *The African Queen*, Katherine Hepburn was paid to toss Gordon's Gin overboard. The global product placement industry is estimated to be worth as much as $40 billion.

FOR DISCUSSION

The James Bond film franchise has grossed more than $3 billion worldwide since Dr No in 1962. This makes it the most successful series of films ever made, reaching millions worldwide through cinema release and in-home media.

Die Another Day's Los Angeles and London premieres followed years of complex negotiations between the film's producers and scores of international brands. The strategic placement of products in the film as well as subsequent promotional spin-offs, is rumoured to have gone a long way towards subsidising its $100 million production budget.

Brands featured include:

British Airways
Kodak
Omega watches
Samsonite luggage
Finlandia vodka
Aston Martin
Jaguar
Sony

(*Burt*, 2002)

In Casino Royale, Omega watches capitalised even further on the Bond franchise. Other films where product placement has been highly visible are Tom Hanks' Castaway which heavily featured FedEx, and Jerry Maguire, a film about sport sponsorship which provided ample opportunity for placement. The chocolate brand Galaxy used placement in an integrated way when they used the second Bridget Jones' Diary film. The chocolate bar featured heavily in a key scene and was followed-up with a sampling activity where cinema-goers were handed a bar as they left the film.

Activity 5

Look out for example of programme sponsorship on TV and radio and product placement in the cinema, on TV and radio. Identify how they are being used and how appropriate their use seems to be. How effective do you think your examples of programme sponsorship and product placement are and in what ways do you think the sponsors have benefited?

Activity 6 **(20 minutes)**

Collect a direct response press or magazine advertisement or a piece of direct mail. Using the AIMRITE framework, critically appraise the media choice made. How could the communication be improved?

7 SPONSORSHIP

Sponsorship can be defined as a contribution to an activity or organisation by another. Although sponsorship may be purely altruistic, it is normally undertaken with the expectations of achieving benefit for the sponsor, eg in achieving corporate or marketing objectives.

7.1 Growth of sponsorship

The growth of sponsorship as a form of marketing communication can be attributed to a number of factors. These include:

(a) Concern over traditional promotional methods, ie media fragmentation and clutter

(b) Creation of favourable associations

(c) Overcome linguistic/cultural barriers

(d) Wide/multiple target audience appeal

(e) Overcome legal barriers

(f) Selective targeting

FOR DISCUSSION

Where legal constraints prohibit the promotion of products (eg tobacco) using other forms of marketing communications, sponsorship can be used to overcome some of their limitations.

7.2 Benefits and risks of sponsorship

One of the benefits attributed to sponsorship is that it can be more efficient than other forms of marketing communication because it can generate both audience appeal and link the values of the sponsored entity to the sponsor.

Other benefits may include community image building where a small business may sponsor a local football team by providing their strip emblazoned with their logo.

Sponsorship also appeals to corporations as a marketing communications medium because it can be tied to other marketing activities, eg providing a free sample of a sports energy drink at a sponsored event. Corporate sponsorships of many art and cultural events and sports such as Wimbledon are frequently used for corporate hospitality opportunities

---

FOR DISCUSSION

It is important to select the appropriate sponsorship deal to ensure synergy between the sponsor and the sponsored. Sponsorship deals, particularly with individuals, can go wrong due to unforeseen circumstances.

The potential risks associated with sponsorship include negative associations where perhaps a sports team does not perform well. Clutter is a particular issue in sports such as Formula 1 where a vehicle may have a number of different corporate sponsors. Sponsorship is also risky because any benefits are difficult to evaluate.

FOR DISCUSSION

Using celebrity association to develop brand personalities is a common but high risk tactic. When Angus Deayton, presenter of the BBC's popular Have I Got News For You, was announced as the new face of Barclaycard advertising in April 2001, he was described by the marketing directors as 'the perfect match for Barclaycard – intelligent, understated, yet always commanding respect'. But this respect proved to be short-lived. In October 2002 he was finally sacked from the high profile TV show following a series of Sunday Tabloid newspaper allegations of drug taking. *(http://news.bbc.co.uk)*

Kate Moss is another celebrity dropped by sponsors following reported allegations of drug use. Her raised and more successful exiting profile, however, meant that not all sponsors distanced themselves from her at the time of the allegations although Burberry and Chanel did.

Why do you think Burberry and Chanel dropped Kate Moss following drug allegations but Rimmel and Virgin didn't?

7.3 Sponsorship developments

Three aspects of sponsorship which have grown markedly in recent years are broadcast sponsorship, product placement and cause-related marketing.

A programme is deemed to be sponsored if any or part of its costs of production or transmission is met by an organisation or person, other than the broadcaster or producer. This is exemplified by Harveys' sponsorship of Coronation Street. Radio sponsorship has also increased. Pepsi took over as sponsors of The Network Chart Show in August 1993 from Nescafe, with a complete overhaul of the original show's format. After 9 successful years, in late 2002, Pepsi announced the termination of their sponsorship of the show.

In January 2003, the show became Hit40UK, and coincided with launch of the ill-fated rival chart show: the Smash Hits! Chart. On 14 June 2009, Hit40UK became The Big Top 40 Show, powered by iTunes.

Organisations have a long history of giving to charitable causes. This type of sponsorship (sometimes referred to as CRM – cause related marketing), involves a firm aligning itself to a particular charitable cause or foundation, and supporting it either financially, or donating staff time and/or product. CRM allows firms to portray themselves as caring.

7.4 Ambush marketing

Ambush marketing involves a firm, often a competitor, attempting to deflect attention from another sponsor onto itself.

Definition

> **Ambush marketing** is the term used to refer to a company's intentional effort to weaken or ambush its competitor's official sponsorship by engaging in promotions or advertising that seek to confuse the buying public as to which company really holds official sponsorship rights.

There are various ambush strategies that a firm can employ. The first is to sponsor the media coverage of the event but not the event itself. Second, they could sponsor a sub-category within a particular event, eg a horse race on Gold Cup day and then heavily market the association. They could sponsor an individual such as a footballer and then run advertisements during the main event. Finally, a company could run an advertisement campaign that features the type of activity being sponsored but not the actual event.

FOR DISCUSSION

The major reason for event sponsorship is to indulge senior management in their favourite pastime. Is this a valid opinion?

---

8 EXHIBITIONS

Exhibitions and trade shows provide a temporary forum for sellers of a product category to exhibit and demonstrate their products to prospective buyers. Some exhibitions exist as marketplaces where buyers and sellers meet, other exist purely as promotional vehicles, eg London Motor Show. Some exhibitions are open to the public, eg BBC Good Food Show, while others are business-to-business vehicles, eg Concrete Today. These events can take many forms from in-store tasting demonstrations, to conferences, to very large international trade and consumer shows such as the International Spring Fair at the National Exhibition Centre in Birmingham.

8.1 Reasons for exhibiting

One important role of exhibitions and trade shows is to increase sales either directly on the stand or through follow-up activity. Other reasons include:

- Enhance company image
- Interact with customer
- Promote existing products
- Launch new products
- Obtain competitor intelligence
- Enhance personal morale
- Interact with distributors

8.2 Planning exhibitions

Although exhibitions can be expensive activities, many firms do not put adequate time and effort into planning. Here are the recommended stages.

1. Set objectives
2. Select which exhibition to attend
3. Plan for staffing the stand
4. Plan support promotions
5. Decide stand layout and currents
6. Plan follow-up activities
7. Plan the project-logistics
8. Evaluate and follow-up

FOR DISCUSSION

Sharwoods, the Indian, Thai and Chinese food manufacturer, sells into both retail and wholesale channels and uses exhibitions as an integral part of its strategy. For each show, it sets specific, measurable targets and the main priority is to encourage tasting for retail and consumers, an experience that is difficult to achieve through any other medium. The Chef demonstrations are very powerful for attracting visitors to the stand, as is free tasting. It attends fine food and ethnic food fairs as well as consumer events, with the aim of showcasing new products and generating new sales from the new trade contacts made.

Activity 7

Visit an exhibition. Carefully observe and evaluate all the activities that are going on. Consider the organisation of the exhibition as a whole; the number of stands, layout, visitor attendance, exhibitor attendance, promotional materials, atmosphere and all supporting services, eg catering. Evaluate the event from a visitor's perspective.

9 CORPORATE IDENTITY

The situation analysis may have uncovered issues concerning the way the organisation is perceived by a range of stakeholders, or **negative attitudes** towards the organisation, perhaps as a result of an **ethical issue or crisis that struck the company** and the associated **media comment**. In these circumstances part of the objectives of the marketing communications strategy will be to correct or adjust the perception or attitude influential stakeholder audiences have of the organisation.

EXAMPLE

Brand: North West Water
Client: John Drummond

Agency: BDH-TBWA
Authors: Belinda Miller
Katherine Dinwoodie

Despite the fact that key stakeholders (customers, employees, community groups, opinion leaders, and the company's most hostile critics, the press) attacked the company for high costs, research revealed extreme ignorance of actual prices. The brief was to achieve measurable improvements in customer satisfaction, ensuring that North West Water was repositioned as a customer orientated company that delivered value for money services. The campaign highlighted the range of services provided, at an average daily cost of 60p.

As a result of the campaign:

- Over a third of customers became aware of the 60p figure
- Value for money perceptions increased by 22%
- Customer satisfaction reached 78%
- Loyalty increased – 75% of customers claimed they couldn't switch
- 75% of key stakeholders viewed the company as socially responsible
- Agreement that 'community expectations are met-exceeded' increased from 54% to 70%
- Employees were optimistic in the belief that customer perceptions would improve further
- Levels of job satisfaction increased by 10%
- 87% of customers believed that bills should remain the same or rise.

Source: *Reproduced with kind permission of IPA*

A profile communication strategy therefore addresses the needs of how the corporate entity is perceived by a range of stakeholder audiences. For example, it is quite common for an organisation to develop a communications campaign that is targeted at the financial markets and the Stock Market in particular. This is referred to as investor communications. This happens because the company feels the share price undervalues the organisation or fails to reflect the true worth. It may be that the company wants to inform the financial markets of profit results, changes in senior management or prepare the way for merger and acquisition activities, all of which can seriously affect a companies standing unless handled in the appropriate way.

EXAMPLE

Some web pages are designed to counter negative stories and views expressed by unofficial or even anti-lobbying group sites. Shell has to contend with a host of highly critical sites over its environmental record and its involvement in Nigeria. It now uses both special web-based discussion lines and campaigns, along with a free flow of information, to counter some of the allegations that are not actionable.

From its home page on *www.shell.com,* the visitor can click onto TellShell, a series of open discussion forums that are uncensored, other than for legal necessity. Anyone can contribute anything, whether it is critical of Shell or not. Shell will also put its own point of view, entering into the debate as it evolves. As Bowen (2002) describes it, it is 'a clever way of being transparent while getting its own views across'.

9.1 Corporate identity, corporate image

Corporate identity and **corporate image** are two different facets of the profile development strategy. Increasingly organisations are adopting the phrase corporate branding as a substitute for corporate identity.

Corporate identity is about the way an organisation communicates with its audiences. There are two main forms of communication, those that are planned and pre-determined by the organisation, and those that are unplanned and unexpected

The individual communication methods that make up these planned and unplanned communications are referred to as cues. Examples of planned cues are letterheads, logos, signage, product quality and the behaviour and level of knowledge of its employees. Examples of unplanned cues are media comment, the cleanliness of the company's vehicles and any actions taken by competitors and consumer groups that may reflect or directly relate to the organisation.

Activity 8 **(30 minutes)**

Identify three corporate communication campaigns and the cues used by each to communicate with the different audiences.

The way in which these cues are perceived, frames the way an individual sees and understands an organisation and helps form the image they have of an organisation. Monsanto developed a strong corporate campaign in order to raise the social and scientific arguments related to genetically modified foods. This attempt at being perceived as fair minded and concerned about these issues was articulated using two-sided arguments and invited comment and discussion.

Corporate identity therefore is about how an organisation presents itself. Corporate image is what an audience believes an organisation to be as a result of their understanding of the cues. Sometimes the perception of these cues is correct and sometimes they are not correct. This may be because corporate communications are good or because corporate performance is not good.

Corporate reputation is an extension of corporate image. Corporate reputation refers to the individual's reflection of the historical and accumulated impacts of previous identify cues, whether or not they have been influenced by transactional experiences.

9.2 Corporate communication strategy

As well as communicating about its individual products and services, the company may wish to pursue a corporate communication strategy. This can take either of two forms. First it can be a simple corporate communication campaign aimed at improving the company's identity and subsequently its image. Second, it may be a campaign whereby the company associates itself with a current and topical social issue.

Activity 9 **(30 minutes)**

Identify two major companies who have developed corporate campaigns related to social issues. What do you consider to be the benefits and potential problems associated with such a strategy?

9.3 Crisis communications

Closely allied to corporate identity is the field of crisis management (communications). Company image and reputation can be severely tarnished or even ruined if a response to a crisis is deemed inappropriate.

EXAMPLE: MERCEDES

The initial response by Mercedes when its then prototype vehicle the A-Class rolled over when driven by journalists was to deny that there was a problem. That denial, which lasted eight days, turned into a crisis as 3,000 orders were lost and the media refused to let go of the problem. The reputation of Mercedes was challenged for the first time in a long time and only the acceptance of the problem and a public statement on the actions the company was to take with regard to production and design, alleviated the pressure on the company.

Some crises can be anticipated perhaps because of the nature of the business environment in which an organisation operates. For example, hospitals can plan for bed shortages due to epidemics or local rail/traffic accidents. Airlines plan meticulously to cope with air accidents although their incidence is relatively rare.

10 GUERRILLA MARKETING

Definition

> **Guerrilla marketing** is unconventional marketing intended to get maximum results from minimal resources.

Guerrilla marketing is all about surprise and eliciting interest in the product and for maximum effect should be highly targeted. It is a marketing discipline which is growing with a number of specialist agencies now trading. This form of promotion is considered to be one of the most effective for small businesses with limited resources. A small bicycle lock manufacturer for example chained a bike using one of its locks to a set of railings in Cambridge, next to it they placed a half stolen bike with a sign pointing to the complete cycle stating that the owner should have chosen their lock as that bike was still there.

One of the most famous (and visible) examples of a guerrilla tactic was FHM projecting an image of a naked Gail Porter onto the Houses of Parliament in order to launch the magazine's poll of the 100 sexiest women. Clearly this was not authorised by MPs. Often the controversy which ensues guerrilla tactics is just as important to the campaign in order to gain a high level of awareness. Sometimes companies take a huge risk because not all of these tactics are strictly legal!

EXAMPLE

In July 2007 pagans were moved to perform 'rain magic' to wash away an 80ft doughnut-wielding Bart Simpson which appeared overnight next to the Cerne Abbas chalk giant in Dorset. The giant is a pagan fertility symbol and the appearance of the cartoon character was painted to coincide with the launch of the latest Simpsons film.

Definition

> **Viral marketing** refers to marketing techniques that use pre-existing social networks to spread advertising messages. The process uses word of mouth, forwarded emails and often blog content.

Chapter roundup

- Choice of promotional tool can be affected by factors such as time available, budget constraints, stage of the product life cycle, target market and the product or service's characteristics.
- The sales force provide a vital function to the organisation as they form a direct link to buyers.
- Not only does the salesforce act in the capacity of salespeople, in an indirect way so do other employees.
- Sales promotion encompasses a range of techniques appropriate for targeting consumers, trade and the sales force.
- Below the line communications make use of non-commissioning paying media.
- Sales promotion objectives can include increasing awareness, encouraging brand switching, giving incentives to consumers, increasing display space and developing a consumer database.
- Packaging is a marketing tool that encompasses graphic design with marketing concepts to create an identity for the brand.
- Merchandising can be defined as the range of sales promotions activities intended to ensure that products are easily available and prominently displayed.
- Public relations is defined as the planned and sustained effort to establish and maintain goodwill and mutual understanding between an organisation and its publics.
- PR embraces a range of activities including advice, employee relations, community and interest group relations, lobbying and monitoring public opinion.
- Four PR models exist and the ideal one is the two-way symmetric one.
- PR techniques can be utilised to communicate with consumers, other businesses, employees, external publics and finance.
- Direct marketing is the planned recording, analysis and tracking of customer behaviour to develop relational marketing strategies.
- Relationship marketing is a view that emphasises the importance of the relationships developed between an organisation and other parties including customers, partners, suppliers and the trade.
- Sponsorship is a contribution to an activity or organisation by another, usually with the expectation of achieving benefit for the sponsor.
- Sponsorship can be more efficient than other forms of communication as it can generate both audience appeal while linking the values of the sponsored entity to the sponsor.
- Ambush marketing involves a firm, often a competitor, attempting to deflect attention from another sponsor onto itself.

Chapter roundup continued

- A profile communication strategy addresses the needs of how the corporate entity is perceived by a range of stakeholder audiences.
- Corporate identity is about the way an organisation communicates with its audience.
- Exhibitions and trade shows provide a temporary forum for sellers of a product category to exhibit and demonstrate their products to prospective buyers.
- **Corporate identity** is about the way an organisation communicates with its audiences.
- Guerrilla marketing is unconventional marketing intended to get maximum results from minimal resources.

Quick quiz

1. Define personal selling.
2. What roles can the salesforce be involved in?
3. What activities can the salesforce be involved in?
4. Define sales promotion.
5. What is the advertising to sales promotion ratio?
6. List four consumer and four trade sales promotions activities.
7. What are the potential emotional and psychological benefits of packaging?
8. What are the key packaging features?
9. What is a planogram?
10. What are publics?
11. What are the four models of PR?
12. Define two-way symmetric.
13. What is a database?
14. List four direct marketing media.
15. What does AIMRITE stand for?
16. What factors have contributed to the growth of sponsorship?
17. What are the potential risks associated with sponsorship?
18. What are the three main developments in sponsorship?
19. List four reasons for exhibiting.
20. What are the two main forms of communication concerned with corporate identity?

Answers to quick quiz

1 The presentation of products and associated persuasive communication to potential clients, which is employed by the supplying organisation.

2 Order collecting, order taking, pre-order caller, order supporter and order getter.

3 Prospecting, communicating, selling, servicing, information gathering, allocating and shaping relationships.

4 A range of tactical marketing techniques, designed within a strategic marketing framework, to add value to a product or service, in order to achieve a specific sales and marketing objective.

5 30:70

6 Consumer: coupons, money off, loyalty schemes, merchandising
Trade: allowances, contests, sampling, free gifts.

7 Aesthetically pleasing, expression of brand values, visual impact, added value, a reminder, loyalty cues and creation of an emotional link.

8 Colour, typography, logo, type/material, shape and structure, label or mark and size.

9 Diagrams or plans showing store and shelf layout.)

10 Refers to the many target audiences that communications may be focussed towards, eg customers, influencers, media, employees, pressure groups etc.

11 Press agency/publicity, public information, two way asymmetric and two way symmetric.

12 Direct dialogue between a sender and receiver of communications.

13 A collection of data, usually on a computer, shared to provide useful, convenient and interactive access to information.

14 TV, radio, direct mail, telemarketing.

15 Audience, Impact, Message, Response, Internal Management and End results.

16 Media fragmentation, favourable associations, overcome linguistic and cultural barriers, wide appeal, overcome legal barriers (eg tobacco) and allows for selective targeting.

17 Negative associations, clutter and evaluation difficulties.

18 Broadcast sponsorship, product placement and cause-related marketing.

19 Four from: enhance company image, interact with customers, promote existing products, obtain competitor intelligence, launch new products, enhance personal morale and interact with distributors.

20 Planned, ie pre-determined by the organisation and those that are unplanned and unexpected.

Answers to activities

1 The answer to this activity will depend on the items you have chosen.

2

Stage in the PLC	Promotional activity
Introduction	High profile activities to raise awareness and encourage trial eg TV and poster campaigns as well as sampling (either door drops or in-store)
Growth	Need to build brand preference and loyalty using promotions such as competitions and free offers as well as advertising to create long term image
Maturity	A high degree of customer understanding so need to encourage greater consumption by reminding and reinforcing through print media and mass advertising
Decline	Need to attempt to control the rate of decline by rewarding loyalty through promotional activities which are low cost

3 You will need to research the answer to this activity yourself, by obtaining the relevant literature.

4 The answer to this activity will depend on the items you have chosen.

5 There is no specific answer to this activity.

6 The answer to this activity will depend on the items you have chosen.

7 The answer to this activity will depend on the exhibition you have attended.

8 The answer to this activity will depend on the companies you have chosen.

9 The answer to this activity will depend on the companies you have chosen.

Chapter 4 :
INTEGRATED PROMOTIONAL STRATEGY

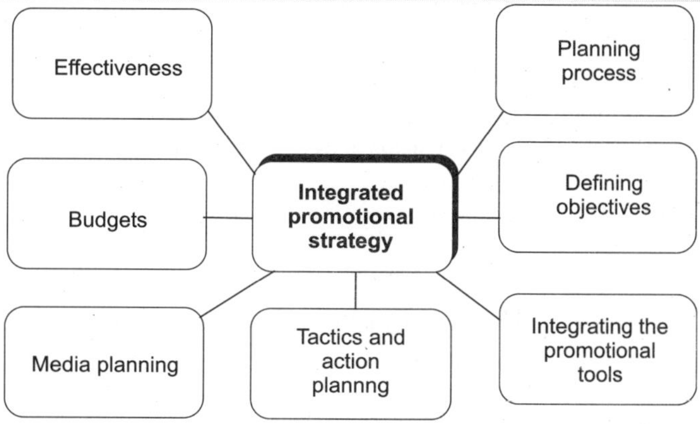

Introduction

Planning is the process by which one establishes objectives, strategy and tactics. This chapter will begin by considering the purpose and process of marketing communications planning. Objectives are necessary for planning operations at all levels of business, and marketing communication objectives typically refer to the goals the marketing communications have in affecting the mind of the target audience.

The third section will consider the factors that have encouraged the development of integrated marketing communications as well as the associated barriers. Tactics refers to the individual actions that combine to achieve the promotional objectives. The relative advantages and disadvantages of key media are discussed when reviewing the media planning process.

The chapter concludes with a revision of budgeting approaches and a final section is concerned with the tools and techniques of marketing communications evaluation.

Your objectives

In this chapter you will learn about the following.

(a) The role of planning in developing successful marketing communications

(b) The importance of devising SMART objectives to facilitate evaluation

(c) The factors which have contributed to the increasing recognition of the benefits of integrated marketing communications

(d) An overview of action planning and the development of tactics

(e) The importance of effective media planning

(f) The principles underlying the key budgeting approaches

(g) The range of effectiveness measurement methods and tools

1 THE PLANNING PROCESS

1.1 Overview

It is important to realise at the outset that the planning of marketing communications is an integral part of much wider and more comprehensive business planning and marketing planning processes.

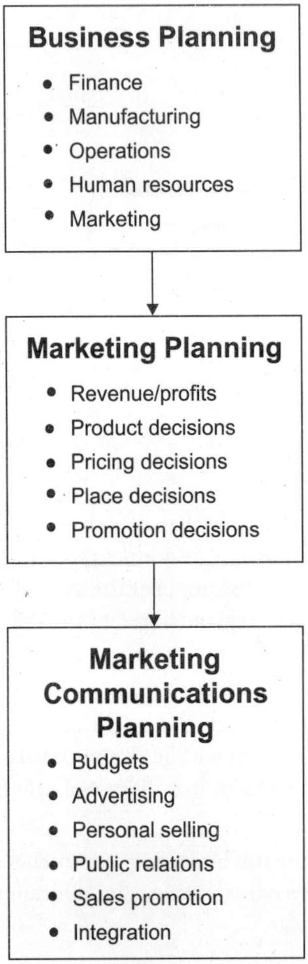

Figure 4.1: Integration of business and promotion planning

Definition

Marketing communications plan: document that summarises the main issues and details of marketing communications activities, including relevant background information and marketing communications decisions.

Activity 1 **(30 minutes)**

For your own organisation, or an organisation of your choice, set out your understanding of how business planning, marketing planning and promotion planning are carried out and integrated.

It may be necessary to consult your own managers or other senior managers to get them to describe the process.

It will be useful to chart the process.

Suggest ways in which the process might be improved

All planning at what ever level may be summed up as a process of answering three basic questions.

(a) Where are we now?
(b) Where do we want to go?
(c) How do we get there?

These are powerful questions and indicate the dynamics of planning; that is the answers should enable a firm sense of direction to be established and a number of specific steps defined to take an organisation forward.

Whilst these questions are powerful it is necessary to build a more comprehensive and structured process that can be easily understood, easily remembered and easily applied both in practice and also in examination situations. There are many different approaches to building a marketing plan or, more specifically, a marketing communications plan. There is no single common approach, but there are essential elements that every plan must have.

SOSTAC is a simple mnemonic that helps managers to recall the key components of a marketing communications plan. SOSTAC can be applied to any kind of plan – corporate, marketing, marketing communications, direct mail or even a personal plan.

Situation analysis	(Where are we now?)
Objectives	(Where do we want to go?)
Strategy	(How do we get there?)
Tactics	(Details of the strategy)
Action	(Implementation)
Control	(Measurement, monitoring researching and modifying.)

Smith and Taylor (2002) suggest a process based on a mnemonic.

SOSTT

+ 4Ms

These letters then provide the standard elements of a promotions plan.

Situation	(Where are we now?)
Objectives	(Where do we want to go?)
Strategy	(How do we get there?)
Tactics	(Details of strategy)
Targets	(Target markets/audiences)
+	
Men	(and women required to do the job)
Money	(financial resources/budget)
Minutes	(timetable of activities)
Measurement	(monitoring effectiveness)

The order of the letters represents the logical order of the planning process.

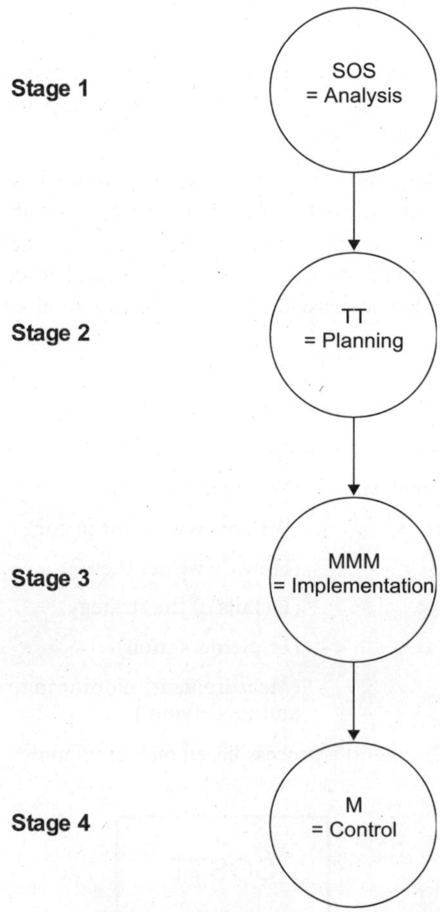

1.2 Audit

The 'situation analysis' is sometimes called a 'marketing audit' and occasionally an 'environmental analysis'. It is worth repeating that what we are concerned with is primarily promotional planning but this must be seen within the broader context of business and marketing planning.

2 DEFINING OBJECTIVES

Having arrived at a comprehensive and structured list of strengths, weaknesses, opportunities and threats it is now possible to set about the key task of defining marketing communications objectives. Again it is very important to remember that communications objectives cannot be generated in isolation as they are part of a hierarchy of objectives.

Definition

> **Objective**: The goal or aim or end result that one is seeking to achieve.

Hierarchy of objectives

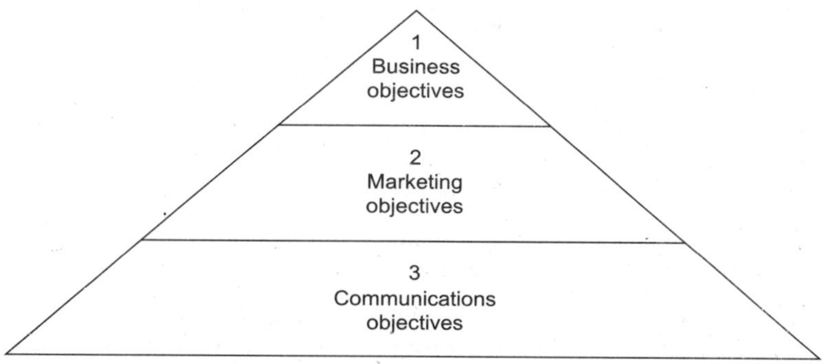

Business objectives are typically concerned with profitability growth and organisation improvements and will normally be of a longer-term nature. **Marketing objectives** are typically concerned with increasing sales, increasing market share and with all the elements of the extended marketing mix: the twelve P's. Of the extended marketing mix only one P is devoted specifically to promotion. However communications can have an important impact on many if not all of the other elements.

An alternative powerful way of generating communications objectives is to consider the individual elements of one of the communication models such as AIDA.

(a) **Awareness.** Promotion is almost always designed to increase the awareness of an organisation's products or services among its target audiences.

(b) **Interest.** Besides generating awareness, promotional strategies, and therefore objectives, must also be concerned with creating specific interest.

(c) **Desire.** Though valuable precursors, awareness and interest objectives are not in themselves sufficient. Other promotion objectives must be established with a view to increasing the desire for an organisation's products or services.

(d) **Action.** The final stage is getting the customer or potential customer to purchase the company's products or services. Therefore promotion objectives must be concerned with bringing about these actions.

Communications objectives like business objectives and marketing objectives are not simple wish lists but are concrete examples of a determination to succeed. They provide milestones against which to judge future performance and they are also the key to the integration of business activities. The characteristics of objectives can usefully be defined using the mnemonic SMART. Thus all communications objectives must be SMART.

Specific	Promotion objectives must relate to specific end results and not be so generalised as to be useless.
Measurable	Promotional objectives must, wherever possible, be quantified and therefore capable of being measured.
Achievable	If objectives are not capable of being reached they can be demotivating. They should be challenging but also achievable.
Relevant	All business objectives are about making choices between priorities in the use of resources. It is therefore important that the chosen promotion objectives are relevant to the overall marketing strategy.
Timed and targeted	To measure whether an objective has been achieved it is necessary to set agreed timescales. The T also refers to the need to target objectives at particular groups of customers or market sectors.

Some specific examples may be helpful. These are mainly taken from articles in the marketing press. (Details of timescale and measurability are not generally explicit, though there is no reason why they should not be.)

(a) 'BBC 2 is mounting an advertising campaign for the first time in its history *to boost its profile among a younger, less middle-class, more female audience*'.

(b) ' ... *to promote Stella Artois's Belgian heritage and premium ingredients* ... last year's campaign aimed *to persuade consumers that it was worth splashing out for a Stella Artois*.'

(c) 'Late-night slots on Channel 4 are the best way *to reach 17-year-olds. We want to intrigue them so that they will call in*, and from there decide whether De Montfort is right for them. The University needs *to stand out in an increasingly competitive environment*, and *to confront historic prejudices against the former polytechnics*.'

3 INTEGRATING THE PROMOTIONAL TOOLS

3.1 What is integration?

Strategy must be communicated in such a way that the messages are consistent through time and targeted accurately at appropriate stakeholder audiences. Each organisation must constantly guard against the transmission of **confusing messages,** whether this is through the way in which the telephone is answered, the impact of sales literature, the way sales persons approach prospective clients or the transparency of an organisation's overall corporate activities.

Marketing communications is about the promotion of both **the organisation** and its **products and services.** An increasing number of managers recognise the growing role the organisation plays in the marketing process and the impact that organisational factors can have on the minds of consumers.

It is logical to conclude that, if there are different audiences, many of them exist inside and outside the organisation, and some of them actively contribute to the source of some communications (eg marketing communication agencies). It is **important to bring corporate and business strategy together with marketing strategy** so that at some point, in some way, all these elements can be integrated, as is necessary if communication, marketing communication, is to be effective.

EXAMPLE

Red Bull is an example of a brand which uses integrated marketing communications very well. The drinks company integrate guerrilla marketing tactics, their website, TV and press ads with their high profile sponsorship of a range of extreme sports such as F1 racing and events such as the Red Bull Air Race. The Red bull music academy is a more recent addition to the promotional strategy, heavily targeted to a young audience. The company also sponsors university students as Red bull Gliders. These 'super kid on campus' students are employed at £6 per hour to promote Red bull and drive around in branded cars generating sampling occasions. The core brand message is all about providing energy. This message is consistently applied throughout its marketing activities.

Definition

A dictionary definition says that **integration** is 'combining parts into a whole'.

Immediately it can be seen that integration of marketing communications is possible at three levels.

(a) Integration with business strategy

(b) Integration with marketing strategy

(c) Integration of the promotional tools

FOR DISCUSSION

For integrated marketing communications, more than one creative treatment – message or image – may be used, but where more than a single treatment is employed, they should be mutually consistent.

FOR DISCUSSION

Cadbury's Text'n'win was an interesting interactive sales promotion using text messaging. The promotion primarily targeted 16- to 24- year-olds, who are familiar with texting as a means of communication. Codes were printed inside Cadbury's chocolate bar wrappers which the consumer had to text to a given telephone number to find out whether or not they had won. The promotion was supported by radio advertising and internet activity. In eight weeks, 2.3m entries were received, representing about 3.5% of consumers and almost twice the response of previous comparable promotions, allowing Cadbury's to capture detailed customer data that can be used in more targeted campaigns in the future.

Integrated marketing communications (IMC) means different things to different people, but is more likely to occur when organisations attempt to enter into a co-ordinated dialogue with their various internal and external audiences.

Definition

> **Marketing Communications** is 'a management process through which an organisation enters into a dialogue with its various audiences. To accomplish this the organisation develops, presents and evaluates a series of co-ordinated messages to identified stakeholder groups.
>
> The objective of the process is to (re)position the organisation and/or their offerings, in the mind of each member of the target audience in a consistent and likeable way. This seeks to encourage buyers and other stakeholders to perceive and experience the organisation and its offerings as solutions to some of their current and future challenges *Fill* (*2002*).

The word dialogue is used deliberately. Communication theory tells us that feedback is important. Of course, it is important to use feedback constructively and good marketing communications allows for the development of a circle of information between an organisation, its customers and interested stakeholders. Promotional messages should encourage target audiences to respond to organisations (or products/brands). This response can be immediate through, for example, purchase behaviour, registering on a website, using customer care lines or even through storing information in memory (or a file or desk) for future use. Creating and maintaining a dialogue therefore is a critical aspect of marketing communications.

The communication tools used in this dialogue and the messages conveyed should be **internally consistent with an organisation's strategies**. The target audiences should perceive the communication and associated cues as coordinated, likeable and timely. In addition, members of the target audience(s) should, at some time, be sufficiently motivated to want to respond to the communication and encourage future messages.

The word **positioning** is used in the definition as well. The manner in which an organisation (product or brand) is perceived relative to other competing products can be important to the level of success an organisation might enjoy. Therefore, the way in which a product is perceived by its various audiences is influenced by the marketing communications (stimuli) that are received by the audience.

Management pursuit and development of IMC involves the totality of an **organisation and all those with whom it interacts**. Because of the range of activities, the customer/audience focus, the breadth of the organisation and cultural shift involved in developing IMC, this concept is regarded as a strategy. This is important as IMC is too often depicted as just the co-ordinated impacts of the tools of the promotional mix.

FOR DISCUSSION

Where integration is not applied, there are potential dangers of marketing communication dysfunction in which the activities and effort become counter-productive.

3.2 The development of IMC

There are a number of reasons why organisations are seeking to establish IMC. The following table sets out some of the drivers behind this growth (Fill, 2002).

Organisational drivers for IMC

- Increasing profits through improved efficiency
- Increasing need for greater levels of accountability
- Rapid move towards cross-border marketing and the need for changing structures and communications
- Co-ordinated brand development and competitive advantage
- Opportunities to utilise management time more productively
- Provide direction and purpose

Market based drivers for IMC

- Greater levels of audience communications literacy
- Media cost inflation
- Media and audience fragmentation
- Stakeholder's need for increasing amounts and diversity of information
- Greater amounts of message clutter
- Competitor activity and low levels of brand differentiation
- Move towards relationship marketing from transaction based marketing
- Development of networks, collaboration and alliances

Communication-based drivers for IMC

- Technological advances
- (Internet, databases, segmentation techniques)
- Increased message effectiveness through consistency and reinforcement of core messages
- More effective triggers for brand and message recall
- More consistent and less confusing brand images
- Need to build brand reputations and to provide clear identity cues

As with any new development or attempt to advance an organisation, there will inevitably be those who wish to resist any change to their accepted pattern of life and understanding of their world. IMC is resisted for many reasons.

Failure to establish IMC as a total concept may be for one or other of the following reasons.

- Financial structures and frameworks
- Reluctance to change
- Traditional hierarchical management and brand structures
- Attitudes and structure of suppliers and agencies
- Perceived complexity of planning and coordination
- Lack of experience

Overcoming these different forms of resistance can be tricky and partly because of the enormity of the task, especially in global organisations, there are few examples of truly rooted IMC. Here are some of the ways in which the restraints can be overcome.

- Adopting a customer focused philosophy
- Using training and development programmes
- Appointing change agents
- Planning to achieve competitive advantage
- Developing an incremental approach

The diagram below sets out a model of IMC and demonstrates the way in which the different elements of an organisation's activities need to be brought together if IMC is to flourish (Fill, 1999).

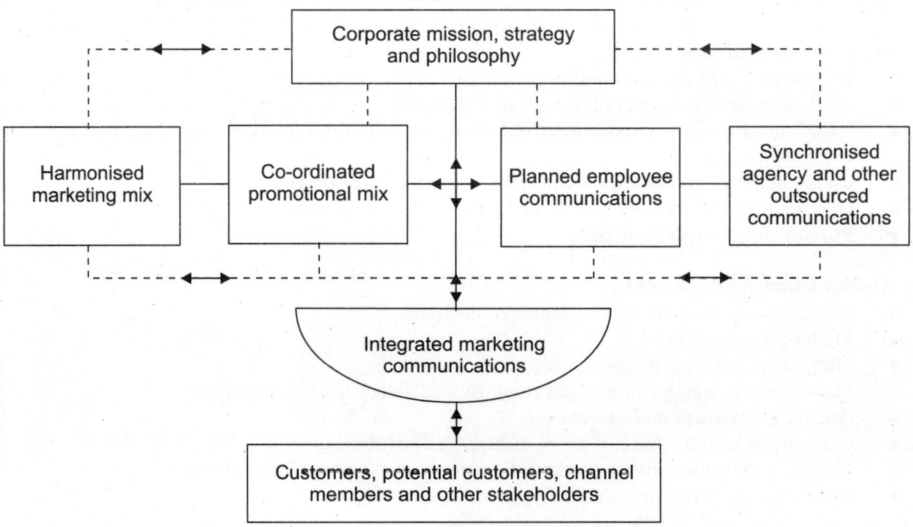

Figure 4.2: Integrated marketing communications

3.3 Benefits of integrated marketing communications

The principal benefit derived from the integration of marketing communications is synergy. By bringing together the various facets of marketing communications in a mutually supportive and enhancing way then the resulting 'whole' is more than the simple sum of its parts.

Benefits of integrated marketing communications include:

- Creative integrity
- Consistent messages
- Unbiased marketing recommendations
- Better use of media
- Greater marketing precision
- Operational efficiency
- Cost savings
- High calibre consistent service
- Easier working relations
- Greater agency accountability

3.4 Barriers to integrated marketing communications

Integration is not easily achieved and while the associated problems are not insurmountable, they are significant for a variety of reasons. These include:

- Mind set
- Taxonomy and language
- Structure of organisations
- Elitism
- Magnitude of task
- Adequacy of budget
- Manager ability
- Agency remuneration systems
- Dimensions of integration

Definition

> **Mind set:** A particular way of thinking or view held.

Many of the reasons encouraging the growth of integrated marketing communications are externally driven – they are factors outside the control of organisations, clients and agencies. Factors inhibiting integration are frequently internally, organisationally driven which are typically within the control of management to overcome, if there is a will to do so.

> **Activity 2** **(30 minutes)**
>
> You are a newly appointed marketing executive and your marketing director has asked you to produce a report that can be presented at the next board meeting. You should succinctly highlight the issues the company might have to face when first attempting to improve the integration of their marketing communications effort.

3.5 Push and pull strategies

Brassington and Pettitt (2006) note that within a push strategy, the manufacturer chooses to concentrate communications activity on the member of the distribution channel immediately below. In contrast the pull strategy requires the manufacturer to create demand for the product through direct communication with the consumer. The retailers will perceive this demand and, in the interests of serving their customers' needs, will demand it from the manufacturer. This bottom-up approach pulls the product down the distribution channel, with communication flowing in the opposite direction from the product.

4 TACTICS AND ACTION PLANNING

Having decided the promotional objectives and the broad promotional strategy it is now necessary to decide the individual actions to be undertaken (tactics). This requires a great deal of creativity on the part of the marketing team, their advertising agencies and other supporting agencies. A number of steps can be taken in deciding actions, including the following.

(a) **Review the conclusions of the situation analysis,** and consider how to build on strengths, overcome weaknesses, grasp opportunities and avoid weaknesses.

(b) **Consider the achievement of promotional objectives.** What promotional methods are most appropriate?

(c) **Evaluate the promotional tool kit.** Evaluate each of the promotional tools, above the line methods and below the line methods, to see which can make a contribution.

(d) **Consider the promotional budget.** The size of the promotional budget may eliminate the more expensive promotional media such as television advertising.

(e) **Integrate together into a schedule.** Having decided the most appropriate and cost efficient forms of promotion it is necessary to weld them together into an overall schedule of activities.

It will be extremely useful to construct an overall promotions plan and timetable, usually expressed in the form of a Gantt chart, as shown below. This serves to focus the minds of the planners on the contribution of each promotional element and how they may be integrated. It also provides a method of communicating the plan effectively and can be used for monitoring actual achievement against that planned and budgeted.

Activities	Jan	Feb	Mar	Apr	May	Jun	Jul	Aug	Sep	Oct	Nov	Dec	Cost £000s
1 Initial research	■	■											30
2 Corporate design			■	■									50
3 Trade advertising					■	■							700
4 Launch event						⊗							100
5 Editorial coverage						■	■						50
6 Special promotions								■	■				100
7 Consumer advertising									■	■	■		1000
8 Monitoring effectiveness												⊗	20

Total cost £2.05 million

Figure 4.3: Timetable for a promotions plan

5 MEDIA PLANNING

The concept of segmentation, which leads on to targets and positioning, is an essential part of marketing theory and practice. Segmentation is the process of dividing up large heterogeneous markets with similar needs. The ultimate, of course, would be to address the needs of every individual customer directly and specifically. This may become possible in future with the growth of electronic home shopping using the telecommunications superhighway.

Variable	**Example**
Geographic	Continent (Europe) Country (United Kingdom) Region (South East) County (Lancashire) Town (Manchester) Postcode (WA14)
Demographic	Age (over sixty) Sex (male, female) Status (married) Family size (3,4,5) Income (under £20,000) Occupation (lecturer) Education (degree) Religion (Protestant)
Psychographic	Social class (A B C1 C2 D E) Lifestyle (upwardly mobile) Personality (ambitious)
Behavioural	Benefits required (quality, service, price) Usage rate (light, medium, heavy) Loyalty status (strong)

Definition

> **Psychographic segmentation:** Based on psychological dimensions such as values, lifestyles, attitudes, interests and opinions.

Once the market has been divided into segments it is necessary for the marketing manager to make the correct target decision. Three broad options are possible: undifferentiated marketing, differentiated marketing and concentrated marketing.

(a) **Undifferentiated marketing.** Segments can be ignored and one marketing strategy offered to all customers. There are certain cost advantages to this approach and perhaps the most famous example is that of Henry Ford who introduced the Model T Ford in any colour you wanted as long as it was black!

(b) **Differentiated marketing.** A company can operate in two or more segments and offer a unique marketing mix to each. This is quite common among larger companies who may employ several different brands in the same market.

(c) **Concentrated marketing.** In undifferentiated marketing the whole market is attacked and in differentiated marketing, marketers go for two or more segments. In concentrated marketing the concentration is on a single market sector, for example Rolls Royce in the luxury car market.

Next it is necessary to select a strategy to position the product or service in the minds of the consumers of the selected segments. Positioning can be undertaken using one of the segmentation bases.

- By benefit or attribute
- By price and quality
- By use or application
- By product user
- By competition

Definition

> **Positioning:** the relative perceptual position of one brand compared with competing brands.

5.1 Media planning concepts

There are a number of concepts associated with media planning and an understanding of these (and the jargon) will help you to appreciate some of the strategic issues associated with this important aspect of the communication process.

Reach

When a new product is launched or a new variant introduced to the market, the communications objective is very often to generate high levels of awareness. The complementary media strategy is called a reach (or coverage) strategy. This means ensuring that as many people in the target audience have an **opportunity** to see/hear the message during the relevant time period/campaign.

Frequency

The ability of people to retain (and of course forget) information varies widely. In view of this, **advertising messages need to be repeated.**

Definition

> **Frequency** is used to refer to the number of times a person is exposed to the message, within a particular campaign or period of time.

FOR DISCUSSION

Frequency is important because promotional messages usually have to be seen more than once to create a meaningful effect.

The word exposure in the preceding paragraph is important. Calculations in media planning are based upon an individual's **opportunity to see** (OTS) the advertisement. This means seeing the media vehicle (*Marie Claire*, *FHM*) which, of course, is not the same as actually seeing or reading a particular advertisement.

The relationship between reach and frequency is important. All campaigns need to generate a certain number of OTS and these are determined and measured by what are referred to as ratings (or Gross Rating Points). Ratings are the multiple of reach and frequency.

Reach × Frequency = Ratings (in television these are known as TVRs)

Definition

> **TVR (television rating points**: An estimate of the audience for a TV advertisement and are determined through BARB data (covered shortly). They are in effect index numbers that represent the proportion of the potential viewing audience.

One of the important tasks of the media planner is to determine the number of times the target audience should be exposed to the message. This is referred to as the **level of effective frequency**. There is no set answer and a debate about whether it should be 1, 2 3 or 10 times in any one purchase interval, continues. Without wishing to trivialise an important issue there appear to be two main views.

(a) Effective Frequency state that the answer is three.

(b) Regency Planning argue that one exposure per purchase interval is all that is necessary.

You need to be aware of the issue and be able to justify your media schedule when preparing a marketing communication plan.

5.2 Developing the media plan

Many of the initial considerations in media planning will be identical to those which apply when starting communications planning.

Market background

Market size, shares and trends must all be taken into account. If a client is trying to break into a highly competitive marketplace, such as washing powder, perfumes or confectionery, then heavyweight multi-media advertising may be the only way of making a presence felt. On the other hand, if a small advertiser is trying to establish himself in the market for a highly specialised service (for example, genealogical research services for the family historian), a tightly targeted campaign through a specialist medium will probably suffice.

Although some advertisers are forced into specific media choices in order to mirror and offset the actions of their competitors, other advertisers may choose a little-used medium in order to capitalise on 'stand out value'.

Media must be able to deliver the target market required. Some audiences are more difficult to deliver than others, owing to their media viewing habits. Young adults tend to be light television viewers and may be best targeted with cinema advertising. Mass media will rarely deliver niche audiences, special interest magazines being a more appropriate media vehicle.

Activity 3 **(15 minutes)**

Suppose you work for a cinema chain. What information might it be useful to collect to help potential advertisers decide when and whether to use some or all of your cinemas as an advertising medium?

Product/service background

The role which advertising is to play for the product or service will to some extent dictate media strategy. If the campaign's objective is to ensure that the audience is constantly **reminded** about the product being advertised, then media may be used continuously in a low key manner. If the objective is to inform about a new product or service, then a mass media launch will be more suitable.

Budget

Clients should always specify the amount of money that they intend to spend on media, as opposed to the production budget for a campaign.

The budget can prove to be a media constraint. A budget of £100,000 would tend to dictate a campaign that runs on a local basis only, or a national campaign which utilises only one medium (for example, a national press campaign with a limited number of titles). A budget of £2m would allow for a limited national campaign across a mix of media. As previously stated, you should try to get a feel for this by reading the marketing press.

Media characteristics

Media choice is also governed by a number of factors arising from the different properties of the various media options.

The nature of the medium in its own right is an important consideration. People purchase magazines for their entertainment value, or because they serve as an information source.

The **positioning of adverts within television, radio or cinema contexts** can make a difference to how they are perceived. An advert scheduled in the middle of a TV game show will deliver an audience with a different mind set from one scheduled in the centre break of a documentary. Take notes next time you watch either on commercial TV.

Another consideration is **how people use media**. For instance, many popular radio stations are used as a background to other activities (driving a car, talking to friends, carrying out activities at work or in the home). People are generally unlikely to be giving their main attention to listening to the radio (unless it is 'talk radio').

The amount of time spent with the medium can be a factor. Daily newspapers are a relatively quick read in the busy environment of the working week.

Booking and production lead times may rule out the use of certain media. Monthly magazine space is generally booked months in advance. Television and cinema commercials with high production values will take months to prepare, film and edit.

As well as taking into account the inherent features of each medium, **media channels must be evaluated quantitatively** for their ability to deliver against criteria such as coverage, frequency and cost.

Coverage (also called reach or penetration) is a measure of the percentage of a particular target audience reached by a medium or a whole campaign. Frequency is the number of times the target audience has an opportunity to see (or hear) an advertising message. Cost will not only be measured as an absolute, but also in terms of the cost per thousand contacts of the target audience.

Media planners will use recognised media research sources such as the National Readership Survey, Target Group Index and BARB to calculate media efficiency.

Definition

> **BARB – Broadcasters' Audience Research Board.** This body is jointly owned by the BBC and ITV and is responsible for producing information on TV viewing activity. Electronic meters and diaries from over 4,400 nationally representative households are used to record the information.

Client preferences

Clients may have their own specific reasons for dictating or declining the use of specific media options. One company booked a poster site directly opposite one of their main competitor's head offices on an 'until cancelled' basis. Every morning and evening, employees were greeted with the sight of their rival's latest advertising campaign.

Media scheduling

As the media planner works through the available choices, a media schedule begins to evolve. This is the formal listing of which adverts are to appear where. Media schedules can be constructed for short term campaign bursts or for a whole year's advertising cycle.

Budget will be a major determinant in the seasonality of advertising. A very small budget may dictate that advertising is limited to certain key times of the year (eg pre Christmas; peak sales periods). A large budget that allows for year round advertising is usually allocated in one of two ways.

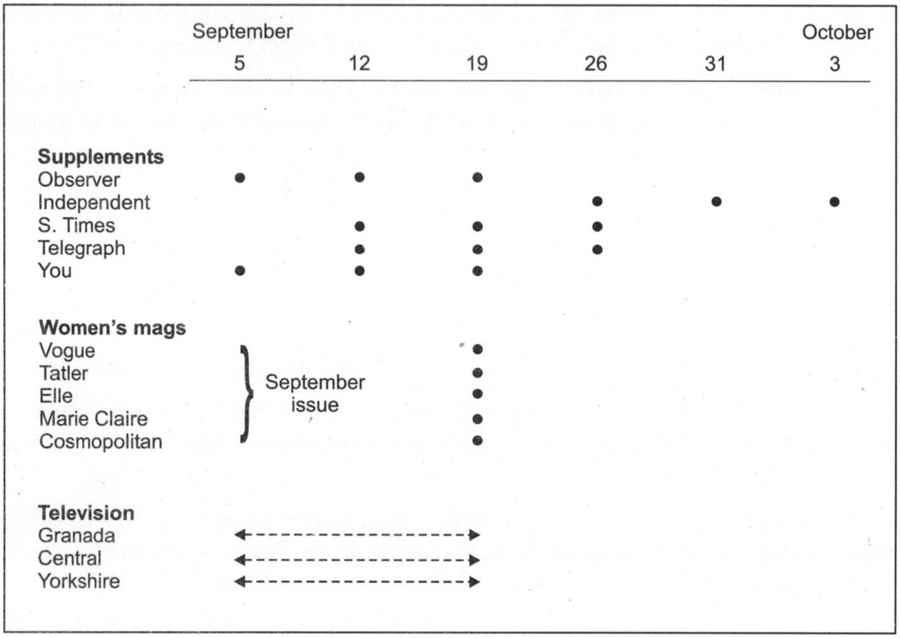

Figure 16.4: Example media schedule

Definitions

(a) A **burst campaign** concentrates expenditure into promotional bursts of three or four weeks in length.

(b) A **drip campaign** allows for a continuous but more spread out presence.

FOR DISCUSSION

Media planning requires that consideration is given to target audiences beyond the target market.

5.3 Key media characteristics

Medium	Advantages	Disadvantages
Newspapers (daily metropolitan/ national)	• 'Mass' medium: large audience in single exposure • Targeted sections (auto, home, computers etc) • Reader navigation: seeking news, information • Short lead time for production: accept ads 24 to 48 hours before publication	• Circulation does not mean readership: wasted circulation paid for • Print/image reproduction of variable quality • No exclusivity: ad may be next to competitor's • Costs loaded for preferred positions
	• Flexibility of ad size • Tangibility of ad (can be torn out and kept) • Multiple readers/users • Allows detailed information (prices, phone numbers etc) • Allows (still) images • Allows response mechanisms (eg captions)	• Short life-span of news
Newspapers (local/free)	• Low cost • Geographical targeting • High local readership • Special sections (especially local real estate, entertainment etc)	• Circulation of free papers/weeklies not always monitored/audited • Variable editorial content • Subject to weather and junk mail rejection if letterbox dropped
Magazines	• High circulation (major titles) • Targeted audiences (special) • High quality reproduction (colour photography etc) • Potential high prestige (vogue, time etc) • Reader motivation (selection, subscription) • Long shelf life and multiple use/readership • Tangibility, detail, images, response mechanisms (see newspapers)	• High costs of production • Hyper-segmentation (by interest and geography, may be insufficient circulation to support local outlets) • Long lead times: copy/artwork required 1 to 3 months before publication, can be inflexible

Medium	Advantages	Disadvantages
Television	• 'Mass' medium: large audience at single exposure, almost universal ownership/access • Detailed monitoring of exposure, reach, viewer habits • Allows for high degree of creativity • Realism: impact of sound + sight + movement • High-impact visual images reinforce retention • Allows demonstration • Flexibility as to scheduling • Allows association with desirable products	• Most expensive of all media costs • High production costs • Lack of selectivity (except via programming) of audience • Lack of opportunity/: does not reach commuters/workers • Long lead times for booking and production: penalties for withdrawal: inflexibility • Passive, unmotivated audience: 'zapping' by video fast-forward and remote controls erodes reach
Radio	• 'Mass' medium: wide coverage/access • Audience selectivity (local/regional) programme style/variety/content) • Opportunity: radio is portable – in-home, in-car, on public transport, shops, offices – even jogging • Function: high usage for morning news, home 'companionship', background • Personal (+ potential for participation through talk-back) • Highly competitive costs of air time and production • Can be backed by personal DJ promos	• May be passive 'background' noise: low attention, retention • May be 'cluttered' by announcers/DJ promotions • Sound only: no tangibility (pressure on retention of message), no shelf-life or 'pass on' circulation, no demonstration, no coupons, limited details etc
Outdoor media (poster sites bus stops, buildings etc)	• Flexible: sites, duration of lease • Comparatively low cost • Opportunity: exposure to commuters, shoppers	• Difficulty of verification of exposure/response • Subject to weather • Opportunity: site specific • No audience selectivity (except by site)
Cinema	• Glamorous • High impact (large size, highly visual, loud sound, high quality) • Captive audience (no TV 'zap' factor) • Can segment by local area	• High cost • Opportunity: site/time specific • Poor verification of response • Limited number of people reached per exposure

The following bar chart compares the media actually used most to advertise different products, suggesting that consumers look to different media for information about different products – or that advertisers (perhaps, your competitors) think they do.

The following is a broad SWOT analysis comparing major media.

Medium	Applications	Targeting	Testing	Cost per contact	Response speed	Response %	Response volume
Press	– Lead generation – Direct sales – General awareness – Support for other activities – Boost store traffic	Medium	Medium	V low	Fast	Low	High
Radio	– Awareness – Store and event traffic boost – Lead generation (high ticket business-to-business)	Medium to poor	Poor	High	Medium	V low	Low
TV – general	– Awareness – Store traffic boost	Medium to poor	Poor	High	Fast	Low	Low
TV – direct response	– Lead generation (high ticket items) – Direct sales (low ticket items) – Support for other activities	Medium	Poor	Low	Fast	Low	Medium
Posters	– Awareness – Store traffic boost	Poor	Nil	V low	Slow	Nil	Nil
Inserts	– Lead generation – Direct sales (especially non cash-with-order sales	Good	V good	Low to medium	Fast	Medium to low	High
Direct Mail	– All (weakest where prospects 'cold', no suitable list available)	V good	V good	V high	Medium	High	Medium

The principal task in using media is to reach the right people, the right number of times, with greatest effect, with the least waste, at least cost, without distorting the message. The watchwords in media are reach, frequency, impact, economy, efficiency and effectiveness.

6 BUDGETS

The mechanics of budgeting are covered in Chapter 9, as part of Unit 20, Sales Planning and Operations.

6.1 How to decide budgets

Activity 4 **(30 minutes)**

As a marketing manager, write a short article for inclusion in a company magazine suggesting how the amount of money spent on marketing communications might be strategically important. Use examples to illustrate your article.

Your article will probably have highlighted that without investment in marketing communication, brand awareness (therefore sales) will fade over time. However, the expenditure the company is prepared to commit to supporting marketing communications will depend on its strategy including the corporate plan, the actions of competitors, life cycle stage and profitability.

Your article will probably also have referred to how different levels of expenditure would be required for a particular type of marketing communication strategy – does the message have to be put across through a particular (high or low cost) medium, locally or nationally or integrated across a number of media? The tendency for the cost of advertising media to rise is called **media inflation**. The rate of media inflation has tended to exceed wider inflation in advanced economies, causing firms to control their budgets with great care.

(a) What variety of **marketing communications** is to be used?
(b) What **tasks** are to be undertaken?
(c) How **competitive** is the market place?
(d) How **well known** is the organisation?
(e) Are there any **special requirements**?

To some extent your strategy will also determine which combination of the theoretical approaches to budgeting your company is likely to adopt. Revise the eight methods below before tackling the exercises.

- Completely arbitrarily
- All you can afford
- Historical basis
- Matching the competition
- Percentage of sales
- Experiment and testing
- Modelling and simulation
- Objective and task method

FOR DISCUSSION

When using the affordable method, extra care has to be exercised in particular situations such as when launching a new product or operating with declining sales.

EXAMPLE

The European Central Bank (ECB) was faced with a huge challenge in planning a large pan-European campaign to launch the euro on 1 January 2002. A mix of PR, direct marketing and above-the-line advertising was required to inform individuals and organisations about the changeover arrangements in the Eurozone countries as well as ensuring that the look, feel, size, denominations and security features of the new currency would be recognisable to everyone. A PR campaign was running throughout 2001 along with a public information leaflet drop to 300 million Europeans. The mass media campaign centred around the slogan, 'The Euro. Our Money', and a single campaign was translated into eleven languages rather than trying to develop a different campaign for each country. Publicis was the agency which developed the campaign in liaison with the ECB, national central banks, government finance ministries and other bodies. The agency had 70 staff working on the project, including 30 at a specially opened 'Euro Buro' office near the ECB headquarters co-ordinating teams at other Publicis offices across Europe. The objectives of this integrated campaign were non-negotiable and had to be achieved if the euro launch was going to run smoothly. The campaign was designed around those objectives and the cost is reported to have been between £50 and £80m. *(www.euro.ecb.int)*

FOR DISCUSSION

Two primary decisions have to be made in setting budgets using the percentage of sales method – what percentage to use and what sales period to use.

Activity 5 **(30 minutes)**

To demonstrate the logic and difficulty of the objective and task method choose a marketing communications problem with which you are familiar.

(a) Define the precise marketing communication objectives.

(b) Determine the tasks necessary to achieve these objectives.

(c) Cost out the problem both in terms of the individual tasks and in total.

FOR DISCUSSION

It is difficult to operationalise the objective and task method because it is not possible to guarantee that by undertaking a particular marketing communications task, or combination of tasks, a specified outcome will be achieved. Nor is it possible to know if the tasks were conducted in the most efficient way. There could be significant over-spending as a result of being over-cautious in using this method.

Activity 6 **(15 minutes)**

Compare the advantages and disadvantages of the various methods that can be used to determine the appropriate levels of marketing communication budgets.

6.2 Advertising to sales ratios (A/S Ratios)

One of the important factors that always needs to be considered is the amount spent on communications by competitors. It can be difficult determining the amount spent by competitors on below-the-line activities, although accurate guesstimates can often be made by those actively involved in the market.

Above-the-line activities can be measured (data bought from various marketing research agencies) and can be used to gain an insight into possible strategies.

The A/S ratio for an industry provides a benchmark against which it is possible to determine how much should be spent or stimulate consideration of why certain amounts have been spent.

Definition

The **A/S ratio** is different for each market sector. It is calculated by working out the total amount spent on advertising (usually at rate card cost) as a proportion of the sales in the market. Therefore, if sales in a market are valued at £150 million per year and the amount spent on advertising is £14 million then the A/S ratio is said to be 9.33%.

Part of the strategic decision is to decide whether an individual company's A/S ratio should be higher or lower than, or the same as (at equilibrium with) the industry average.

(a) **Reasons to spend more** might be that a **new product or variant** is being introduced to the market so greater effort is require to **develop awareness** (reach) and then perhaps knowledge and or establish brand values.

(b) **Reasons to underspend** the industry average might include trying to maintain an established market position or **directing spend to other products** in the portfolio or deciding to **put more work below-the-line**.

6.3 Share of voice

Definition

Share of voice: Within any market the total of all advertising expenditure (adspend), that is, all the advertising by all the players, can be analysed in the context of the proportions each player has made to the total.

If one advertiser spends more than any other then more of their messages will be received and therefore stand a better chance of being heard and acted upon. If a brand's **market share (SOM)** is equal to its **share of voice (SOV)** an equilibrium can be said to have been reached.

It is possible that organisations can use their advertising spending either to maintain equilibrium (SOV = SOM) or to create disequilibrium.

The following matrix shows how different spending strategies are appropriate depending on your competitors' share of voice and your own share of market.

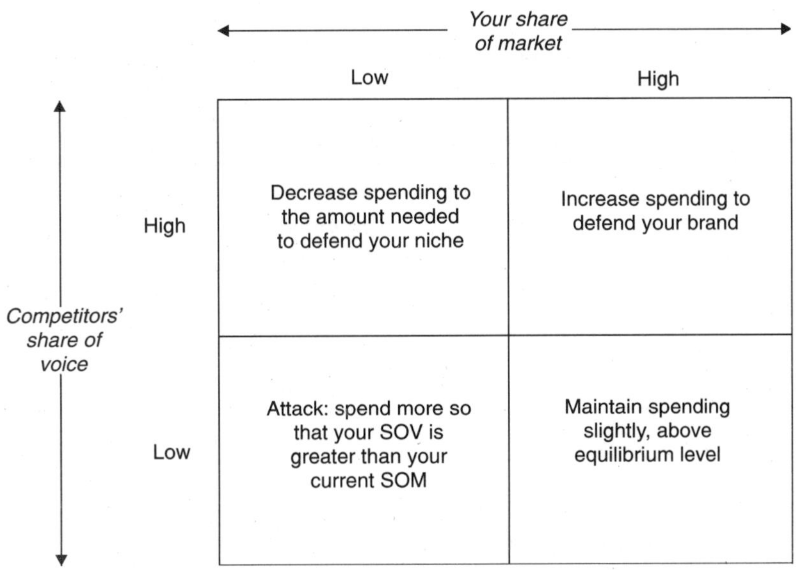

Figure 4.4: Shroer matrix

Note that careful monitoring of the fortunes of competitors is needed: if you know that a competitor is spending large sums on restructuring, say, they may not be in a position to retaliate to a sudden advertising burst by your company.

6.4 Controlling the budget

Marketing communication budgets may be very substantial and have a major effect on profitability. Firms will generally seek to make promotional spending as effective as possible (known in the trade jargon as 'maximising media spend'). Careful integration of a range of promotion techniques can be an important means of achieving this. Controlling the effectiveness of the budget may be difficult if not impossible. What *is* possible is to use normal budgetary control techniques in marketing expenditure and to review its effectiveness regularly even if this is only by means of informed judgement. A simple way of representing this twin track is shown below.

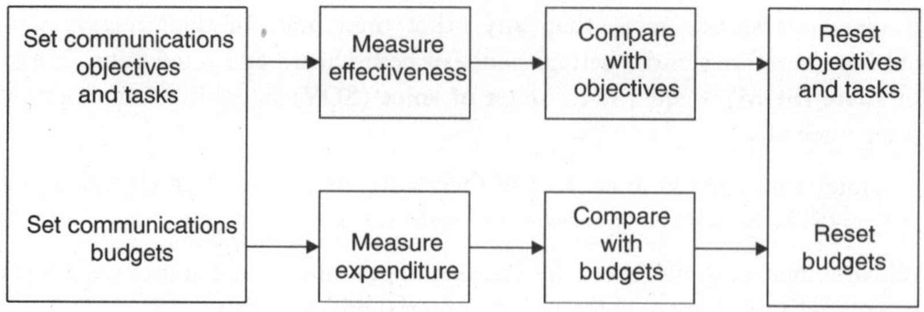

Figure 4.5: Controlling the budgets and effectiveness

The difficult part is measuring the effectiveness of the marketing communications process. The following are some possible techniques.

Marketing communications methods	Examples of measurement
Personal selling	Sales targets
Public relations	Editorial coverage
Direct marketing	Enquiries generated
Advertising	Brand awareness
Sales promotion	Coupons redeemed
Exhibitions	Contacts made

6.5 Software

Software has been developed to assist with the task of media planning and control. Typically, the software will provide for planning advertising, buying media and tracking each ad insertion or exposure and its cost. Functions will include listing, searching and analysing ads and media suppliers.

7 EFFECTIVENESS

7.1 Effectiveness

The effectiveness of promotion can only be measured in terms of the objectives that were set for it to achieve. Typical objectives for advertising will include increases in awareness, the creation of specific brand values and increased take up of offers of trials. Objectives for sales promotion will obviously relate to increased unit sales. Such objectives will properly be expressed in detail and in measurable terms such as percentages of the target segment population or absolute values or quantities.

Most of the research techniques used specifically to measure the effectiveness of marketing communications employ methodology which is used much more widely in all kinds of research. As such only a brief list will be discussed.

- Sampling
- Questionnaires (and so analysis)
- Ad hoc and continuous research
- Panels and audits
- Pre and post testing

7.2 Measures for advertising

We may divide performance measures for advertising into two main groups: basic measures and performance measures. Basic measures have already been described in our earlier discussion of budgets and include such measures as cost per thousand.

Performance measures

(a) **Exposure**. Exposure can be measured in terms of frequency (eg the number of times a TV advertisement is screened) and audience share (the number of potential customers reached). One TV advertisement might reach two million people; by repeating the advertisement, the intention would be to reach people who missed the advertisement previously, but also to reinforce the message through repetition to people who have seen it before.

(b) **Awareness**. Awareness of the existence of a product, or awareness of certain particular features of a product. Awareness could be measured by recall tests or recognition tests.

(c) **Sales** (volume and/or revenue). Advertising is often intended to increase sales, the effect of advertising on sales is not easy to measure. Why?

   (i) Advertising is only one part of a marketing mix. Other factors influencing sales might be price changes, whether intermediaries have stocked enough of the products to meet an increase in demand, and competitors' actions.

   (ii) Advertising might succeed in **maintaining** a firm's existing market share, without actually increasing sales.

(d) **Profits**. The difficulties of measuring the effect of an advertising campaign on profits are therefore the same as those described in (c) above. Breakeven analysis might be used to calculate the volume of extra sales required to cover the (fixed) costs of the advertising. In monitoring the effects of a campaign, management might be able to judge whether this minimum increase in sales has or has not, in all probability, been achieved. However, advertising might be necessary to 'build' a brand or for management to 'invest' in it.

(e) **Attitudes**. The aim of a campaign might be expressed in terms of 'x% of customers should show a preference for Product A over rival products'.

(f) **Enquiries**. Advertising might be aimed at generating extra enquiries from potential customers. Where possible, enquiries should be traced to the advertisement. For example, a customer reply coupon in a magazine advertisement should be printed with an identification number or label, identifying the magazine and date of its issue.

It is difficult to measure the **success of an advertising** campaign, although volume of sales may be a short-term guide.

(a) A campaign to launch a new product, however, may have to be judged over a longer period of time (ie to see how well the product establishes itself in the market).

(b) Advertising's main purpose in the communication mix is to create **awareness** and **interest**.

(c) The effectiveness of advertising is therefore usually measured by marketing researchers in terms of **customer attitudes** or **psychological response.** Most of the money is spent by agencies on **pre-testing** the given advertisement or campaign before launching it into national circulation. Relatively less tends to be spent on **post-testing** the effect of given advertisements and campaigns.

Post-testing involves finding out how well people can **recall** an advertisement and the product it advertises, and whether (on the basis of a sample of respondents) attitudes to the product have changed since the advertising campaign.

EXAMPLE

When financial service brands such as Virgin Direct and Goldfish were launched they failed to convert high levels of awareness into new business.

'The brands, supported by estimated ad budgets of about £5m and £10m respectively and featuring Richard Branson and Billy Connolly, were ever-present on TV at the end of 2000, with Goldfish securing 30 per cent brand awareness for its credit card and Virgin 13 per cent for its products. But neither converted that awareness into new business, according to exclusive research on new financial service and loyalty schemes conducted by the RSL Strategic Initiatives Monitor.

Its survey showed that less high-profile brands such as MBNA's credit card, which had an awareness of only ten per cent, achieved a holding of two per cent – outstripping its higher spending rivals.

Significantly the reasons for changing suggest that credit card holders are looking for immediate benefits rather than the promise of rebates in the future from their cards. Over a third of new cardholders mention low APR (annual percentage rate – broadly, interest rate) and a quarter 'no annual fee' as reasons for taking new cards. In contrast only six per cent were attracted by points or tokens offered, while five per cent claim to have switched because they banked with the card issuer.

In 2007 Skoda ran a very popular TV ad campaign which featured a lifesize model of a car being made out of cake. The ad created widespread awareness for the brand but ad industry sources were mixed in their view as to whether awareness could be converted into sales increases.

7.3 The effectiveness of sales promotions

There is often a direct link between below-the-line advertising (sales promotions) and short-term sales volume.

(a) The **consumer sales response** to the following is readily measurable.

- Price reductions as sales promotions (for example introductory offers)
- Coupon 'money-off' offers
- Free sendaway gifts
- On-pack free gift offers
- Combination pack offers

(b) It might also be possible to measure the link between sales and promotions for industrial goods, for example special discounts, orders taken at trade fairs or exhibitions and the response to trade-in allowances.

(c) However, there are other promotions where the effect on sales volume is **indirect** and not readily measurable, for example sponsorship, free samples, catalogues, point-of-sale material and inducements.

(d) Promotions may go hand in hand with a direct advertising campaign, especially in the case of consumer products, and so the effectiveness of the advertising and the sales promotions should then be considered together.

A manufacturer can try to control sales promotion costs by:

(a) Setting a **time limit** to the campaign (for example money off coupons, free gift offers etc must be used before a specified date).

(b) **Restricting the campaign** to certain areas or outlets.

(c) Restricting the campaign to **specific goods** (for example to only three or four goods in the manufacturer's product range, or only to products which are specially labelled with the offer).

7.4 Channels of distribution

Some organisations might use channels of distribution for their goods which are unprofitable to use, and which should either be abandoned in favour of more profitable channels, or made profitable by giving some attention to cutting costs or increasing minimum order sizes.

It might well be the case that an organisation gives close scrutiny to the profitability of its products, and the profitability of its market segments, but does not have a costing system which measures the costs of distributing the products to their markets via different distribution channels.

A numerical example might help to illustrate this point. Let us suppose that Biomarket Ltd sells two consumer products, X and Y, in two markets A and B. In both markets, sales are made through the following outlets.

(a) Direct sales to supermarkets
(b) Wholesalers

Sales and costs for the most recent quarter have been analysed by product and market as follows.

	Market A			*Market B*			*Both markets*		
	X	*Y*	*Total*	*X*	*Y*	*Total*	*X*	*Y*	*Total*
	£'000	*£'000*	*£'000*	*£'000*	*£'000*	*£'000*	*£'000*	*£'000*	*£'000*
Sales	900	600	1,500	1,000	2,000	3,000	1,900	2,600	4,500
Variable production costs	450	450	900	500	1,500	2,000	950	1,950	2,900
	450	150	600	500	500	1,000	950	650	1,600
Variable sales costs	90	60	150	100	100	200	190	160	350
Contribution	360	90	450	400	400	800	760	490	1,250
Share of fixed costs (production, sales, distribution, administration)	170	80	250	290	170	460	460	250	710
Net profit	190	10	200	110	230	340	300	240	540

This analysis shows that both products are profitable, and both markets are profitable. But what about the channels of distribution? A further analysis of market A might show the following.

	Market A		
	Supermarkets	*Wholesalers*	*Total*
	£'000	*£'000*	*£'000*
Sales	1,125	375	1,500
Variable production costs	675	225	900
	450	150	600
Variable selling costs	105	45	150
Contribution	345	105	
Direct distribution costs	10	80	90
	335	25	360
Share of fixed costs	120	40	160
Net profit/(loss)	215	(15)	200

This analysis shows that although sales through wholesalers make a contribution after deducting direct distribution costs, the profitability of this channel of distribution is disappointing, and some attention ought perhaps to be given to improving it.

Chapter roundup

- The planning of marketing communications is an integral part of much wider and more comprehensive business planning and marketing planning processes.
- Marketing communications objectives should be specific, measurable, achievable, relevant, timed and targeted.
- In its simplest form, integrated marketing communications is concerned with the integration of all elements of the marketing communications mix across all customer contact points to achieve greater brand coherence.
- The development of IMC has been encouraged by factors such as lack of real growth in advertising expenditure, a growth in media independents and a growth in international communications.
- Failure to establish IMC may be down to financial structures, reluctance to change and lack of experience.
- Positioning can be undertaken by benefit, price and quality, use or application, product user or competition.
- When developing a media plan a number of different factors need to be taken into consideration. These include market background, product/ service background, budget, media characteristics and scheduling.
- Media planning requires that consideration is given to target audiences beyond the target market.
- The watchwords in media are reach, frequency, impact, economy, efficiency and effectiveness.
- Budgets are both a resource and a constraint and increasing emphasis is being placed on being able to justify them in the light of marketing communications performance.
- In determining budgets it is important to clearly identify what they are to be used for because what is included and excluded varies between companies.
- A variety of basic budgeting methods are available but there is no single best method.
- Performance measures for advertising include exposure, awareness, sales, profits, attitudes and enquiries.

Quick quiz

1 What should be included in a marketing communications plan?

2 What does the SOSTT + 4Ms mnemonic stand for?

3 To what does AIDA refer?

4 What is an integrated marketing communications strategy?

5 How can IMC be encouraged within an organisation?

6 Name four key benefits of IMC.

7 Define psychographic segmentation.

8 What is meant by the term reach?

9 What does TVR stand for?

10 What do BARB do?

11 What are the three key disadvantages of magazines?

12 Name three advantages of using outdoor media.

13 Why is the percentage of sales the most commonly used method of setting a budget?

14 Define the term share of voice.

15 List five types of research that could be undertaken to determine effectiveness.

Answers to quick quiz

1 It should summarise the main issues and details of marketing communications activities, including relevant background information and marketing communications discussions.

2 Situation, Objectives, Strategy, Tactics, Targets + Men, Money, Minutes and Measurement.

3 A communications model concerned with Awareness, Interest, Desire and Action.

4 Marketing communications is a management process through which an organisation enters into a dialogue with its various audiences.

5 Adopting a customer-focused philosophy, using training and development programmes and developing an incremental approach.

6 Benefits include creative integrity, consistent messages, better use of media and cost savings.

7 Psychographic segmentation is based on psychological dimensions such as values, lifestyles, attitudes, interests and opinions.

8 A measure of how many members of the target audience are reached by a medium or collection of media used in a campaign.

9 Television rating point.

10 The Broadcasters' Audience Research Board is responsible for producing information on TV viewing activity.

11 High production costs, hyper-segmentation and long lead times.

12 Flexibility (of sites and lease duration), comparatively low cost and opportunities to see.

13 Ease of calculation, ability to be precise, can be quickly monitored, appears logical and is low risk from a financial perspective.

14 Within any market the total of all advertising expenditure can be analysed in the context of the contributions each player has made to the total.

15 Sampling, questionnaires, *ad hoc* and continuous research, panels and audits, pre and post testing.

Answers to activities

1 This will depend on the organisation you have chosen.

2 Notes for a report highlighting the issues the company might have to face when first attempting to improve the integration of its marketing communication effort:

- The development of clearly defined marketing objectives which are consistent with other organisational objectives
- A planned approach which covers the full extent of marketing communications activities in a coherent and synergistic way.
- Identify a range of target audiences – not just confined to customers or prospects but include all selected target audience groups
- The management of all forms of contact which may form the basis of marketing communications activity
- Effective management and integration of all promotional activities and people involved
- Incorporate all product/brand and corporate marketing communications efforts
- Range of promotional tools/messages/media need to be consistent

3 Number of screens
Policy on screen usage: are some always eg used for children's films?
Foyer facilities: café or bar available
Type of customer: local or from a wide area
Type of film shown eg very cultural, or just mainstream
Foreign language films shown

4 Some suggestions are given in paragraph 6.1.

5 This will depend on the issue you chose. You probably found this quite challenging.

6 **Arbitrary method**

Advantage: Uses experience
Disadvantage: Based on intuition and so not recommended

Affordable method

Advantage: Relatively easy to undertake

Disadvantages: Product rather than marketing orientated as not based on market analysis

Not useful for new products where little may be considered to be 'left over' for promotion

Lacks flexibility and an appreciation of situations such as declining sales

Competitive parity method

Advantage: Useful to recognise competitor activities so could be useful in conjunction with other methods

Disadvantages: Need to consider a number of factors including size of the competitor and its market position

Looks at averages and so does not appreciate industry variations

Cannot react to competitive activity, nor differing objectives

Objective and task method:

Advantage: Based on objectives

Disadvantages: Need to ensure that objectives are appropriate and this can be problematic

Difficult to implement

Percentage of sales method

Advantages: Most popular approach

Links marketing communications expenditure directly to levels of sales

Flexibility in that it can be based on future sales, historic or averaged sales

Disadvantage: Need to ascertain what percentage to set and how turnover should be determined

Part B

Sales Planning and Operations

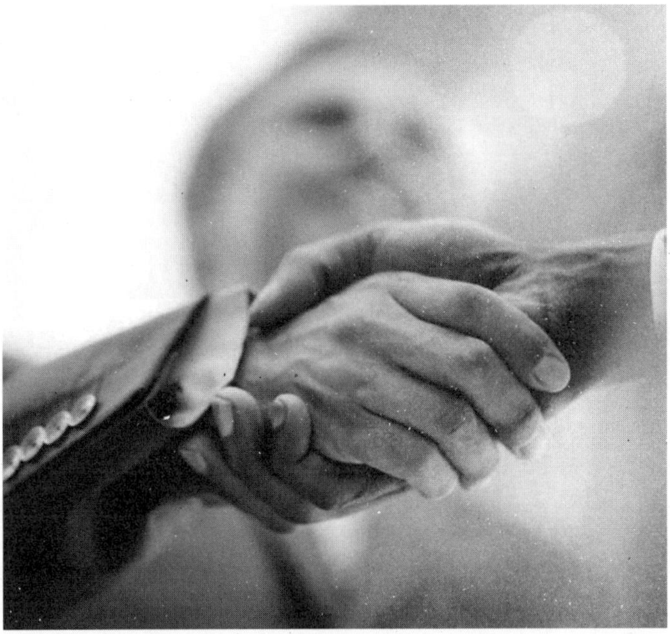

Chapter 5 :

SELLING AND THE PROMOTIONAL MIX

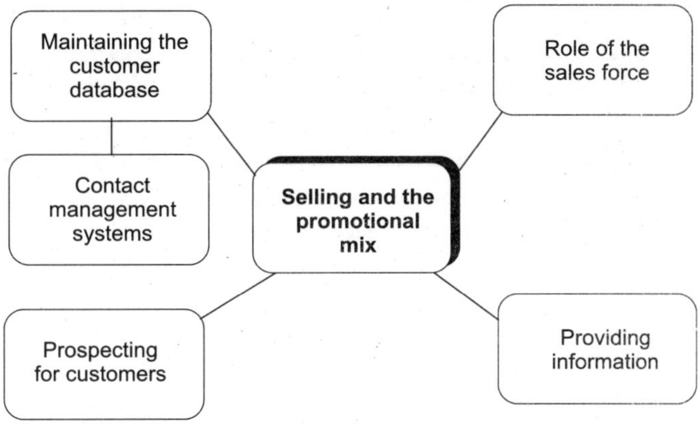

Introduction

Personal selling is part of the overall promotional mix, but is more relevant to some activities and products than others. This chapter will cover the role of selling and how it fits into the marketing mix, how information is gathered to help in sales planning and prospecting for customers and the importance of maintaining an effective customer database.

Your objectives

In this chapter you will learn about the following.

(a) The role of personal selling in the communications mix

(b) The components of the selling task

(c) The importance of information gathering by and for sales personnel

(d) How customer databases can be managed

The Unit details describe the role of selling in the promotional mix. The overall promotional mix, and the need for integration were described in Chapters 3 and 4. Review those chapters if you feel you need context.

1 THE ROLE OF THE SALES FORCE

1.1 Personal selling

Personal selling was covered quite extensively in Chapter 1, as part of Unit 18 on Advertising and Promotion.

Definition

> **Personal selling** is a direct and face-to-face form of communication which uses demonstration of the product, persuasion and negotiation to make the sale.

Each individual probably has his or her own ideas of the 'typical' salesperson, but it is interesting to consider the wide range of face to face sales activities which exist. **Types of selling** include:

- **Delivery people** who also sell (eg a milkman).
- **Salespeople** within the premises of the sales organisations (eg a shopkeeper or store assistant).
- **Travelling sales** representatives, who require limited technical knowledge (eg soap, food and drink, etc).
- Salespeople who need **technical expertise** to sell their product, probably selling to a small number of potential industrial customers (eg sales representatives for IT hardware or software systems).
- Salespeople who need to **create a sale** through their selling methods where an established market does not exist (eg door-to-door selling of Cable TV).
- Sales people acting as **consultants** to consumers (eg financial services).

Personal selling is still important because it is both personal and interactive.

	Personal?	*Interactive?*
Advertising	No	No
Sales promotion	No	No
Public relations	No	No
Personal selling	Yes	Yes
Internet selling	No	Yes

> **Activity 1** **(5 minutes)**
>
> Take note of the next time you have an encounter with a salesperson. How much advice did they give you, how interactive was the process?

Advertising is a message directed to customers in aggregate. Sales promotion is driven by the consumer. Selling is the only activity that is genuinely personal although customer care – post purchase – should also be personal.

The reasons why an organisation might decide that a personal sales element in the communication mix is worthwhile are likewise diverse. They include the following.

(a) The need to **demonstrate** a technical product (especially in the sale of industrial goods). Retailers may employ store assistants with some technical knowledge of the products on sale, but a manufacturer's own sales force is likely to be given specialised product training.

(b) The need to **explain a complex product** or service.

(c) **A lack of active selling by intermediaries and the desire to improve sales.** Wholesalers and retailers will try to sell; all the products they handle, and will not favour one manufacturer's products. Even dealers are sometimes lethargic in trying to sell their products.

(d) An **inability to persuade intermediaries** to accept products (there is often resistance by wholesalers and retailers to new products).

(e) **High intermediary profit margins** affecting the final sale price to customers. These costs of intermediate stages in the distribution channel mean that direct selling in some cases will be cheaper.

(f) A **small market** with only a few target customers may make direct selling cheap (and a dealer network impracticable).

EXAMPLE

Business to business marketers in technical markets, such as computers or specialist machinery, will take the time to explain the product benefits or be involved in the design of the product (or service, such as computer software) with the client.

(g) As a means of maintaining **good relations with end customers**, and obtaining feedback (ie market research information) about what the customer likes and does not like about the current products, or what new product developments the customer would wish to see happening.

1.2 The task of selling

Even in an organisation with a market orientated philosophy, there will be a need for a persuasive sales force. The need to convince the customer will arise because the customer's needs are unlikely to be **satisfied** exactly by any one product on offer. The sales task is to offer the most suitable product. For instance customers might need some reassurance that they are getting what they want. For example, a customer for a domestic household appliance might want to be certain that it can do everything he or she wants it to, and customers in DIY stores or garden centres often seek similar 'technical' advice from sales assistants. Another reason is that it may not be economically or technologically feasible to satisfy a customer's needs exactly. This is especially true in mass production industries. Customer tastes might have changed since the decisions about designing a product were first made, or expertise may be needed, for example in financial services so selling is a very important element of the promotional mix.

FOR DISCUSSION

Selling an intangible service such as life assurance is difficult, as the benefits of the service are difficult to communicate.

The task of selling involves:

(a) **Communicating the advantages** of a product to the customer

(b) **Securing a sale**

(c) **Prospecting** for additional customers. This involves searching for prospective customers, perhaps visiting them several times, and then making a sales 'pitch'.

(d) **After-sales service**. Queries and complaints will arise and must be dealt with to the customer's satisfaction, in order to win repeat sales.

(e) **Gathering information** about what the customer wants

EXAMPLE

Many holiday companies will send or give a customer a questionnaire after the holiday. This can be used to assess customer satisfaction and to gather important market research information that can be used by sales staff.

The detailed tasks involved in selling can and do vary substantially but have been listed to include:

(a) Product delivery (eg the milkman)

(b) Order taking inside the seller's store

(c) Order taking 'outside' by a field salesforce

(d) Order taking by telephone

(e) Building up goodwill (eg merchandising work)

(f) The provision of technical or engineering advice to customers, perhaps in helping a customer to draft specifications for a product

(g) 'Creative' selling of tangible products

(h) 'Creative' selling of intangible products (eg people involved in the sale of services such as banking, or insurance)

(i) Recommending credit

(j) Collecting payment and avoiding bad debts

(k) Researching the market providing new prospects and up-to-date information for management

FOR DISCUSSION

Given that the term 'salesperson' covers such a wide range of selling activities, it may be apparent that the desirable personality of the salesperson is likely to vary from one type of selling to the next.

Activity 2 **(5 minutes)**

Professional services such as medical services can also be marketed. What characteristics would a salesperson in this market need?

Making sure that the right person is selected for the right sales job is an important element of the sales management task. Successful selection and recruitment starts with a thorough and careful analysis of the job description.

Salespeople can be required to have many skills besides the obvious ones of presentation, communication and negotiating competence. They may be required to speak other languages, drive and have technical expertise as well. It is important that all these necessary attributes are recognised and built into the job description.

On many occasions, personal selling is used in combination with other aspects of the marketing and promotional mix. We discuss this in the next section.

For the most effective use of the sales resource, it has **to be supported by other activities in the organisation, particularly marketing. The external focus** of the sales team, their apparently independent **work** culture and some misplaced envy for the travel and entertaining (often an integral part of the sales role) can easily lead to a 'them and us' attitude developing between sales personnel and their colleagues in other departments.

Management have an important task in preventing such barriers developing. They need to ensure the sales staff are recognised as being at the sharp end of a team effort, a position which can often be both uncomfortable and lonely. Support provided from the centre not only makes the salesperson's task easier, it makes the whole team effort more effective.

The role of the **sales support activities** should be to:

(a) Maximise the proportion of sales time spent in face to face client contact

(b) Provide direction, and to ensure sales resources are targeted at the market segments and leads offering the greatest potential

(c) Provide the necessary backup to help the sales person ensure a continuing relationship with a satisfied customer

Sales promotion activities are temporary changes in the marketing mix, used to achieve tactical objectives. They can take many forms like free gifts and competitions, temporary price offers or extra volume.

Sales promotions can be designed to influence three distinct groups.

(a) The **sales team** themselves, where promotions are incentives to encourage extra effort in promoting a new or sluggish product line etc.

(b) **Intermediaries**, like wholesalers or retailers, where promotions are designed usually to encourage some brand loyalty in their recommendation to the customer, to win extra shelf space or to encourage increased volume sales.

(c) To the **end user**, where promotions are designed to create interest or remind the customer of the product and its benefits.

Sales promotions need to be devised to meet specific objectives. These can be to help sell more in a quiet sales period, eg the January post Christmas store sales. Sales promotions can be used to encourage trials of a new product, like smaller sizes, test period offers, demonstrations and so on. A product positioned in a competitive growth market needs promotions to encourage brand loyalty and repeat purchases. 'Collect six box tops for a free gift' would help to achieve this. Mature products rely on promotions like competitions to generate interest. Promotions of products in decline are used to clear end of line stocks.

The distributor and supplier have a shared interest. Both will benefit from increased sales. The intermediary, however, is unlikely to be concerned about **which** brand customers choose to buy. Either way a sale is made. The distributor may actually make a higher margin on another brand, perhaps an 'own' brand.

1.3 Converting awareness to action

Sales and marketing have to be co-ordinated in the joint objective of **easing customers through the decision making process from awareness to action.**

One role of marketing is to provide sales with a flow of **qualified leads**. These should represent potential customers who are aware of the company and/or product, are already interested in it and who have or have begun to have a positive attitude to its purchase.

(a) The **conversion rate** of contacts already this far down the decision-making process is likely to be higher than if the buyer has to be introduced to the product or company by the salesperson.

(b) The salesperson can concentrate on the **action stage** of selling, where it is particularly effective. This reduces the amount of non-selling time spent generating leads etc.

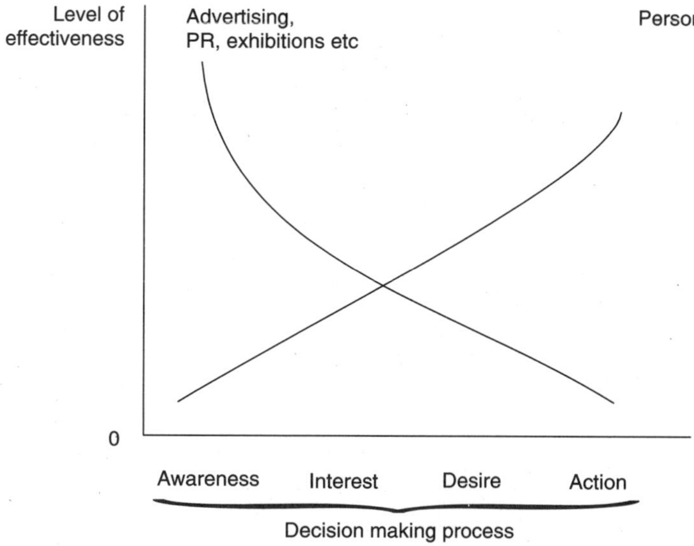

Figure 5.1: Converting awareness to action

Each of the promotional tools of marketing have their own particular strengths and weaknesses.

(a) **Advertising and public relations** are good at generating awareness and interest, but poor at action.

(b) **Personal selling** on the other hand is too labour intensive and expensive to be very good at generating awareness and interest, but it is very good at building **desire, changing attitudes and converting this to sales.**

Used in combination, the promotional tools ensure the maximum number of customers are moved through the decision making process at the minimum cost.

Communication objectives should therefore be written and results measured, in specific terms. Advertising should not be judged in terms of actual sales, but in terms of awareness or attitude. The advertising may be working, generating awareness and interested but if they are not being converted to sales by the sales team, then this is the element of the communication mix which needs reviewing.

The precise combination of marketing activities used to generate quality sales leads will vary from industry to industry. In consumer markets media advertising, offering brochures may be a means of identifying precisely those who are interested. In industrial markets the exhibition may be a more appropriate means of generating qualified leads. Direct mail and telephone selling are also likely to be used to provide the sales team with qualified sales leads.

FOR DISCUSSION

Collect examples of direct mail. Discuss/evaluate how effective they are at generating sales.

Whatever combination of communication tools is used, the contribution of each to achieving eventual sales must be quantified and evaluated. Marketing managers need to recognise that it is often more cost effective to **increase the conversion rate** of interested contacts into sales, than to increase the numbers of people who are **aware** of the product. Getting the balance right between the selling effort and other promotional support is critical to the effectiveness and efficiency of the overall marketing effort.

2 PROVIDING INFORMATION

The support activities are needed to provide the sales team with the information that will make the sales activity more effective. In return, the sales team should be providing a stream of **information and feedback** about sales, customers and the marketplace. This information will aid managers in their future marketing and sales decision-making.

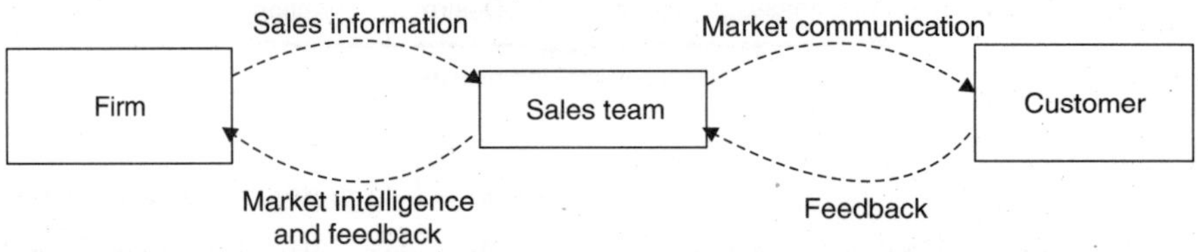

Figure 5.2: Information provision process

The sales team can be seen to hold a special place in the flow of information and communication between the firm and its customers. It is clearly important that the sales personnel have the skills to perform these functions accurately, without distortions and omissions.

FOR DISCUSSION

Sales personnel need training to be effective information gatherers.

Providing the sales force with adequate technical and functional training to perform their role is one way management can support the sales effort.

2.1 Sales research

Information is often an undervalued resource within the organisation. Yet it can provide considerable competitive advantage if managed and used well. In the context of selling, good information can both reduce sales costs and help to increase sales revenues generated by the same sales team.

Feedback information can be analysed by sales managers to enable them to **diagnose weaknesses** in the sales activity and identify the most rewarding targets.

(a) Profiling the 20% of customers who generate 80% of the business provides segmentation information, which means more customers of the same type can be identified and targeted.

(b) Analysis of the sales effort enables managers to give advice about:

  (i) The most profitable balance of new to old calls
  (ii) The most effective call rate per day
  (iii) The best use of presentations and demonstrations etc in a sales call
  (iv) The most effective frequency of sales calls

When it is recognised that the average sales person often spends less than 10% of his or her time in direct customer contact, it can be seen that any improvements either in the amount of effective selling time or the effectiveness of the selling process, can generate significant improvement in performance. Information provides the clues which enable managers to facilitate these incremental improvements.

The salesperson's perspective of the market place is perhaps unique. Of all people in the organisation the salesperson is most likely to see the company as the customer sees it – from the outside in. Others look at the business from the inside out. This different perspective should not be undervalued. It can contribute to both sales forecasting and business planning, but the flow of information needs to be encouraged and nurtured.

2.2 Customer and competitor intelligence

Good salespeople are ones who know their customer's business. This means not only knowing who they are competing with for the contract, but also who their customers are competing with.

This knowledge of a market is built up over a considerable period. It is one of the reasons why organising sales forces by industry or sector can be very effective and it also explains why sales people often specialise in a sector even when they change companies.

Now it is only necessary to reinforce the importance of building up and maintaining a good database of intelligence about both customers and competitors. Communicating this information to the sales force is the second but equally important step in this process.

New technology provides the systems to both store and retrieve rapidly such information. Sales teams should be able to access an up to date record on a company, immediately before a sales visit. This should record:

(a) Sales contacts made, including those made by other sales teams from the company

(b) Orders received, value, frequency etc

(c) Current financial standing, including overdue accounts

(d) Any intelligence on changing personnel in the company, new business won, contracts signed, plans announced etc

This information would supplement the sales persons own personal records and would provide a more macro view of the client company.

Knowing what your competitors are up to is of course a continuing concern for the marketer. As already indicated, the sales team may be an important early warning system in this respect. Equally, providing the sales teams with early information about proposed special offers, or new products being launched by competitors, helps the salesperson be better prepared when negotiating with a customer.

FOR DISCUSSION

Both information and intelligence are only of value if they are shared and used.

2.3 Measuring sales potential

Both specific sales information about calls and sales actually made, and market intelligence about customers and competitors, provide managers with an insight into sales potential.

If the sales resource is regarded as both valuable and scarce, it must be used with care. Maximising its value to the organisation means using it in areas where the sales potential is perceived to be greatest. This analysis of potential would then be a matter of policy, which would be implemented to guide the salesperson's allocation of effort and time.

Whilst it is possible to identify a number of factors likely to influence sales potential, it should be remembered that sometimes the greatest opportunities are not the most obvious and the customer who seems to offer they least potential may in fact offer the greatest. Too narrow an approach, prescribed by managers, may hinder the salesperson's ability to identify new sales opportunities.

Sales potential can be affected by a number of issues, as indicated below.

(a) **Competition**. It can be more profitable to concentrate activities on a part of the market with a lower total potential because there is less competition. This is the concept of **niche marketing**. It is often harder to win a small share of a big cakc than to gain a larger share of a small one.

(b) **Future forecasts.** Sales potential should not be judged only on a short-term basis, but should also be assessed on a forecast of the longer-term future. A company in a mature industry wishing to place a very large order now, may offer a lower potential in the long term than a smaller company operating in a growth market, which today only requires a small order.

(c) **External factors**. All business is influenced by its external environment. Suppliers should assess the both factors which affect their business, but also those which affect their customers.

Activity 3 **(20 minutes)**

What factors have increased the mobile phone market over the past few years? How does this affect the sales function in mobile phone companies?

(d) **Marketing strategy.** The company decision about product range, service levels and pricing policy will all have an impact on the sales potential of an area or customer. It is worth remembering that sales revenue can be increased either by:

(i) Increasing the number of customers or by
(ii) Increasing the average spend of the existing client base.

The strategies to support either of these approaches will influence the effectiveness of the sales activity.

Market forecasts and business plans need to be informed by consumer information. Their basis can usually be found in forecasts of sales and market potential.

(a) Market potential data usually comes from the market researchers' assessment of a particular market segment.

(b) Sales potential estimates (the amount of expected sales which can be achieved profitably within the market segment) will be provided by the sales department.

When evaluating the sales potential of an area or territory it should be recognised that not all clients will be of equal value or potential. Looked at in terms of a life cycle it can be seen that the salesperson's portfolio of clients will be made up of:

(a) New customers with low current value but high potential;

(b) Growing customers with greater current value but only limited future growth potential;

(c) Mature clients with significant current value but no growth potential;

(d) Declining clients with only the potential of diminishing sales, but whose current value may still be worthwhile.

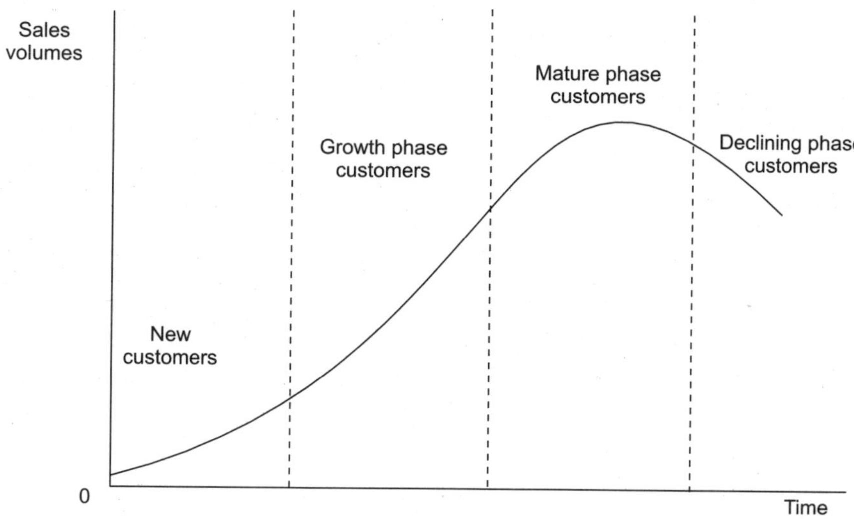

Figure 5.3: Customer life cycle

This analysis shows how it is possible for 20% of customers to generate 80% of sales, because their sales values are not equal.

FOR DISCUSSION

Sales effort is often concentrated on new customers to the detriment of existing customers.

The dilemma for the sales team is the trade off between current sales value and future sales potential. How much time should be allocated to the declining customers whose orders are still valuable and how much to the currently less valuable new accounts?

3 PROSPECTING FOR CUSTOMERS

3.1 Need for new

Whatever the organisation, the need for new customers is ever present. This does not just apply to profit earning producers of goods and services. Political parties require new supporters, charities new contributors and celebrities new fans and sponsors. This means that prospecting for new customers is an ever present part of the job for all those involved in selling.

New customers are needed for two reasons.

(a) To facilitate the **growth and expansion plans** of the organisation.

(b) To **replace 'lost' customers** who, through retirement, death, liquidation, take-over, or who have moved to a competitor, cease buying.

Successful sales staff are those who are always aware of the need for expanding their list of qualified prospects. The ability to locate new prospects is therefore a fundamental sales skill.

Definitions

Defining what is meant by the term **prospect** is quite important. A list of possible customers not screened in any way, for example, taken from a phone book or a list of visitors at an exhibition are known as **leads**. Leads may be potential prospects.

When leads have been screened or assessed against specific criteria, like their need for a product, ability to pay for it or interest in it, then they are qualified prospects.

It is then possible for the sales team to qualify leads according to their potential value and the likelihood that they might make a purchase. This approach means priority can be given to the strongest leads or prospects and it is an important procedure for ensuring the most effective use of the sales resources.

3.2 Locating new leads

The professional sales person is always on the look out for potential new clients and leads, but there are a number of sources which can help in this process.

From the marketing effort

In a marketing-oriented organisation other elements of the marketing and communication mix will be active in generating awareness and creating interest amongst new potential clients and customers. For example, an advertising campaign or direct mail drop, with a freephone number or an offer of further sales information or brochure, will generate a list of interested clients. Similarly an exhibition stand should also generate a list of qualified prospects.

From other parts of the company

Where the organisation has several divisions or the sales force activity is organised around products rather than customers, it is likely that potential prospects may already be contacts of the organisation.

(a) The mail lists and customer details from other sections and sales teams will consist of people who already have a relationship with the organisation.

(b) Similarly lists of past clients may also be capable of being reactivated.

(c) Service engineers are often well aware of clients who may be in the market for a new product. They are not always trained to sell, but they can be encouraged to pass on these qualified leads to the sales team.

Networking for leads

The best leads are often those which come along with a personal recommendation from an existing client. This adds the powerful dimension of word of mouth communication to the formal sales approach. Seeking and obtaining such leads from current customers and forming a network of clients, perhaps within the same business or area, can be very useful.

Leads from an industry

Becoming an industry watcher is also an invaluable source of leads. Trade journals and associations provide names of key decision-makers, news of moves and new strategies can all be monitored and responded to proactively. It is also possible to purchase mail lists of key personnel in specific industries. The problem with such purchased lists is that they may be out of date and they are unqualified leads.

Leads from other firms

The activities of competitors can also be tracked by observation, informal meetings at industry events like trade fairs and trade association meetings, and through the industry press. It is also worthwhile striking up relationships with the sales staff of noncompeting firms. They will know the key decision-makers and policies of their clients and exchanging such information can benefit both sales teams.

Cold call canvassing

Despite all the sources of qualified prospects and the support provided by the rest of the marketing activity, cold calling for new leads is still important in many sales departments. The use of telephone books, newspapers, membership lists, or just knocking on doors in an area, are all well established methods of cold calling. Often firms will provide telephone sales support to their representatives in order to undertake the cold calling more cost effectively and **qualify leads** to ensure that sales staff contacts the person who:

(a) Is the key decision-maker with the authority to pay
(b) Has a need for the product
(c) Is able to pay.

This preparation ensures that the sales time spent giving a presentation is not wasted.

It is worth the sales team remembering that, a sale is only a book entry until payment has been received. Getting credit references about prospective clients is best done before sales effort is expended on the lead and many firms have departments or access to credit rating services like Dunn & Bradstreet who can undertake this routinely.

4 MAINTAINING THE CUSTOMER DATABASE

Definitions

In theory, a database is simply a coherent structure for the storage and use of data. It involves the centralised storage of information, which provides:

(a) **Common data** for all users to share.

(b) Avoidance of **data duplication** in files kept by different users.

(c) **Consistency** in the organisation's use of data, and in the accuracy and up-to-dateness of data accessed by different users, because all records are centrally maintained and updated.

(d) **Flexibility** in the way in which shared data can be queried, analysed and formatted by individual users for specific purposes, without altering the store of data itself.

Such structure could be fulfilled by a centralised file registry or library, or a self-contained data record like a master index card file. In practice, however, large scale databases are created and stored on **computer systems,** using **database application packages** such as Microsoft Access.

4.1 Features of databases

Computer database packages allow data to be stored in a coherent structure in one place.

(a) **Data** are the raw components of information: names, dates, item descriptions, prices, colours, addresses and so on.

(b) **Fields** are the labels given to types of data. A customer database, for example, might include fields such as: title (data = Mr), first name (data = Joseph), last name (data = Bloggs), Company (data = Anon Ltd), Address, Phone Number, Fax Number, Contact Type (data = customer), interests (data = widgets) and so on.

(c) **Records** are the collection of field relevant to one entry. So all the above data fields for a particular customer (Mr Bloggs) make up one customer record.

(d) **Tables** (or database files) are collections of records that describe similar data. All the customer records for a particular region or product may be stored in such a file.

(e) **Databases** (catalogues) are collections of all the tables (and other formats which can be created from them) relating to a particular set of information. So your customer database may include tables for various regions, customers, product customers, customer contacts and so on, plus various reports and queries that you use to access different types of information.

Basic features of database packages

(a) **Find particular records**, using any data item you know

(b) **Sort records alphabetically**, numerically or by date, in ascending or descending order

(c) **Filer records**, so that you 'pull out' and view a selection of records based on specified criteria (all addresses in a certain postcode, for example, or all purchasers of a particular product)

(d) **Interrogate records**, generating the selection of records based on a complex set of criteria, from one or more linked tables. (For example, you might specify that you want all customer records where the field 'City' equals London or Birmingham and where the field 'Product' equals Widget and where the field 'Purchase Date' is between January 2009 and January2010. The query would generate a table consisting of customers in London and Birmingham who purchased Widgets in 2009.)

(e) **Calculate and count** data entries. (For example if you wanted to find out how many customers had purchased each product, you could run a query that asked the database to group the data by the field 'product' and then count by field 'customer ID' or 'last name': it would count the number of to 'sum' or add up all the values in a field: total number of purchases, or total purchase value.)

(f) **Format** selected data for a variety of uses, as reports, forms, mailing labels, charts and diagrams

Activity 4 **(30 minutes)**

Find out what type(s) of database your organisation (or college) uses, and for what applications. If possible, get access to the database and browse through the index, directory or switchboard to see what databases/catalogues contain what database files or tables, queries, reports and forms, with what fields. If you can't get access to a database at work, try the local library, where you may find that the 'index card' system has been computerised as a database. Or use an Internet search engine or browser to interrogate some online databases.

Our interest in databases is simply a user interest, because databases can provide valuable information to sales personnel.

(a) Computer databases make it easier to collect and store more **data information.**

(b) Computer software allows the data to be **extracted** from the file and **processed** to provide whatever information management needs.

(c) Developments in information technology allow businesses to have access to the databases of **external organisations.** Reuters, for example, provides an on-line information system about money market interest rates and foreign exchange rates to firms involved in money market and foreign exchange dealings, and to the treasury departments of a large number of companies.

(d) The growing adoption of technology at **point of sale** provides a potentially invaluable source of data to both retailer and manufacturer.

(e) Increased **sales and/or market share** (due to enhanced lead follow-up, cross-selling, customer contact)

(f) Increased **customer retention** (through better targeting)

(g) Better use of **resources** (targeting, less duplication of information handling)

(h) Better **decision-making** (from quality management information)

4.2 Building a database

A comprehensive customer database might include the following.

(a) **Customer titles**, names, addresses and contact (telephone, fax, (e-mail) details

(b) **Professional details** (company; job title; responsibilities), especially for business-to-business marketing

(c) **Personal details** (sex, age, number of people at the same address, spouse's name, children, interests, and any other relevant data known, such as newspapers read, journals subscribed to)

(d) **Transaction history** (what products/services are ordered, how often, how much is spent)

(e) **Call/contact history** (sales or after sales service calls made, complaints/queries received, meetings at shows/exhibitions)

(f) **Credit/payment history** (credit rating, amounts outstanding, aged debts)

(g) **Current transaction/details** (items currently on order, dates, prices, delivery arrangements)

(h) **Special account details** (membership number, loyalty or incentive points earned, discount awarded), where customer loyalty or incentive schemes or valued customer cards are used.

Each of these items will be in a separate field (and, in a relational database, perhaps separate tables) in your database.

Contacts databases

As well as a database of existing customers, the organisation may wish to build a database of sales leads, prospects and other contacts as a **mailing list.**

(a) **Contact titles**, names, addresses and contact (telephone, fax, (e-mail) details

(b) **Professional details** (company name, address, contact details, job title) in a business-to-business context

(c) **Contact 'type'** – exhibition visitor, referral, engineer, 'cold' contact, bought-in list

(d) **Contact's interests** in a particular product/service area

(e) **Contact history** (whether called/mailed, whether responded, whether followed-up, whether purchased)

EXAMPLE

Sources of contact or mailing list information

(a) Recommendation and referrals from customers (whether spontaneous or through 'introduce a friend' schemes or referral requests)

(b) **Enquiries** for further information, in response to advertising, promotion and PR (via telephone, mail, 'hits' on web site)

(c) Enquiries compiled at exhibitions and fairs

(d) **Leads** brought back by salespeople, not yet converted into sales

(e) Details provided in response to **promotional competitions**, prize draws and incentives. Every 'send in for your chance to win' or 'send in to claim your discount' coupon should be a vehicle of capture of mailing list data: this will often be their primary purpose

(f) Relevant **secondary sources**

(g) Specialist **mailing list suppliers**. Lists can be hired or bought from commercial list owners: they can often be appropriately segmented (we discuss this further below)

(h) The **in-house database** of non-competing organisations in the same market, who may be willing to swap or rent lists. If you buy anything by post, you end up on a mailing database, and are often given the opportunity to receive, or decline to receive, information on related products.

4.3 Maintaining the database

If the customer database is linked to **on-line transaction processing** (for example, via EPOS), purchase data will automatically be updated with each new transaction. However, a typical contacts database will have to be regularly and systematically **maintained**.

(a) Contacts who become customers should be transferred to the customer database and deleted from the contacts database in order to avoid duplicated mailings.

(b) Any up-dated or altered information should be entered in the database such as changes of address or customer status.

(c) Additional information obtained from contacts should be added to the relevant records.

(d) New names and records should periodically be added to the database, and names which have received no response should be deleted.

(e) 'Undeliverable' items are returned to the sender, often marked with reason for non-delivery. If the mailing list has been bought or rented, any undeliverables should be returned to the owner or broker so they can update their database. If the mailing was based on an in-house list, addresses and names should be checked (common errors include misspelt names, missing lines of the address, wrong company name) and if no error can be readily identified, the record should be erased.

(f) Requests from customers or members of the public to have their details erased from the database should be honoured.

(g) New fields can be added to the database design as new types of information become available.

A customer database which allows purchase frequency and value per customer to be calculated indicates to the marketer who the potential heavy users are, and therefore where the promotional budget can most profitably be spent.

By tracking purchases per customer (or customer group) you may be able to identify:

(a) **Loyal repeat customers** (who cost less to retain than new customers cost to find and attract, and who therefore need to be retained

(b) '**Backsliding**' or lost customers, who have reduced or ceased the frequency or volume of their purchases (These may be a useful diagnostic sample for market research into declining sales or failing customer care.)

(c) **Seasonal** or local purchase patterns (heavier consumption of soup in England in winter, for example)

(d) **Demographic purchase patterns**. These may be quite unexpected. Grey Advertising carried out studies in the US which showed that many consumers behave inconsistently to the patterns assumed for their socio-economic groups. Lower income consumers buy top-of-the-range products, which they value and save for. Prestige and luxury goods, which marketers promote largely to affluent white-collar consumers, are also purchased by students, secretaries and young families, which have been dubbed 'Ultra Consumers' because they transcend demographic clusters.

(e) Purchase patterns in response to **promotional campaigns** (Increased sales volume or frequency following promotions is an important measurement of their effectiveness.)

4.4 Identifying marketing opportunities

More detailed information (where available) on customer likes and dislikes, complaints, feedback and lifestyle values may offer useful information for:

(a) **Product** improvement

(b) **Customer care** and quality programmes

(c) New **product development,** and

(d) **Decision-making** across the marketing mix: on prices, product specifications, distribution channels, promotional messages and so on

Simple data fields such as 'contact type' will help to evaluate how contact is made with customers, of what types and in what numbers. Business leads may be generated most often by trade conferences and exhibitions, light users by promotional competitions and incentives, and loyal customers by personal contact through representatives.

Customers can be investigated using any data field included in the database: How many are on e-mail or the Internet? How many have spouses or children? Essentially, these parameters allow the marketer to **segment** the customer base for marketing purposes.

EXAMPLE

'Newcomers to database marketing have to make a mental leap from viewing the database as a collection of names to seeing it as an engine for driving truly personal marketing, says Melanie Howard, head of direct marketing studies at the Henley Centre.'

"Companies must understand the database is not a way of marketing, but it facilitates the personal marketing approach. They must be careful. It they think they are doing personal marketing just because they have a name and address they have a problem." They must understand what will win consumer loyalty.

'Analysing the data properly and using it effectively will separate the winners from the losers, argues Edwina Dunn-Humby, working for the company involved in running Tesco Clubcard. "Manufacturers have learned that that data about purchasing is valuable and if they can link it to names and addresses that is even more valuable. Not many are grasping the deeper meaning of that. The few that do are forward thinking and visionary," she says.

'She puts Tesco in that category. Its Clubcard collects purchasing information at the swipe of a card. The card can be used in any store, enabling marketers to build a picture of individual habits. Because the Tesco system is about collecting points then sending out vouchers, the retailer has a valid reason to write to customers.

'Being in the forefront of database marketing will take more than up-to-date technology and marketing skills, Dunn says. It will demand a third skill which she thinks has been left out of the database marketing equation: statistical analysis. "We are not bringing statisticians into the world of marketing. The bridge building is being done between marketing and IT. The big bridge that needs to be built now is between statisticians and marketing. That will separate out people who know what to do with the data."

Marketing Business

4.5 Using database information

The following is a summary of the main ways in which database information can be used.

(a) **Direct mail** used to:

- (i) Maintain customer contact between (or instead of) sales calls
- (ii) Generate leads and 'warmed' prospects for sales calls
- (iii) Promote and/or sell products and services direct to customers
- (iv) Distribute product or service information

(b) **Transaction processing**. Databases can be linked to programmes which generate order confirmations, despatch notes, invoices, statements and receipts.

(c) **Marketing research and planning**. The database can be used to send out market surveys, and may itself be investigated to show purchasing patterns and trends.

(d) **Contacts planning.** The database can indicate what customers need to be contacted or given incentives to maintain their level of purchase and commitment. A separate database may similarly be used to track planned and on-going contacts at conferences and trade shows and invitation lists to marketing events.

(e) **Product development and improvement.** Product purchases can be tracked through the product life cycle, and weaknesses and opportunities identified from records of customer feedback, complaints and warranty/guarantee claims.

(f) The **Data Protection Acts 1984 and 1998** provide that data users (organisations or individuals who control the contents of files of personal data and the use of personal data) must register with the Data Protection Registrar. They must limit their use of personal data (defined as any information about an identifiable living individual) to the uses registered.

4.6 Data mining

With a good database of information, companies undertake **data mining** for information that can be used for marketing purposes. Data mining can identify target customers for appropriate campaigns. The term **online analytical processing (OLAP)** is often used now to describe the analysis of huge amounts of data by **data warehouses**, creating a major source of information for marketing decisions.

EXAMPLE

Recording and keeping an electronic database memory of customers and prospects and of all communications and commercial contacts helps to improve all future contacts.

The explosion in personal **text message** usage has led to mutterings and ripples of excitement amongst researchers because of the new opportunities it represents. The growth in texting has been dramatic, reaching near saturation in some segments: 80% of 18 to 24 year olds use mobile phones, added to this, over 90% of this group use text messaging.

What started as a personal consumer-to-consumer pursuit, is increasingly moving towards a range of business-to-consumer activity. One rapidly emerging area is text-based advertising, whereby third parties use the 160 characters available on screen to communicate with their target market.

To achieve this, companies need to build **large databases** of mobile phone owning individuals, which ideally contain **detailed profiling information** to allow them to target their offerings precisely.

---

5 CONTACT MANAGEMENT SYSTEMS

Contact management systems are increasingly being used within sales and marketing departments in order to keep track of the interactions between its sales force, internal sales office staff and customers. This software if used correctly can become a central element to a management information system with all customer details being kept up-to-date including sales figures. Typical features include correspondence tracking, phone call logs, email filing, purchase history, quotation details, forecasts and links with EPOS together with information and details for the sales force to be able to manage the relationship.

Chapter roundup

- Personal selling is an important aspect of the communications mix.
- The task of selling involves communication, securing a sale, prospecting for potential customers, after sales service, information gathering.
- Sales personnel are in an important position in the flow of information between the customer and the organisation.
- Sales people are useful in gathering information on customers and competitors.
- Information about sales, customers and competitors can be used to give an indication of sales potential.
- The Product Life Cycle (PLC) can be evaluated in terms of sales potential and customer characteristics.
- Prospects are potential customers who have been screened or assessed.
- Managing customer databases is an important and growing area of sales management
- Database information can also be used strategically, for example to give indications on product improvements and customer care programmes.

Quick quiz

1. Why might an organisation decide to incorporate personal selling in its communications mix?
2. Personal selling is important because it is both personal and interactive. True or False?
3. Is personal selling good for raising awareness of products?
4. What type of information can sales personnel gather?
5. How can sales revenue be increased?
6. In terms of the PLC, who makes up a salesperson's clients?
7. Where might a salesperson get new customer leads from?
8. What type of information might an effective customer database include?

Answers to quick quiz

1 To demonstrate a technical product, explain a complex product, improve sales, to persuade wholesalers and retailers to stock products, if it is a small market or if direct selling may be cheaper.

2 True.

3 Usually advertising is better to raise awareness; personal selling is too expensive and labour intensive. The exception may be if the market is specialised and small.

4 Sales, consumer characteristics, competitor information.

5 By either increasing the number of customers or increasing the spending of existing clients.

6 New customers, growing customers, mature customers and declining customers.

7 From marketing efforts (eg advertising, direct mail), from within the company (eg lists of past customers, mailing lists), from networking, from industry sources, other firms or cold calling.

8 Customer titles, professional details, personal history, transaction history, contact and payment history, current transactions and special account details.

Answers to activities

1 There is no specific answer to this activity. It depends upon your own experience.

2 Knowledge and understanding of the profession
Professionalism
An 'unpushy' approach
Technical excellence
Good communication skills

3 Reductions in price
Third generation licences; greater accessibility
Fashion and popularity
Better technology; Internet access, photos, video
Better technology; smaller handsets

It is currently very 'easy' to sell mobile phones, especially at Christmas. The sales function is probably of little importance at the moment, although there is a high level of competition.

4 There is no specific answer to this activity. This is not really something you can learn from books – just have a go!

Chapter 6 :
THE SELLING PROCESS

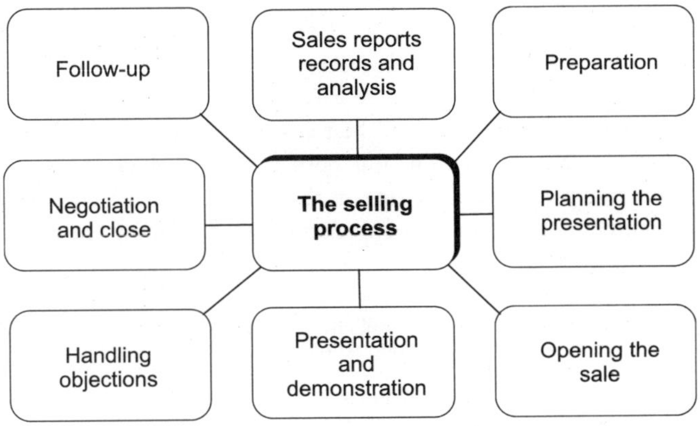

Introduction

This chapter will describe the selling process and the stages for effective selling. This includes planning and preparing the presentation, how to present the offer, handling objections and closing the sale. Follow-up and record-keeping are also of importance to the sales function and are discussed in this chapter.

Your objectives

In this chapter you will learn about the following.

(a) The importance of having a process of selling

(b) How to plan and conduct a presentation or demonstration

(c) Ways of dealing with objections

(d) The process should continue with follow-up procedures necessary after the close of a presentation

1 PREPARATION

As with so many activities, the key to success in selling lies in the preparation and planning. In this chapter we will examine the groundwork which the professional salesperson needs to do in terms of sales preparation before embarking on the sales call.

1.1 The role of the seller

Today's sales representatives need much more than a bag of product samples and a well 'rehearsed' pitch of the company's offering. As the sales effort becomes more and more integrated with marketing activities, so the role of the seller has changed. Expectations amongst buyers are that the supplier will be represented by an 'expert' able to diagnose problems and help in their resolution. For both the supplier and the buyer, then, the sales person represents a very valuable link in the communication channel – responsible for transmitting much more than just promotional messages about the product.

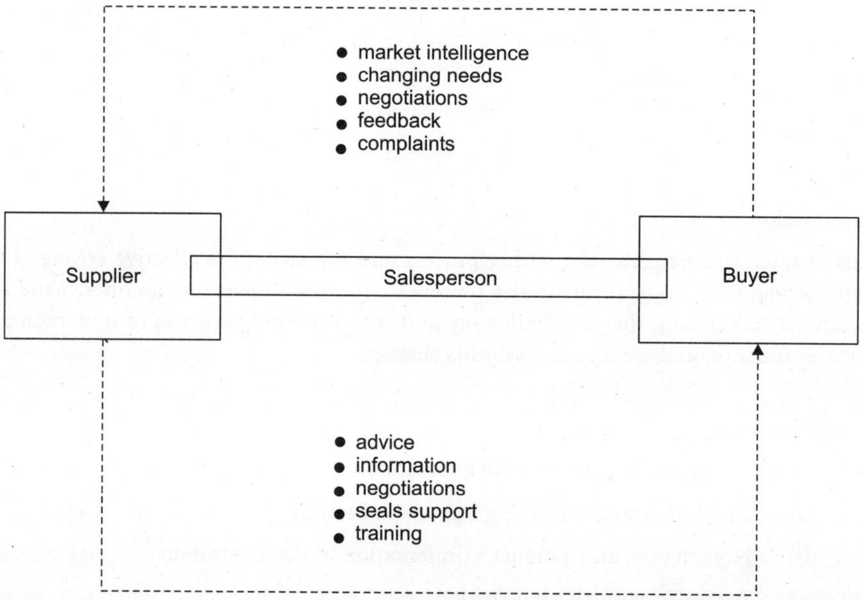

Figure 6.1: Role of the salesperson

The salesperson facilitates a two-way flow of communication and information between buyer and supplier. The value of that information is enhanced by adequate planning and training for the sales team.

As expectations of the sales team increase, their customers become increasingly sophisticated and educated and the products being sold more complex. The need for preparation becomes ever more important, as expectations of sales teams increase. Customers needs become more sophisticated, customers' education is enhanced, and products themselves become more complex.

The well prepared salesperson needs to know about the:

(a) Company or organisation
(b) Industry and competition
(c) Products
(d) Customers.

Activity 1 **(10 minutes)**

Before moving on jot down a list of the ways in which you think information about points (a) – (d) above might help in the selling situation.

1.2 What you should know about your employer

To the customer, the salesperson personifies the company, although in fact he or she only **represents** it. The well informed sales representative needs to be aware of company policy, key personnel and be able to answer any questions with confidence. The following is not an exhaustive list of what the sales team should know, but it is a starting point.

(a) The history and current company organisation. How long has the firm been in operation? Why, when and how did it originate? What new or unusual products has it been involved with, has it done anything especially worthy of note, for example awards, prizes etc?

(b) What is the standing of the firm in the industry? What is its reputation? Market share? Standing in the stock market, if it is a listed company? How many employees does it have? What countries does it operate in?

(c) Who are the senior managers in the firm? Who are the non-executive directors? Are any of them well known for other activities?

(d) What are the general policies of the firm? (Policies reflect the culture of the organisation and can be important.) How does the firm stand on equal work opportunities? Does it employ disabled people? What is it doing to promote environmentally friendly production methods? How does company policy promote customer satisfaction? What is its policy on refunds, guarantees and warranties?

(e) Does the company operate within politically sensitive areas, for example trading with developing economies? What are its policies for such activities?

(f) Specific policy areas which are likely to be of direct interest to buyers include:

(i) Policy on pricing and discounts;
(ii) The granting of credit facilities and the basis of contracts;
(iii) Delivery promises;
(iv) Periods of notice and basis for termination etc.

The sales staff must not only be familiar with these specific issues, but also be able to interpret their implications for a particular customer.

Although much of this information will be provided through induction and sales training, keeping up-to-date and extending the base of company knowledge will often be the individual's responsibility. Annual reports are a useful source of background information as are staff newsletters and other sources of internal briefing. A sales person working away from base for much of the week has to make a special effort to keep up with changes in personnel, new policies and the firm's projects within the community.

Activity 2 **(1 hour)**

In your organisation (or one you are familiar with) gather the type of information above that it would be useful for sales personnel to know.

1.3 What you should know about the industry and competition

Knowing what share of a market your firm controls is important, but it is equally important to know about the industry as a whole.

(a) What is its history? What developments are forecast? What is the size and standing of the industry when compared to other industries?

(b) What type of customers typify the industry? How are they changing?

(c) Who are the key suppliers in the industry? Who are the closest competitors? What are their strengths and weaknesses?

(d) Are there any likely newcomers to the industry? If so who are they? Who are the key players in overseas markets and are they likely to compete with you in the future?

(e) How are products and services distributed and promoted within your industry?

Information about the industry and competitors can be found in a number of places. Trade associations and industry publications can provide valuable background information.

Activity 3 **(15 minutes)**

Answer the questions (a) – (e) above for an industry of your choice.

(a) They are a useful source of updates on new developments, and forecast changes.

(b) Company reports and surveys are also useful as they indicate in broad terms a company's strategy, and its financial health.

(c) Customers may also be in regular contact with competitors sales teams.

1.4 What you should know about the product

The sales representative is expected to know about the company's products, what and, how they are made, what they can do, why they are different or better than the competitors. What really is a product though?

To the customer, the product **is a tool for solving a problem**. It is the package of benefits which the supplier is offering as a solution to that problem. The 'product' is therefore more than simply a bundle of physical attributes, it also features the intangible elements of its image, and reputation, the after sales service promise, and the price.

EXAMPLE

Endowment policy and pensions providers faced criticism that on many occasions they sold policies that were not suitable for clients.

1.5 How much benefit is on offer, and at what price?

The salesperson needs to know how to present the product's features in such a way that the product provides the buyer with relevant and valuable benefits. This requires extensive knowledge of both the product and all its attributes, possible uses and varieties. A retail salesperson requires extensive knowledge of the alternative products available and their relative strengths, weaknesses and attributes.

Particularly in industrial markets, it is increasingly the case that the complexity of the product requires the expert knowledge of a technical sales force. In these markets the process of gaining credible product knowledge is likely to take years, so instead of training the sales staff about the product, technical experts such as engineers are given sales training.

1.6 What you should know about the customers

Customer knowledge is essential to the sales preparation process. In general terms it is useful as has already been indicated, to know about the type of firms who are buyers from your industry. It is also helpful to know about their activities and how these are changing.

Specific customer information can hardly be too extensive. Prior knowledge of a client's business, organisation and interests demonstrates good customer care and interest. Information which indicates the customers current supplier, and the value of potential sales is particularly useful as it assists sales staff in assessing the priority each prospect should be given.

Customer information can also be obtained from published sources as indicated above. Trade associations and publications as well as annual reports provide a good basic framework of customer data. To this can be included in-house and industry market research surveys which may have profiled typical customers and their buying behaviour and any customer data base information available to the company.

Across a number of sectors and industries the increased availability of computerised information systems is providing more and better data on past and present customers. Sales teams need to make use of these new sources of up to the minute market intelligence.

2 PLANNING THE PRESENTATION

Preparation for a sales call requires much more that knowing about your company and products and identifying who you are going to visit. Planning how you will approach the client, what benefits you need to present and the best approach for communicating them, are all essential elements of the preparation process.

2.1 Deciding an approach

Sales presentations are like any other form of communication. To work, there must be a number of elements in place. Preparation of these elements is key to success.

The sales representative

The sales representative personifies the supplier. The degree of preparation undertaken will give credence to the professionalism of the organisation and the importance and seriousness with which the customer is credited. Preparation for a sales visit includes not only the preparation discussed earlier in this chapter, but also a planned approach and, of course, personal preparation.

Knowing the objectives

Finding the right approach and preparing effectively depends on clarifying the sales visit objectives. Objectives can vary widely according to the nature of the product, requirements of the supplier and the relationship with the customer. Certainly different objectives will be best achieved with different approaches. Objectives could be:

(a) Get a meeting and arouse the client's interest, or to win the opportunity of making a sales presentation.

(b) Come away with an order for new business or a commitment to put you on a shortlist of suppliers.

(c) Win a routine reorder or to simply ensure awareness of a new product.

(d) Fulfil any number of secondary objectives, for example collecting feedback on product performance or attitudes to a competitors recent initiative.

FOR DISCUSSION

A different approach needs to be made to companies depending on the sales objective.

The buyer

The buyer may be representing others, the family in the case of a consumer purchase, or a company in a business to business market. However, before making a sales presentation to him or her, you have to first attract the buyer's attention.

Appointments

Ensuring you have the buyer's attention is often easier if you have arranged an **appointment**, especially if the sales presentation requires concentration and the undivided attention of the audience.

The problem with asking for an appointment is that it invites the opportunity of being turned down. Getting through the front door, past battalions of gatekeepers in the form of receptionists, telephonists, secretaries and assistants can be a daunting task. Using the right approach can increase the chances of success.

Gaining an appointment depends on quickly attracting interest, which means:

(a) Introducing yourself and your company.
(b) Briefly outlining the benefits you and your product can offer to the company.
(c) Ask for a specific appointment date and time.

This formula can be more easily guaranteed by letter. There are no interruptions but of course it is more difficult to ensure a letter will reach its intended audience and there has to be a follow-up call to confirm the arrangement for an appointment.

EXAMPLE

Some attention grabbing approaches include the following.

(a) **Solution approach**
Mrs Holmes, this is Jo Seller of XYZ Company. Our recently launched Gold system has been designed to halve the administrative paperwork of companies your size. I am in the area on Thursday next week. Would it be convenient to show you how this saving can be made, or would Friday be better?

(b) **Endorsement approach**
... We have recently installed our new system at WXZ Company and they are delighted with the results. Their Mr Smith thought you would find the system a great benefit to your operation ...

(c) **Congratulations approach**

... Mrs Law, congratulations on the forthcoming wedding of your daughter which I saw announced in the paper today. Our special brides' wedding service can take the headache out of the arrangements and save you money ...

Whichever approach you use, whether by phone or letter, make sure it is:

- Personal
- Clear
- Positive
- Concise
- Interesting

It is not always practical to make appointments in advance (eg when selling door to door). However, you have to be prepared for the customer to be out or too busy to deal with you. In some sectors, customers may be happy for the sales representative just to 'pop in'. However most people resent time wasting so only call if you have a clear purpose and objective, something new to offer or discuss.

Increasingly, as the real cost of selling is recognised, making the most of sales time is also being given a higher priority. Appointments help to ensure sales time is spent with contacts who are genuinely interested, reduces the 'waiting time' to see buyers and increases the 'quality' of sales time by reducing the number of interruptions.

Whether a sales presentation is made as the result of an appointment or not, it is important to remember that sales communication can only be effective if it is made to the right audience and that listener is receiving the message clearly.

2.2 The message

A message's clarity can be adversely affected by a variety of factors including an audience which does not listen properly, and also by the way the message is constructed and communicated (ie encoded).

Preparation is important in this stage and depends on knowing the audience. Using technical jargon to a non-specialist buyer is unlikely to have a positive impact, but neither is talking down to an expert. Concepts which are hard to express verbally may be easily communicated with an illustration or diagram.

Successful sales messages are those which are based on identified customer needs and clearly present **relevant user benefits**. Then the message appears relevant and is much more likely to be acted upon.

Standard or variable messages?

One way of controlling what salespeople say is to encourage them to deliver a standard or set sales presentation. This is often the case for telephone selling.

(a) The 'word perfect' sales pitch, more suitable for delivery by phone (when the buyer's cues to interrupt can be more easily ignored) is much less common today than in the past.

(b) It fails to maximise the real value of the salesperson – the ability to respond to customer needs and worries, and to judge the mood of the sales negotiation. It takes away the benefit of two way sales communication and turns the salesperson into another media for delivering a standard message just like the TV or radio. Such an approach cannot really provide for individual customer needs, and is unlikely to maximise sales opportunities.

EXAMPLE

Some companies such as McDonald's have scripts that sales personnel follow when dealing with members of the public. Business to business markets are much less likely to have scripts, as negotiations are usually two way.

Providing sophisticated sales aids which present key product features and benefits is a less rigid approach to standardising the sales presentation. Visual presenters, short videos and computer and slide presentations can enhance the professional image of the presentation and can help to communicate fundamental aspects of the product or service.

The sales representative planning a structured sales presentation is aware of the need to take the buyer through the stages of the AIDA decision process.

Awareness

Interest

Desire

Action

The **action** stage should not necessarily be seen as making a sale. It needs to be considered in the context of the original objectives – if that was to be invited to make a full presentation, then that is the action to be targeted.

2.3 The formal presentation

In some industries the 'interested' customer will invite the supplier to make a formal proposal or presentation of what they can offer. In industries like computers, consultancy and advertising this formal presentation may well be at the end of a detailed evaluation of the clients needs and present position. It can take the form, as in the advertising world, of specially produced multi media presentations. It can involve many individuals on both sides and can be very expensive to mount. It is worthwhile only when the potential business is substantial and should only be undertaken on the basis of the most thorough preparation.

A good presentation will display the following attributes.

(a) It should be flexible – able to be adapted to the interests, needs and wants of the prospect.

(b) It should be clear

(c) It must be credible and relevant

(d) It should clearly describe the product or service and the *benefits* it offers the prospect

(e) It should arouse and maintain interest

(f) It should motivate the prospect to action, set by the sales objective.

2.4 The unspoken message

Sales professionals have to pay attention not only to their preparation of the spoken selling message, but also the unspoken one. Body language is the term given to the visual clues, which we are all expert at picking up and often translate at a subconscious level, eg a salesperson lacking the confidence to look a buyer in the eye may be perceived to be dishonest and untrustworthy. The professional seller must become a skilled communicator both spoken and unspoken messages.

2.5 Feedback

The final element in sales communication is feedback. If the advantage of selling is its ability to be a two-way communication channel, then the 'receive' button on the sales person has to be tuned in!

3 OPENING THE SALE: AWARENESS AND INTEREST

The actual sales interview is often the culmination of hours or even weeks of preparation and planning. How long it lasts is not important, it is the **outcome** that matters.

Every word and action will have a bearing on the eventual outcome, and on the long-term relationship between the two.

3.1 First impressions count

The buyer will begin to assess the seller before a word has been spoken. The manner in which the interview was set up, the appearance, posture and body language of the sales person will all contribute to vital first impressions.

(a) The approach phase has a clear responsibility in this structure – to gain and hold the attention of the buyer. Most sales professionals consider this **initial phase** as being the most **crucial** of a successful sales visit. It is the first moments which set the tone for the whole meeting.

(b) The worst first impression can be made by keeping the customer waiting. Appointments made must be kept punctually. That means allowing adequate time between sales calls and knowing in advance where you are going and how to get there. Unavoidable delays must be communicated as soon as possible to the prospect.

The sales person has a number of points which need to be covered in the approach phase of the interview.

(a) Personal introductions should reinforce the buyer's conviction that it is worth spending time on this meeting.

(b) The sales person therefore has to **sell himself** or **herself** before anything else. They must convince the prospect of their credibility. They can then move on to selling **their products** and **their organisation**.

(c) Gain and retain the prospects' interest and win their trust so they will enter into a dialogue about their needs., problems, concerns etc.

The first minutes of a meeting are really about selling the rest of the interview.

Activity 4

Set yourself a project related to a major purchase you are planning/hoping to make in the future. This might be a new washing machine, car or stereo system, a holiday in the sun, or a new camera. Take the time to identify a range of potential suppliers and then approach them for information about the product you are considering. Pay particular attention to the approach the sales staff use and their presentation or demonstration of the product.

- Which sales person was best?
- Why?
- If you were responsible for training the sales staff you encountered what suggestions would you make for improving each individual's effectiveness?

4 PRESENTATION AND DEMONSTRATION: INTEREST AND DESIRE

The stage of presentation and demonstration should be designed to help change the attitude of potential customers from 'not purchasing' towards a conviction 'to purchase'.

Showing or demonstrating the product, its features and benefits is particularly useful in maintaining the buyer's interest because it involves the buyer's **other senses in addition to hearing.** They are no longer just listening to the seller, they are looking at the visual aids or trying out the product.

4.1 Questions

During this second stage the salesperson will continue to ask questions and listen to answers which will build a more and more complete picture of the customer's needs and requirements.

(a) **Open questions**

Using open questions like who, when, why, how and what, are good for encouraging the customer to enter discussions and reveal preferences and buying motives.

> For example:
> Q: Do you like this red model?
> A: No
> A better question is:
> Q: What colour do you like best?

(b) **Focus**

Questions can **help focus the buyer's attention** on an issue he or she had not previously considered or a problem not yet recognised.

> Q: Have you considered how much heat is lost in a typical flat-roofed factory?

(c) **Involvement**

People **become more involved** when they are asked questions. Questions are part of the whole process and satisfactory answers provide further evidence of the product's benefits.

(d) **Clarify**

Questions can also be used to **check understanding** and encourage the customers to clarify or answer their own objections.

> Q: Are you clear how this system works?
> Q: Have you any questions about the products performance?
> Q: What don't you like about this new lever operated mechanism?
> Q: Why do you prefer the old style?

Although anyone can ask questions, it takes a well trained and professional salesperson to:

- Ask the right question
- Listen to the answers
- Interpret their implications in terms of the sales situation.

4.2 Turn features into benefits

The object of the exercise is to present the product in a way which is meaningful for the prospective buyer. It is worth reiterating the concept you met much earlier – of the product as a tool for solving a customer's problem. Without a need, there will be no purchase.

The process the sales person has to go through can be illustrated as shown below.

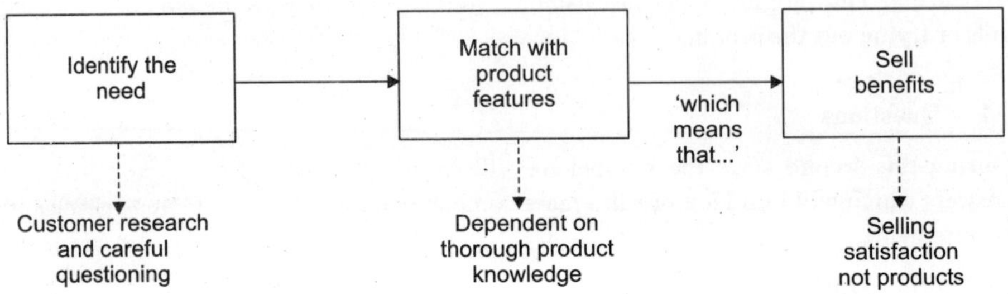

Figure 6.2: Sales process

Firms develop specific features to give them a competitive position in the market place, but features belong to the product (product orientation). Customers buy benefits not features (ie what those features will do for them). Turning features into benefits demonstrates a customer-oriented approach. This is easy to do by taking the feature and adding the phrase – '... which means that ...'.

Feature		*Benefit*
This model has five doors	*which means that ...*	... it is very easy to load shopping and children!
The compact design of this model	*means that ...*	... it is very easy to park.

The benefit offered should be relevant and important to the customer. **This is why the preapproach research and questioning are so important.**

An effective sales presentation will:

- Be complete
- Be clear and concise
- Highlight features and benefits relevant to the prospective buyer
- Cover and eliminate as many questions and objections as possible
- Handle the question of competition and thorny issues like price.

The process of making a sale is not simply a matter of routinely going through a series of rehearsed stages and steps. It actually requires motivating the customer to want to buy. This process requires skill and patience and depends on:

(a) Customers recognising, accepting or convincing themselves they have a need;

(b) Customers believing that the benefits being offered satisfy their buying motives;

(c) Customers believing that the potential benefits/value of the product justifies its price, in other words, that there is nothing better to buy with the same money. (*Note*. This is not just **direct** competition, but also indirect competition from other types of product or service, eg a family may buy a new car **or** have a special holiday abroad. The family might have a finite amount of resources, and a variety of choices.)

4.3 Using sales aids

Sales aids have already been mentioned in the previous chapter. Extended and highly programmed aids can risk making the sales person redundant to some extent, but developed creatively and designed for flexible use, they can do just what they are intended to do which is to **aid selling.** Sales aids in the form of brochures, presentation kits and demonstration models can help to:

(a) Add tangibility to a service or product not available for demonstration at the point of sale

(b) Add interest and variety to the sales presentation

(c) Make it easier to explain key selling points or complex products

(d) Show the products in use and customers benefiting from them

4.4 The role of training

The sales person's success in selling is very dependent on the skills demonstrated throughout the sales presentation. Questioning techniques to uncover needs, handling different types of customers and presenting products can all be enhanced by training, particularly the use of role play scenarios.

The ability to highlight the various attributes of a product offering, in the light of revealed customer needs, is only developed with practice.

5 HANDLING OBJECTIONS

5.1 Objections are a good thing

Buyers can object to the product or its price, the company or the timing of the offer. Objections should not be seen as negative.

(a) **They indicate the buyer is actually considering the sales proposition** and objections represent the vocalisation of anxieties, obstacles and issues which stand in the way of making a decision to buy. Objections give the sales person the opportunity of finding out more about the buyer and the buyer's needs.

(b) Buying a new product or service often involves change from tried and trusted methods or brands or well known suppliers. It is human behaviour to resist change and to feel more comfortable with the idea of change if convinced and reassured by the sales person. Sales staff should remember that they are in the business of modifying behaviour and changing attitudes – processes which require a raft of motivational and persuasive skills.

5.2 Ways of overcoming objections

Experience and training will provide the sales person with a toolbox of techniques for handling objections. An appropriate approach can then be selected to suit the specific situation and objection.

(a) All these techniques have one thing in common – they must evolve from **careful listening.** Listening is important to convey to the buyers that their views are important and to reduce any resentment from 'being sold to'.

(b) It helps the buyer feel more involved in the process and eventually will lead to him or her owning (taking responsibility for) the purchase decision. At the end of the process the buyer should be able to say '**I bought** this from you' rather than '**You sold** this to me'.

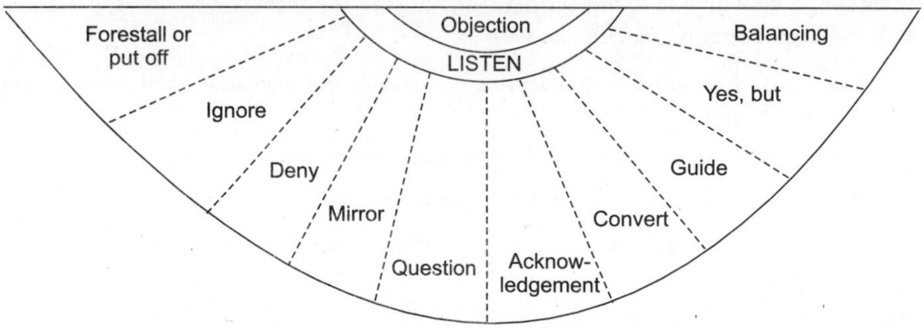

Figure 6.3: Common techniques for handling objections

Technique	Comment
Forestall or put off	**Anticipating objections** and building the answer into the earlier part of the sales presentation is known as forestalling. Putting off handling an objection until later is valid, if you feel it is better dealt with after more of the product's benefits have been demonstrated.
Ignore	This is certainly a technique some sellers use, but it is not to be recommended or used regularly. It can only be valid if the objection is felt to be very weak.
Deny	Denying has to be done tactfully and politely as it can be interpreted as an aggressive response – but if the buyer is claiming something definitely untrue, for example 'your company insists on payments in fourteen days or it imposes a penalty charge', then a direct polite denial would be appropriate.
Mirror	Mirroring is a technique used to give the buyer the chance to consider their own objection as well as an opportunity to clarify your understanding of it. • Your main concern then is • ... Are you saying • ... If I understand you ...

Technique	Comment
Question	Asking for details of the basis of the objection can provide specific instances or examples which can make the objection seem less serious, eg: Buyer: My experience with your company is that they cannot deliver on time. Seller: I am very sorry you have got that impression. Can I ask specifically what problems you have had? Buyer: During the bad weather last winter deliveries were late etc.
Acknowledge	Acknowledging an objection can be seen in the seller's first statement in the example above. It shows the buyer that the objection has been noted sympathetically, recognised but its validity has not been accepted.
Convert	Turning objections into **selling features** is one of the most powerful techniques in the sales persons tool kit. Buyer: We could certainly do with the extra luggage space offered by this bigger five-door model, but my wife must have a car she finds easy to park. Seller: That's what we found many of our customers needed, which is why this model features power assisted steering, and a specially designed rear window making visibility for reversing much easier, which means this car is actually easier to park than many smaller models.
Guide	Guiding is a technique by which the sales person provides a framework to 'guide' the buyer to make their own conversion. It is best used when the buyer has made both positive and negative comments about the product. Buyer: I can see the benefits of this cleaner system, but our old one is still working and I am not sure it is worth the cost of changing. Seller: Have you calculated the weekly costs of the extra cleaning your current system requires? How many hours of production are lost each month while cleaning is done? What benefits do you think a cleaner working environment would give to your staff?
Yes, but	The yes but or yes however approach is based on an agree and neutralise technique. Agreeing shows understanding and sympathy with the objection, whilst providing the chance to demonstrate why the objection is unfounded. Like the 'deny' technique, this can cause offence if not handled with care. Buyers do not like to be contradicted or proven wrong!

Technique	Comment
Balancing	Visualise the pros and cons of the product offering using a simple list technique. This demonstrates the balance of advantages very clearly. *Pros* • Quicker delivery • Less stockholding • More durable • Compatible with existing units *Cons* • Initial start-up costs • Heavier weight

Handling objections is an essential part of the selling role. Experience of customer objections will help the seller be better prepared for future objections, but even the most experienced sales representative can expect two to six objections in a typical sales interview.

5.3 Summarising the key steps in objection handling

- Welcome objections
- Put yourself in the buyer's shoes
- Listen carefully
- Acknowledge and repeat or rephrase the objection
- Investigate any hidden objections
- Ask more questions: what, why and when?
- Choose a technique for handling the objection – but be **tactful**.

Although the sales person must be prepared to meet and respond to new or specific objections it is possible to identify a number of categories or sources of likely objection. Thinking through possible objections means the sales team will be better prepared to handle them and provides the chance to forestall many of those most likely to come up.

Activity 5 **(5 minutes)**

Role play a scenario with a friend where one plays a salesperson and the other a prospective customer at a car showroom

6 NEGOTIATIONS AND CLOSING THE SALE

Changing the customer's attitude towards a product is an important step in the selling process, but by itself achieves nothing tangible. The sales person is ultimately looking for a sale or an order and so the sales interview has to build up to the point at which the sales person asks for the business – the **close**.

Convincing and persuading customers is the job of the sales team and it starts with their own positive attitude and the expectation that they will make the sale.

6.1 Timing of close

There is no single moment when a sale can be closed. It is a mistake to think that all the stages of the sales sequence which we have outlined in this chapter have to be complete before a sale can be confirmed. Sellers must be alert for 'buying cues' or signals throughout the meeting. These are the signals that the buyer is committed to a purchase and they appear at any point.

EXAMPLE

Seller: I wanted the opportunity of showing you the improved features on our model xyz.

Buyer: Yes, I've heard about this model, I think we will need ten.

Seller: Let me demonstrate how it works

Or:

Buyer: Are easy credit terms available?

Seller: I am sure you will enjoy the benefits of the remote control feature.

Buying signals can be an expression of interest either verbal, physically or facially communicated. Whatever form they take the salesperson should attempt a trial close as soon as they are recognised.

FOR DISCUSSION

A trial close loses nothing and acts as a test of the buyer's responsiveness.

There are many techniques for closing a sale. The following table indicates some of the main ones.

Approach	Example
1. **Ask for the order** (Its surprising how many forget to!)	Shall I wrap this one up for you?
2 **Either/or?** (Choice technique)	Would you prefer the green or the blue model? Do you prefer to pay by cash or cheque or credit card?
3 **Assumption** (Based on the belief you will get the order)	As you obviously prefer this model shall I arrange for delivery next week?
4 **Testimonial close** (Using others indirectly as influencers and advisers by listing or showing the orders from other impressive clients)	You know ABC Ltd had their second delivery of this product only last week.

Approach	Example
5 **Tip the scales** Following a summing up of all the relevant benefits and selling points	In view of this attractive offer is there anything stopping you from placing an order now?
6 **Why not close**	You still seem uncertain, is there any reason why you should not buy now?
7 **Emotional appeal** (For use when the purchase decision is likely to be based on emotion or impulse. Insurance can be sold on fear, new cars on pride and charitable giving on guilt)	You look very fashionable in that colour.
8 **Conversion close** (As seen earlier this takes the customers objection and turns it into a benefit)	Buyer: I can't really afford it this quarter. Seller: At this special low introductory price can you really afford to wait?
9 **Concessions close** (Provide a final incentive to help the buyer over the final decision making hurdle – it can be based on the fear of a loss or the chance to make a gain)	I cannot guarantee these prices next month. If you order now I can offer a special discount.

Buyer incentives devised and developed by marketing to support the sales activity can help at the close of the sale. They need to appeal to the buyer and be designed to achieve specific objectives, eg a new product trial or an increase in average order size.

Promotions can take many forms like special terms, advertising support, extra product or seasonal packaging or gifts. Like all promotions they must be ethical and legal and in line with all relevant codes of practice.

6.2 Negotiation of terms

Even when a sale is almost certain, its close can often be determined by the detailed negotiation of the terms of business. As can be seen from above, the sales person may use the flexibility of terms like price or delivery to help close the sale.

Negotiating can take many forms from a minor 'haggling' over price to a major round the table exchange of legal contracts.

The sales team must be well briefed as to the extent of their authority to negotiate terms. The size of discounts acceptable and the ability to deliver service promises should all be known in advance of the sales interview. Confirming availability and delivery dates for products is an important part of the preparation stage of selling.

The degree of autonomy the sales team has in such negotiations is clearly a matter of policy.

- Too much freedom can have considerable impact on the profitability of new business.
- Too little and sales opportunities may be missed simply because of the salespersons inability to move a little on terms.

6.3 Negotiations on price

It is the area of price discounts that causes the greatest concerns for managers. A sales team, with authority to offer discounts, is often suspected of giving these away, perhaps unnecessarily – certainly too easily. The fear is that it becomes too easy to offer inducements. The sales team will use discounts rather than persuasion to motivate a purchase.

Certainly selling on price is a minefield. Lower prices today tend to lead to an expectation of similarly low prices in the future. In consumer markets particularly, price is taken to be the guide to quality, and lowering price can directly impact on product image. Ideally it is preferable to sell added benefits rather than to lower prices and this needs to be borne in mind.

6.4 Agreeing the terms

Marketing is concerned not with simply selling the product but with developing a continuing relationship with the customer. It is increasingly referred to as relationship marketing in industrial sectors and brand loyalty in consumer markets. The measure of success in marketing terms is not simply making the sale, but in ensuring the customer is satisfied.

Negotiating and clarifying all the relevant terms of business are essential first stages in establishing a positive future relationship. Misunderstanding about payment terms, delivery dates or quality of product can all lead to dissatisfaction and lost future business.

It is fundamental to ethical and professional selling that an order is not signed on the basis of 'pie in the sky' promises or unclear terms. Getting it right at this stage is the foundation of good future relations.

6.5 Improving negotiation skills

Negotiation is the process of bringing the buyer and seller together. The objective is straightforward enough: to ensure that both parties are satisfied by the exchange.

EXAMPLE

The sales representative must assess the limits of each party to the negotiation: each will have some idea of their minimum and maximum boundaries.

Buyer: Minimum performance criteria
Maximum price payable for them
Extras that would justify paying a bit more, up to an absolute limit.

Seller: Rock bottom price it will go to
Maximum amounts of concessions

This, according to Brassington and Pettitt (2006), is a delicate judgement, but if the seller can detect when the buyer is close to their absolute limit, then a sale is more likely than if a buyer is pushed over the limit and withdraws from negotiations.

Negotiating and clarifying all the relevant terms of business are essential first stages in establishing a positive future relationship. Misunderstanding about payment terms, delivery dates or quality of product can all lead to dissatisfaction and lost future business.

Activity 6 **(10 minutes)**

You have been asked to advise a colleague who is about to embark on a negotiation with a key client about a continuation of contract. How should she prepare?

A basic **'win-win' approach** to negotiating is as follows.

(a) Map out, in advance, what the needs and fears of both parties are. This outlines the psychological and practical territory.

(b) **Define your desired outcome** and estimate the worst, realistic and best case scenarios. ('If I can pay £500, it would be ideal, but I'd settle for £600. Above £700, it's just not worth my while.') Start with the best case and leave room to fall back to the realistic case. Keep your goal in sight.

(c) **Look for mutual or trade-off benefits**. How might you both gain (for example, by getting a higher discount in return for longer or pre-booked series of ads or providing camera ready copy)? What might be cheap for you to give that would be valuable for the other party to receive, or vice versa?

(d) **Spell out the positive benefits** to the other party and support them in saying 'yes' to your proposals by making it as easy as possible. (Offer to supply information or help with follow-up tasks, for example.) Emphasise areas of agreement and common ground.

(e) **Overcome negativity** by asking questions

- What will make it work for you?
- What would it take to make this possible?

(f) **Overcome side-tracks** by asking questions such as: ' How is this going to get us where we want to go?'

(g) **Be hard on the problem but soft on the person**. This is not personal competition or antagonism: work together on problem solving (eg by using flip chart or paper to make shared notes). Show that you have heard the other person (by summarising their argument) before responding with your counter argument.

(h) **Be flexible**. A 'take it or leave it' approach breaks relationships. (However, saying 'no' repeatedly to sales people is a good way of finding out just how far below the list price they are prepared to go!) Make and invite reasonable counter offers.

(i) **Be culturally sensitive**. Some markets thrive on 'haggling'. Some cultures engage in a lot of movement up and down the bargaining scale (eg Asian and Middle Eastern), while others do their homework and fix their prices (eg German). In the former cultures, much emphasis is placed on building relationships and extending hospitality before getting down to terms.

(j) **Take notes**, so the accuracy of everyone's recollection of what was proposed and agreed can be checked.

(k) Summarise and **confirm the details** of your agreements to both parties (by memo, letter, contract) and acknowledge a mutually positive outcome.

Experience, **knowledge** and **expertise** count in negotiation: they add up to bargaining power, which is important even in a win-win approach. If there is someone in your department who has experience in a particular field (such as advertising sales), or your organisation retains an agency or consultancy, be prepared to let them handle negotiations for you.

Activity 7 **(30 minutes)**

Get together with fellow students (or friends) in pairs or teams to prepare and role-play a negotiation. *Either*:

(a) You are looking to purchase advertising space in (any appropriate) magazine for a colour advertisement for your product. You have not previously advertised in this magazine, but have identified it as one which is targeted for your market and high circulation: it could be the key to your up-coming campaign. The copy deadline for the next issue is approaching and the magazine had an unsold colour page which it needs to fill. Rate card price for the colour page is £2,000 (£2,800 for the inside front cover, £2,500 for the inside back cover highly contested positions), which you would love to secure. Standard discounts include 10% media buyer's commission, 10% for a series of six ads. You pay 5% extra for bleed colour (running off the page edge). You and the magazine representative(s) should separately (without telling each other) decide what your necessary outcomes are: you should decide what you have to spend from your space budget, and how many ads you think you will need; the magazine rep(s) should decide that the minimum price they will accept, given their need to see space filled. Negotiate a deal!

or

(b) You want to go on holiday with the whole family to a coastal resort this summer. Your (role-play) partner wants to have some quiet time at home redecorating the bathroom, knowing that the two teenage (role-play) kids are keen to spend time with friends. These projects are important to both (or all four) of you. Negotiate!

If you really can't find role-play partners, make notes on the possible strategies, win-win potential, and best-realistic-worst positions for all participants.

7 FOLLOW-UP

Understanding about the need for and the value of sales follow-up requires recognition that:

(a) The sales effort is not simply a short-term tactical activity aimed at winning a one-off sale.

(b) The selling process is expensive representing a considerable investment of company resources which is unlikely to be paid back on the basis of just one order.

(c) Even a sale which was not made can be followed up and represents a qualified lead for future business.

It is important that sales staff do not feel that the signing of an order is the end of the sales process. **In many respects it should be seen as the beginning of the seller-buyer relationship**.

7.1 Thank the customer

Thanking the buyer for the order should be done at the end of the sales interview, but it can be reinforced by a phone call or letter. If the sales call has resulted in something other than a firm order, for example the opportunity to submit a proposal or estimate, then the follow-up in writing is important to confirm the details of the brief or agreement. The simple act of thanking the client for the order or opportunity to compete for work is a courtesy, but people do like to feel their business is appreciated and important.

7.2 Check the order has been fulfilled

Checking the order has been fulfilled is the next vital stage in the follow-up. With products, this means a phone call on the day of delivery to ensure the order has arrived. With a service or installation, it is important to check at an early stage that work is under way and the client is satisfied with both progress and performance.

(a) The **client** should be contacted, not the seller's operations or delivery staff, as the customer may have a problem of which they are unaware.

(b) The process of checking directly has positive PR benefits. It the client feels you are interested, it presents an image that the seller and the supplier are concerned and it continues the dialogue, making future sales calls easier. The feeling that the sales representative will take direct personal action to correct any errors or mistakes is very reassuring to a new customer. It has the effect of reducing the risk perceived in both the current and future purchases.

(c) It can lead to an increased order of extra fitments, additional supplier etc.

(d) It provides a solid basis for a long-term relationship.

(e) It represents a proactive approach to heading off possible future complaints.

(f) It represents an ideal opportunity to ask for referrals, contacts and colleagues who might also appreciate the benefits offered by your product.

(g) The easiest sales come from satisfied customers.

8 SALES REPORTS, RECORDS AND ANALYSIS

8.1 Paperwork

Paperwork of all types represents non-productive selling time and as such is often resented and avoided wherever possible by the sales personnel. This same lost sales time should cause sales management to think carefully about what paperwork they really need and what their objectives are in requesting it.

However, despite streamlining, computerisation and rationalisation, it has to be appreciated that the selling job is fundamentally about communication. Communication does not stop at the meeting or interview, but has to be followed-up, confirmed and acted upon by communication in writing. This includes order forms and internal paperwork as well as correspondence with the client.

As we have seen, the sales professional is a medium for communication between the company and the customer. The details of feedback, comments, complaints, offers and selling messages all have to be passed accurately between the two parties. Written records and reports are essential to this process.

8.2 Sales reports

Substitute for supervision

In many organisations the report is treated as a means of controlling the sales staff, on the assumption that if you get staff to put in writing what they were doing, when and where, they must have been using their time productively.

Reports are seen as a substitute for close supervision over staff who are working independently.

Seen in this way the process of reporting is both unproductive and demotivating. It is unlikely to result in effective use of sales efforts and will almost certainly fail to provide managers with a stream of valuable market intelligence and feedback.

Control cycle

Controlling the sales activity is nonetheless a responsibility management has to undertake. But control can only be meaningful if it is preceded by thorough planning. Likewise sales plans are only of use if their outcomes are monitored and controlled. The essential ingredient of plans is of course that they contain quantified objectives or targets, which can be used as a basis for monitoring performance.

Once objectives are established, the function of the report can be seen as providing evidence of performance against set targets, (weekly or monthly etc) and providing information which enables management to analyse any variances between planned and actual results.

Management get sales information from visiting sales staff in the field, from sales results and call reports. Sales results, recording actual sales made, do not necessarily provide very useful insights. A particularly large order, or regional economic fluctuations can distort the underlying sales patterns. Typically the report should contain the information below.

Who?	• New or existing customer? • Name of the contact • Details of the lead source.		
What?	• The objective of the visit • What happened during the visit • Past sales history with the client • Results achieved		
Next	• Any action to be taken	– by sales person – by others	
Other	• Details of time spent in sales interview • Mileage and expenses incurred.		

8.3 Sales records

Records enable the salesperson to keep track of contact details, (eg when, where and who). They ensure that important personal contacts and details are not lost or forgotten.

The record system of the sales person might be a database from which sales activities can be planned. A well maintained customer record system helps ensure the sales person maximises potential business from existing clients.

Organisations often have to take positive steps to ensure they too have access to the **customer database**. Otherwise when a sales person leaves the company not only is there the risk of the clients following the representative, there is also the danger of losing potential business through lack of contact with the existing client database.

8.4 Sales analysis

If information is not going to be used, there is little point in collecting it. Both the sales professional and the sales manager should be analysing information for the same reason – to improve efficiency and performance.

Analysis of the selling activity can be both qualitative and quantitative.

8.5 Qualitative analysis

Qualitative measures are much more subjective than quantitative ones, and are likely to involve an assessment of both the sales techniques and process. This would, for example, form the basis of a field appraisal following a manager's field sales visit. Its role is to provide on the job training which is effective and ongoing as well as motivation and control.

The individual sales person can undertake **qualitative analysis**. This involves a review and analysis of his or her own sales performance, particularly when sales were not made. Critical and routine reflection can help to highlight strengths which can be developed and weaknesses which can be improved. This process of personal improvement is of considerable importance to sales staff, particularly those remunerated in part by commission payments.

8.6 Quantitative analysis

Quantitative analysis provides the objective basis for comparing sales performance of

- The individual over time
- Products within a range
- sales within a region

There are a number of ways in which results can be assessed. Typically, the ratios which might be considered include:

(a) Sales call ratio (ie the number of calls made to produce one sale)
(b) Costs per order
(c) Average order value
(d) Proportion of repeat/new orders
(e) Sales calls per day.

Chapter roundup

- Sales personnel need to know about
  - the organisation they represent
  - the industry
  - the competition
  - the products/services
  - the customers
- Sales calls need to be prepared for and the objective of the call needs to be understood.
- Sales messages have to be constructed and communicated (encoded).
- Awareness and interest in the company's product needs to be developed in the sales presentation, hopefully followed by desire.
- A dialogue between the client and sales person should be developed, asking questions and presenting benefits.
- Objections can be handled with experience, training and techniques.
- Sellers must be alert to 'buying curves' throughout the sales meeting.
- Follow up should include confirmation that the order has been fulfilled.
- Sales reports should be seen as a means of retaining control and imparting information.

Quick quiz

1 Give three internal sources of information that sales personnel could use to obtain information about an organisation.

2 Should sales personnel make appointments or cold call?

3 How can a salesperson make a good first impression with a client?

4 Give examples of sales aids.

5 What are the benefits of sales aids to the sales persons?

6 Give three ways in which a salesperson can overcome objections.

7 What negotiations should be undertaken before closing the sale?

Answers to quick quiz

1 Could include induction, training, annual reports, staff newsletters etc.

2 It is usually better to make appointments.

3 Be on time, take care with appearance, personal introduction, and listening.

4 Brochures, presentation kits, demonstration models, videos, computer generated images etc.

5 Add interest, add tangibility, show products in use and make it easier to explain key selling points.

6 Forestall or put off, ignore, acknowledge

7 Terms and price.

Answers to activities

1 *Company/organisation:* to understand the company ethos and communicate it.

Industry and competition: put the company and its products into perspective.

Products: to focus on the sellable or 'good' points.

Customers: to target the intended purchasers and gear the marketing towards them.

2 The answer to this activity will depend on your selected industry.

3 There is no specific answer to this activity.

4 There is no specific answer to this activity.

5 How good a deal do you think you achieved (a) as a customer, (b) as a car dealer?

6 Find out details of current contract
What has the client liked?
What has the client disliked?
How can we remedy what the client has disliked?
Does the client want to change any aspect?
Do we need to be armed with good ideas for a change?
Is price a factor?
Can we offer a discount?
Do we need a change of personnel on the account?

7 There is no specific answer to this activity.

Chapter 7 :

ORGANISING THE ACHIEVEMENT OF SALES OBJECTIVES

Introduction

This chapter looks at sales strategy in the context of the organisation's overall strategy and the product life cycle (PLC). This is followed by a consideration of how management organises the sales function, the importance of careful journey planning, and finally how management can communicate policies and strategies to the sales force.

Your objectives

In this chapter you will learn about the following.

(a) How sales objectives fit into overall corporate and marketing objectives

(b) The impact of the PLC on sales strategies

(c) How the sales function can be organised by management

(d) The importance of careful journey planning

(e) The ways in which management can communicate with the salesforce

1 SETTING SALES OBJECTIVES

1.1 Level of objectives

Sales objectives are – or should be – set in the wider context of the marketing mix.

EXAMPLE

A Bank wants to increase profits.

(a) **Business objective:** grow profits.

(b) **Strategy:** Increase revenue per customer.

(c) **Tactics:** increasing revenue per customer might not be possible unless customers buy other services form the bank (eg insurance).

  (i) The **critical success factor** will be the number of extra services sold to each customer.

  (ii) A **key task** might involve developing a **customer database** so that the firm can target customers with information about other services more effectively.

  (iii) The **resources needed** might include the services of a system analyst, hardware etc and increased sales force

---

1.2 Marketing objectives

To take an example, let's say that middle managers have been faced with a corporate objective of increasing profitability by x% over three years.

(a) In pursuit of this, **production** could cut costs, reduce stockholdings and trim back production levels.

(b) **Marketing** could be implementing strategies to increase revenue, through higher sales. These two departments would clearly be working **against each other,** although both aiming to contribute to the stated corporate goal.

It is only when armed with clear, quantified corporate objectives and the co-ordinating influence of a corporate strategy that unit managers can develop their own functional plans. The first step is to generate unit objectives.

We can outline a hierarchy as follows.

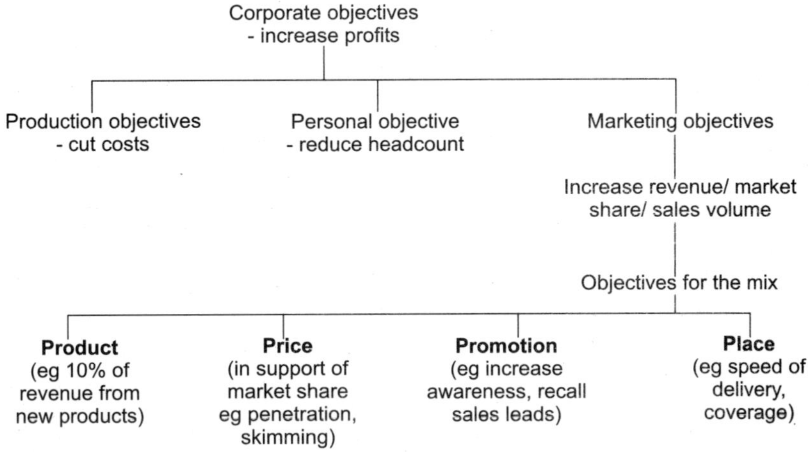

Figure 7.1: Hierarchy of marketing objectives

EXAMPLE

Marketing objectives are often expressed in **sales terms**, for example, market share or revenue or sales volume.

(a) For example A Ltd wishes to increase **market share** to 43% by2010.

(b) This objective can then be further developed by the sales manager who can forecast that 43% in 2010 will equal 1 million cases. In turn the sales manager can then develop the next level of objectives into terms which mean something to those in the sales team: to sell 1,000 more cases per month by 2010.

(c) The individual sales targets or objectives can be set from this. With a salesforce of twenty, each salesperson needs to be selling 50 extra cases per month by 2010.

Objectives can be set for other elements of the mix and for marketing activities.

Mix element	Comment
Product	Although 'marketing' deals with products and markets, marketing objectives for products require the co-operation of the production department and R&D. Marketing can suggest that a percentage (eg 10%) of revenue should come from **new products.**
Pricing	**Distribution** pricing has market share implications (eg penetration or skimming pricing). Distribution can be considered a marketing tool – an objective might be to reduce the time from when the order is received to when the goods are delivered: 'By March 2011, reduce delivery lead times from 5 to 3 days'.

Mix element	Comment
Promotion	Advertising and promotion objectives can be set to shape customer awareness and expectations of the product as well as to generate sales leads. • Recall: How many remember an ad? • Awareness • Interest (eg % of people replying to a mailshot) • 'Share of voice' (compared to other companies' promotions)
Service marketing mix	• People – staff training • Processes – efficiency • Physical evidence (cleanliness of sites).
Customers	• For many firms, repeat business is more profitable than new business – this is the justification behind **relationship marketing.** • A firm might **reposition** its offer to attract a new segment.

EXAMPLE

Most suppliers are involved not only with selling to retailers, but also with working closely with them in terms of point of sale displays.

Activity 1 **(10 minutes)**

The American tobacco company Philip Morris advertised scientific studies which revealed that the dangers of passive smoking (ie inhaling other people's cigarette smoke) have been much exaggerated.

This campaign was widely controversial. Allegedly, the tobacco industry funded the research, but importantly, other research studies contradicted its conclusions. Most people do not understand the niceties of a scientific procedure and are unaware of much of the material on the topic.

What do you think the objective of the campaign was, in terms of the firm's wider strategy?

2 SALES STRATEGY AND THE PRODUCT LIFE CYCLE

The sector of business in which a firm operates is likely to have a significant impact on the role of selling within the marketing strategy. Likewise there are a number of situations where the sales activity may be particularly challenging or important. Of particular relevance is the product life cycle. This was introduced in the previous chapter and will be developed in the next section.

2.1 Selling across the product life cycle

Definition

> You should already be familiar with the concept of the **product life cycle** (PLC). It provides managers with a broad picture of how sales might change over the life of the product, from introduction to decline. Its real value to marketing lies in the awareness that at the various stages of the PLC, the condition of the market, characteristics of the customer and nature of the competition all change and so marketing strategies need to be developed and modified.

Just as the marketing approach needs to change, the various stages represent specific selling situations which the sales person might meet and have to deal with. Although in this section we will examine the roles of sales throughout the PLC it needs to be remembered that in many circumstances the sales person will be offering not just a single product but a portfolio of products at different stages of the PLC.

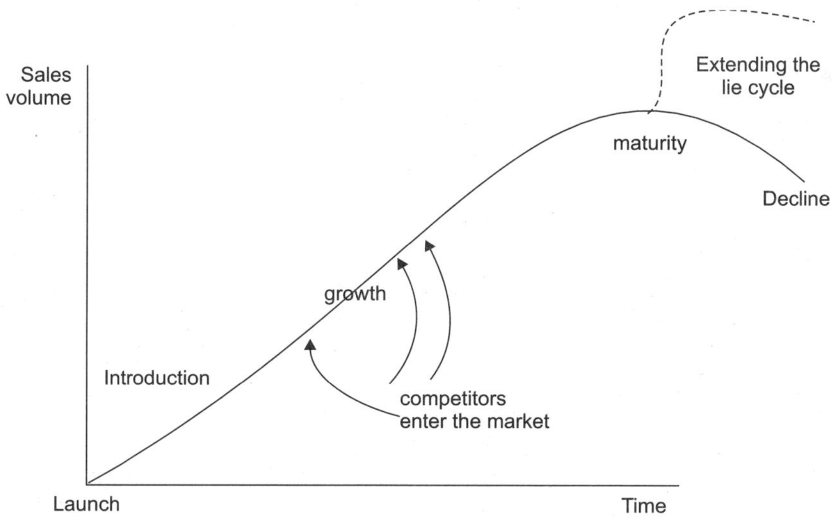

Figure 7.2: Role of sales throughout PLC

The sales team need to be aware of the changing market situation in which they are operating. The marketing support which is provided is also likely to change reflecting the changing needs of potential customers.

FOR DISCUSSION

The PLC is a self-fulfilling prophecy if not used with care, and products can be deleted before the market is ready.

2.2 Selling a new product: achieve a trial

The launch of a new product is the most critical time of its life. Despite rigorous testing and screening at the new product development stage, a very high proportion of products launched still fail to become successful mature products.

The task of the sales force will to some extent depend on the exact situation. Is this a new generic product, or simply an improved model or innovation to a well established range? Is the target market made up of existing customers or new ones? Despite these variations the objective in all cases will be to generate awareness and interest, as quickly as possible, in the target market.

For a really innovative new product, the end users of the product may not be the target group who will be the **main users** once it has been established. Identifying these 'innovators' and influencing the relevant opinion leaders is very important.

The salesperson must make sure that the product is stocked by distributors whose customer profile includes such adventurous clients.

The sales person needs to recognise that **from the customer's point of view, a new product is a risky option**. The greater the perceived risk the more complex and drawn out the decision making process is likely to be. A number of tactics can be used to counter the **risk factor**.

(a) Free trials or tests to demonstrate functional performance.

(b) Guarantees and warranties provided, to 'insure' the continuing performance.

(c) The backing of the company endorsing the product with its image and reputation for:

- innovation
- reliability
- performance
- quality etc

(d) **The advice and recommendation of the salesperson.** This can be very valuable is there is an established relationship of trust between the client and sales representative. The long-term integrity of the individual can be a valuable asset when launching a new product.

(e) In the **resell market**, commitment to a major advertising and promotional launch for a new product, will help convince retailers that the product line will be profitable.

(f) Special offers on **after sales service**, such as training and technical support will reduce the perceived risk.

(g) A lower **introductory price** is a strategy which may be adopted to ensure rapid penetration of the market.

Activity 2 **(5 minutes)**

You work for a shampoo manufacturer who has developed a new line of organic hair products. Give examples of how you could make retailers stock your product and examples of how you could encourage end-users to try your product.

Pioneering

Innovative companies often create new market segments by offering entirely new products. A classic example is the 3M Post-it note. People had no idea that they needed such a product until it was presented to them. The process of introducing such a new product to the market and creating a new segment that buys it is sometimes known as **pioneering.**

The pioneering firm has first mover advantage in that there is no direct competition: it defines the new product standard, sets prices independently, easily establishes consumer loyalty and creates the distribution system. However, pioneering is not easy and the pioneer firm has to work hard to create the new market segment. All marketing activities will be involved in this process, but promotion, and particularly sales, will be especially important. Even more than usual, promotional activities must be carefully integrated so that a single message is passed to the potential market. Potential customer groups must be identified and informed of the features and benefits of the new product. Sales staff will receive special training on the new product and will exploit leads generated by advertising. Prospecting may be centrally organised in tandem with targeted communications via mail, email and telephone.

2.3 Selling in the growth phase: forestall competitors

Selling when sales volume is expanding rapidly is probably the **easiest stage in which to be working.** The new product is by now established and proven, so there is less risk involved in the purchase and more awareness and interest in the product generally.

However, in this stage, new competitors enter the market place, and so marketing activities to ensure brand or company loyalty are likely to be implemented. For the sales team, growth in sales is likely to be depends on reaching the customer before competitors do. It is important therefore, to make a priority of visiting potential customers and to plan sales journeys in a way which fulfils this objective. The growth stage can be protracted or fairly short lived. The nature of the business tends to indicate the likely length each stage of the PLC will last. However, at some point, the growth in sales will level off as the **market reaches saturation.**

2.4 Selling a mature product: account maintenance

At this stage there are few if any new customers and as most sales will be repeat purchases, there is unlikely to be any overall increase in the market size.

(a) The mature stage is usually the longest stage of the life cycle and the sales person's role becomes one of **account maintenance.** Ensuring customer loyalty by providing good quality customer care, easy re-ordering and regular sales contact is the key to maintaining sales at this stage. The sales function at this stage requires a different set of skills than the creative development of 'new' sales at earlier stages of the PLC. Some companies recognise this and the development of new business is the job of a separate sales team to the group who maintain existing accounts.

(b) Alternatively, selling will 'be devoted towards increasing market share.

2.5 Selling to new markets

At the mature stage of the PLC the company may decide to adopt a strategy developed to extend the product life cycle. These modification strategies can be based on the following.

(a) The **product**. Modifications to features and performance are used to:

(i) Attract a more rapid replacement purchase from existing customers, for example, in the car market; or

(ii) Gaining competitive advantage with 'new improved' versions of the product.

This strategy may win a few new sales, and can retain interest and protect existing market share.

(b) The **market**. The product is presented to a new group of customers. **Selling to new markets is a difficult challenge to the sales team.** They will have little knowledge of the market, its needs or key decision makers. This information needs researching and the network of contacts, company reputation and profile will need establishing from scratch. Initially sales visits may be 'cold' calls to people with little awareness of the company or what it can achieve. Again the risks involved for the buyer are high and a supportive strategy needs to be developed to reduce the risk. Publicity and press coverage of the firm's move to the market, advertising, and promotional activities can all be used to generate awareness and interest in the sales call.

(c) **Modify the marketing mix**. This can also result in new customers for the product, for instance:

(i) if price is lowered enabling a different segment of the market access to the product for the first time;

(ii) changing the product's availability can have a similar effect.

Any such strategy needs developing with care as it will reposition the product and may alienate existing customers. The sales team are likely to be the most aware of how customers respond to any such changes.

Activity 3 **(10 minutes)**

Think of examples that fall under (a), (b) and (c) above.

2.6 Selling in the decline stage

Once sales start to decline it is usually means that customers are switching to a new product. This may be a product offered by the same company and so being presented by the same sales team. In this case orchestrating the switch from one to another can be achieved if management provide sales teams with a clear targets and priorities. In such a case resources can be reallocated gradually to the new product, in line with the shifting patterns of demand.

As products enter the decline stage, decisions have to be made about their future. The sales team will be a valuable source of customer feedback and should help to inform managers about the feasibility of withdrawing the product. It may be that, although less profitable, it is seen to be an important core of the range offered, and its existence indirectly encourages sales elsewhere.

The sales person's task if a product is withdrawn is to maintain the business and loyalty of the customer. Handling worries about servicing and spares for existing purchases and helping customers find alternative products are all critical parts of the sales task at this stage.

3 ORGANISING THE SALES ACTIVITY

3.1 Salesforce size

Provided that an organisation has sufficient resources to increase its output and distribution, the sales force's size could be increased up to the point where the marginal costs of extra sales effort begins to exceed the marginal revenue from the incremental sales. Effectively, however, the overall size of the sales organisation is restricted by the resources available to the company and by company policy, and by the balance in the communications mix between personal and non-personal selling.

Every organisation will have some idea about what it can afford to spend on selling. A useful example might be as follows.

(a) Selling expenses should not exceed, say, 10% of sales.

(b) If a salesperson, with selling expenses and commission etc, costs, say £30,000 per annum, then turnover of £300,000 per annum would be required to support one salesperson.

(c) If a company budgets annual turnover of, say, £6 million, then the total sales force should not exceed twenty employees.

These figures are hypothetical, but should indicate to you about how a rule of thumb judgement can be made about the maximum economic size of a sales force, based on annual turnover and selling costs. Obviously, a complex sales force organisation would be inappropriate for a firm with only a relatively low sales turnover!

EXAMPLE

With more efficient sales management techniques and the use of information technology, sales forces in many industries have been reduced substantially over the past few years.

3.2 The selling organisation

The type of selling organisation will be influenced by various factors.

(a) The **intensity of competition**, and possibly the structure of a competitor's selling organisation, will affect a company's own sales organisation structure. If, for example, specialisation appears to give a marketing advantage to a rival product, a company might need to use specialised selling itself.

(b) If it is decided that personal selling by salespeople is the most efficient way to sell, the quantity and quality of the sales force will reflect this decision (ie low dependence on advertising may result in a greater reliance on personal selling).

(c) Wherever possible, specialisation of the sales force should be introduced (whether by function, product, type of customer, outlet or market) but it must be economically justified.

(d) All organisation should be based on functions, not personalities.

(e) Because of the possible social bridge between a 'low status' salesperson and the 'high status' of the buying representative of a potential customer (perhaps its managing director, production or financial director), it may be necessary to use sales management executives to deal with these special cases, (ie to use management as sales people).

(f) The extent to which dealers are used will affect organisation. If a company sells only to a limited number of multiple stores and wholesalers, a small sales organisation will be sufficient.

(g) Generally, there is direct selling for industrial goods but sales are often confined to a few customers, so that the number of orders is small but their value high, and consequently:

(i) the **number** of orders/size of sales force ratio is low; but
(ii) the **value** of orders/size of sales force ratio is high.

FOR DISCUSSION

Specialisation of the salesforce is usually undertaken for high-tech industrial goods.

3.3 Territorial design

Eventually, all large sales organisations involve a territorial breakdown. Where there is no specialisation, the sales organisation may be based entirely on geographical divisions.

(a) There may be a **pyramid organisation** structure with top management at head office, sales supervisors controlling the sales force in a region, and a salesperson or sales force for each territory in a region.

(b) The span of **control of a sales supervisor** is influenced by:

(i) The amount of work to be done.

(ii) The physical conditions under which it is done (eg how much travelling).

(c) The amount of supervision required depends on:.

(i) The initiative which individual salespeople are allowed (if salespeople can arrange delivery dates, price and production possibilities, they must have easy communication access back to their immediate superiors).

(ii) The size of sales commission will determine how much salespeople are willing to work without the need to be supervised.

(d) The size of each sales territory should be such that the amount of time wasted by salespeople in travelling is not excessive; there should be a good 'frequency of call' rate.

The purpose of a territorial salesforce

(a) Reduce travelling time and costs.
(b) Enable the salespeople to get to know their customers and sales areas.
(c) Motivate salespeople by giving them autonomy over their area.
(d) Give salespeople an equal workload or equal sales potential.
(e) Keep the organisation and administration simple.

It is most suited therefore, to the sale of products in a homogeneous range (ie it is important for the salespeople to know their products as well as their customers). If the range of products is wide, and technically complex, it is unlikely that an individual salesperson will be able to learn enough about them to sell them effectively.

EXAMPLES

Organisation structures are not static. They develop and change in response to a variety of needs. Few organisations of any size avoid structural complexity and ambiguity, and changing organisation structures is a task of management.

It is worth taking an historical perspective.

- Until the mid-1980s, many multinationals were organised on a regional basis. The country manager was very important, the gateway to the market. Overseas branches or subsidiaries were often run autonomously.
- In the 1990s, many multinational firms decided to reduce the power of the country managers, and have set up global divisions for certain brands. The relative power of local managers declined significantly: business division bosses were more powerful.
- However, perhaps this necessary change has gone too far, and more power should be handed back to country managers.

Procter & Gamble (P&G)

P&G had cut the country manager role and given power to global divisions. However, it has now modified this. In richer countries, the global division has responsibility for profits and resource allocation. In poorer markets, for example China, regions make the decisions and have more influence over sourcing.

Furthermore, where products are used in each country in similar ways, the global division takes most decisions about production and sales. Where local habits vary (eg in the use of laundry detergents), there are business teams organised by product line and country. *www.pg.com*

Visa

In the Visa organisation, brand, risk and interoperability are centralised in California. The rest is managed on a regional basis. *www.visa.com*

Oracle

Information technology has enabled some organisations to change the way that local and global offices talk to each other. At one time, Oracle France had a different logo and service operation to Oracle UK. Offices in different countries did not communicate. Changing the organisation structure created order.

Oracle may set standard business practices centrally. This allows for more decisions to be taken by country managers. Furthermore, Oracle encourages country managers to learn from each other and to compete with each other. All country bosses are given a daily ranking for their country on revenue per head or expense control.

www.oracle.com

3.4 Specialised selling organisation structures

Specialisation may be introduced into a sales organisation, and may take any of the following forms (or combination of several).

(a) **Specialisation by function:** eg advertising, market research, new production, sales/production liaison, sales training and personnel. This **functional specialisation** is more relevant to the marketing and selling department as a whole rather than to the salesforce itself.

(b) **Specialisation by the nature of goods:** The greater complexity of the goods to be sold and the more knowledgeable the customer, the greater the necessity to employ salespeople with a skilled knowledge of the product.

(c) **Specialisation by the range of goods**

  (i) If a company manufactures a range of goods, its salespeople may specialise in a part of the range, for example, in an office equipment supplier's some salespeople may specialise in calculators and others in document copiers.

  (ii) It is possible to employ product managers who specialise in a product or range of products and who advise the salesforce, who sell the entire range without specialising. This type of organisation has drawbacks because it may be difficult to decide how far product managers should be advisers and how much authority they should be allowed over sales activities.

  (iii) Salespeople must know their products; therefore, if their company's product range is broad and complex, product specialisation may be desirable. Several salespeople would be required to cover the same sales area. Disadvantages of product specialisation are as follows.

    (1) Travelling time and expenses are higher than with a territorial sales organisation.

    (2) One customer buying two different products from the same company might have to deal with two different salespeople.

(d) **Specialisation by range of market:** ie by market segments. Examples of specialisation by market segment are as follows.

  (i) Home and overseas sales.
  (ii) Industrial and non-industrial sales.
  (iii) Male and female markets (eg clothiers).

  The advantage of market specialisation is that salespeople get to know the needs of a particular market segment. The disadvantages of market specialisation are as follows.

(i) Travelling time and costs.

(ii) Potential problems for product designers when different market segments begin to show differing requirements.

(iii) The potentially complex organisation structure; eg possible problems of identifying boundaries between one segment of the market and another, especially when new market segments are evolving.

(e) **Specialisation by range of customers:** In selling industrial goods, a specialised salesforce can be organised so that each salesperson deals with a small number of potential customers in order to foster a better understanding of the customer's business. This is vital for securing large or valuable industrial orders.

The advantages of specialisation by types of customer are as follows.

(i) The salesforce will be more alert to the specific needs of each type of customer.

(ii) In selling industrial goods, knowledge about the customer's industry and needs might be crucial in winning; sales over the bids of competitors.

(f) **Specialisation by range of outlets:** With changing patterns of consumer and wholesale buying, eg the growth of multiple stores and superstores – specialisation by salespeople in dealing with different types of outlet may improve a manufacturer's selling efficiency.

A combination of these different types of salesforce designs can be used. Salespeople might specialise in a type of customer or type of product within a sales area or they might specialise in a type of product for a restricted number of potential customers and so on.

EXAMPLE

Here is a possible organisation of a salesforce for a company manufacturing and marketing upholstered furniture.

The following points can be made about this example.

(a) **Specialisation by product type is probably unsuitable**, because in the case of upholstered furniture there is little or no technical difference between one product and another. Specialisation by product serves no purpose if all products are basically the same, since salespeople will not acquire differences in technical expertise and know-how.

(b) On the other hand, customers for upholstered furniture can probably be divided into distinct categories. Alternatively, distinct market segments might exist.

A possible analysis of customers might be as follows.

Those buying directly, for their own use	*Those buying in order to resell*
Companies (office furniture)	Department stores
Hotels, Theatres, Shipping lines	Retail furniture shops
	Mail order businesses
	Wholesalers
	Discount houses

The total number of potential customers might be quite large, (eg independent retailers, department stores, companies etc); even so, each type of customer might have certain particular characteristics or requirements or buying habits, so that specialisation by customer type would be an appropriate form of salesforce organisation.

Some customers might be buyers in bulk, in which case individual salespeople should be given a number of large accounts to handle.

We do not have enough information about market segments to suggest a form of salesforce organisation based on market specialisation, and so a suggested organisation might be as follows.

(a) **Key accounts**. A number of key account salespeople (perhaps two or three) each dealing with several large customers, and responsible to senior sales executives at head office. A territorial organisation would probably be unnecessary, although it might be convenient to divide key account customers by geographical area, depending on how many of them there are.

(b) If it is considered potentially useful, the rest of the salesforce could specialise by customer type, divided between:

(i) Those selling to direct users;
(ii) Those selling to resellers, including exporters.

Given the large number of potential customers, a territorial salesforce organisation would still be necessary. Since furniture is not a high-volume product, a UK territorial division might be into two or three regions, without the need for sub-division into areas.

Individual salespeople would report to regional managers as follows.

Senior regional sales manager

Regional sales sub-manager (direct users)	Regional sales sub-manager (resellers)
Salespeople specialising in sales to direct users	Salespeople specialising in sales to resellers

However, if the volume of sales does not justify employing a large salesforce, specialisation of the salesforce by customer type would be inappropriate, because its costs would outweigh the benefits obtained.

As with any aspect of marketing and selling, it is the job of marketing management to organise resources so as to maximise the efficiency of selling (and thus to reduce the costs of selling).

Activity 4 **(20 minutes)**

For the organisation you work for or one you have knowledge of (perhaps the management of your college) find out who supplies to the organisation and how they are organised.

3.5 Selling and information technology

Personal selling and management of the selling tasks are expensive activities for an organisation. Information technology is changing the way sales are organised and operationalised. The buying process can sometimes eliminate personal selling using the internet or computerised buying. However, information technology can also be used to make personal selling more efficient and effective. Some applications are as follows.

(a) **Telecommunications**

The use of pagers and mobile telephones means that the sales force can be in constant contact with the head office or clients. Working from home with the use of telecommunications and e-mail is on the increase with less time spent inefficiently travelling. Video-conferencing is also possible, although has been relatively slow to progress.

(b) **Data handling**

Database management has been an important growth area for organisations. It has meant more effective segmentation and targeting of consumers. The effectiveness of various promotional methods can be tracked. Specifically the effectiveness of sales personnel can be assessed more easily. Customer records can be easily kept up to date with personal details stored in the system. Contacts and follow ups can be alerted 'automatically'. In general, if customer information is used effectively then there can be an increase in customer care levels.

(c) **Customer presentations**

The use of IT to tailor presentations to customers and to visually display benefits of the product/service is one of the most exciting developments of IT and marketing. Presentation 'slides' can be tailored and shown on a computer as can product designs.

EXAMPLE

A salesperson for a bedroom furniture manufacturer may have software that can show prospective customers what the furniture would look like in their room in a 3D computer-generated image. Designs, colours etc can all be changed to give the customer the best possible idea of what the product would look like in their own setting.

(d) **Management of the salesforce**

Sales persons' individual performance can be analysed along with the sales force function to assess effectiveness. Spreadsheets can be used to plan sales force activities. Again video-conferencing is an area that can be used here and looks to increase with the development of web cams. This means that meetings can be attended without taking time out to travel to a central location.

A further aspect of sales territory design is sales call planning. Given that a sales area must have adequate sales potential and workload, it should be possible to plan the number of calls a salesperson should be able to make over a period of time. 'Standards' should exist for the average number of calls per day, or average miles travelled per day; and by planning the salesman's workload, it should be possible to prevent time lost through inefficient routing, or spending too long with difficult or reluctant customers etc, we will be looking at sales planning in more detail in a later chapter. We cover journey planning in the next section.

4 JOURNEY PLANNING

The sales resource is both valuable and scarce. Planning how to get the most from it and the best out of the sales hours available is an important element in the preparation process.

The nature of selling makes it not only possible, but actually easy to waste both time and effort.

- Time can be wasted in waiting to see prospects
- Time is spent travelling between appointments
- Time and energy is wasted visiting prospects with little or no likelihood of buying
- Time and energy is wasted visiting existing clients unnecessarily.

4.1 Effective use

Management decisions can have enormous impact on how effectively the salesperson's time will be used.

(a) **Geography**. Decisions on sales organisation and sales territories will determine the proximity of **sales prospects and clients to each other**. Journey times between sales visits can represent a very large percentage of the representative's day.

(b) **Other tasks.** Management makes demands on sales staff to undertake **other routine tasks**, for example, administrative duties, report writing and marketing research. All these reduce the available 'real' selling time. Managers need to be sure that these additional responsibilities are best done by the sales team and are the best use of their time.

(c) **Sales report.** The sales support provided by management can significantly alter the proportion of time the sales personnel can spend with clients. Providing telephone sales support to identify potential prospects, research to screen them and provide background on them and administrative support to make appointments and travel arrangements can all free the sales team from routine and time consuming aspects of their work.

(d) **Objectives.** Managers should provide clear objectives and guidelines to help channel selling activities in a way consistent with overall objectives or strategy. They may produce guidelines on percentage of calls which should be made to potential new clients or the number of times per year existing clients should be visited.

Preparation enables for well-designed journey plans and an organised approach to the sales activities. Set times for being in the office, for example on a Monday morning and Friday afternoon or every day before 10 am and after 5 pm allows queries and callers to be given precise information as to when the sales representative will be available and able to return their call. Now, with the use of e-mail and mobile phones, sales personnel can be contacted much of the time.

Activity 5 **(5 minutes)**

How can administrative support help the salesperson make more effective use of time?

4.2 Call frequency

Sales people, looking to build strong relationships with customers, need to think through the frequency with which they call them, either in person or by telephone:

(a) **too often** and they will be perceived as a nuisance and 'hard seller';

(b) **too infrequently** will allow potentially valuable contacts to lapse and future business opportunities diminish.

Well planned sales activities are based on organised and **targeted cycles of calls and visits.** In some situations the sales management will fix a very rigid journey cycle, with the sales team being allocated a list of customers to be contacted each week. Where sales staff are left to manage their own territory, the journey plan is likely to be based on the desired call frequency.

4.3 How often a customer should be visited.

(a) **Importance of the customer?** (usually in terms of sales value or potential sales value).

(b) **Rate of stock turn and stock levels held by the customer**. Stock turnover and levels will directly influence the order frequency, although where this is a regular occurrence reordering may be done routinely by telephone. The more regularly purchases are made, the more regular the sales contact should be. Products with long life expectancy like capital equipment may be bought infrequently, but a regular if infrequent contact ensures the sales person is well placed to benefit from any expansion plans etc.

(c) **What the buyer wants.** Buyers may specify when and how often they wish to see sales representatives. This may be the case for example with GPs and medical sales staff.

Each customer can be given a rating indicating the frequency with which they should be visited. In this scheme the most time to elapse between calls is six months. By quantifying how many customers the sales person has in each category it is possible to quantify the scale of the journey cycle required.

Customer type	*Frequency*	*Number*	*Calls in six months*	*Total calls*
Category A	Monthly	20	6	120
Category B	Two months	50	3	150
Category C	Three months	90	2	180
Category D	Six months	150	1	150
Existing customers				600

In this example, the salesperson needs to make 600 calls in six months, ie 100 a month. To this total we must add new customer targets. In this case, if we assume management requires each sales person to call on 20 new prospects each month this adds a further 120 calls to the total.

(a) The sales person needs to make 720 calls in six months, 120 calls a month, 30 calls a week (a 4-week month), 6 calls a day.

(b) It is also possible to see that in every month the seller needs to visit:

20 Category A
20 New prospects
25 Category B
30 Category C
25 Category D

4.4 Time

Considerations of location need to be added to this analysis of call targets.

(a) Location indicates how much travelling time needs to be allowed between calls, but simple distance is not an adequate consideration. The degree of congestion, ease of parking and type of road links all need to be taken into account.

(b) A large scale map with key customer categories indicated by different coloured markers helps the sales representative to see at a glance the possible clients who can be visited in any one day. By breaking the whole sales territory down into smaller segments it is possible to ensure that the whole territory is covered and customers within each area seen in a logical and cost effective way.

(c) There is a final dimension which needs to be considered before determining the number of appointments to be made for each day and that is the length of time each sales visit might take. Some will be quick and routine, in others it may be necessary to visit several people or usual to be kept waiting.

4.5 Costing each sale

Once sales activity has been planned out it is possible to assess actual performance against the plan and make modifications to ensure all the targets set are met.

It is also possible to quantify the cost per sales call and the cost per order. If a sales person's salary plus expenses etc costs the firm £1,000 per week and:

(a) He or she makes 20 calls a week each sales call costs £50;

(b) If in an average week he or she takes £10,000 of orders then the sales costs are equal to 10% of sales value.

These sorts of performance analysis provide the basis for setting new performance targets and for measuring the effectiveness of training or new sales aids.

5 KEY ACCOUNT MANAGEMENT

Key account management is an increasingly important role within organisations where major or more strategically important customers have been identified. The role is linked to the concept of relationship marketing and it emphasises the need to develop positive relations with the most profitable 20% or customers. For example, a breakfast cereal manufacturer will probably find that the majority of their sales are to the major retailers such as Tesco, Asda, Sainsburys etc. Owing to the importance and power of these customers, it is likely they would need and warrant a great amount of sales time. For this reason, a key account manager would be assigned to each of these customers in order to better meet their needs, understand their requirements and behaviours such as order patterns and ensure a positive relationship is maintained. Smaller wholesaler groups or independent stores who place orders directly would not necessarily generate enough sales to justify such attention and may be dealt with by a sales office.

EXAMPLE

Even organisations who you may not consider to be in need of a traditional salesforce are able to benefit from the role of key account management. Anglian Water for example employs Business Account Managers to oversee the water consumption of its 'Principal' customers. The company distinguishes between business customers according to whether they are a 'Principal' or 'Major' water users depending on the volumes consumed. Major customers are handled over the phone with two calls a year guaranteed while Principal customers can expect two personal visits a year and access to a dedicated Business Account Manager. The role is also used to ensure that customers do not exceed their agreed levels of consumption and discharge. When agreed levels are exceeded the Business Account Manager works with the customer to find ways of improving water efficiency. In situations where the system requires changing, the key account managers liaise with Process Engineers who work on speciality projects to improve the client's water systems. The Key Account Managers are able in these circumstances to work towards a bonus system. Typical of the rationale for key account management this benefits both parties as it means costs are minimised for the customers and enables Anglian Water to better manage the water supply infrastructure.

---

6 COMMUNICATING WITH THE SALES TEAM

The final link in our communication chain is between the **firm** and its **salesforce**.

6.1 Role of management

The role of management in maintaining not just routine communication, but informative, supportive, persuasive and effective communication, is key to successful sales operation.

(a) The reality is that weaknesses in this area of management activity will show up more quickly and visibly in a sales term than anywhere else.

(b) The sales job is peculiar often isolated and difficult, yet performance can be measured and monitored by the success or not of yesterday's sales calls.

(c) The communication task facing the sales manager is made more difficult by another characteristic of the sales team. They are trained communicators and so likely to see through any insincere messages. If the manager does not believe targets are really achievable, however he or she dresses it up, the sales team are likely to recognise the lack of confidence.

(d) Their performance will reflect the expectation to fail. Attitude effects results and performance and positive communication can change both.

E-mail, mobile phones and video conferencing all have improved day to day communications between head office, clients and the salesforce.

6.2 Sales manuals

Sales manuals and sales bulletins do not represent ideal examples of communicating with the sales team. This is because they represent written communication – one way not two-way processes. It is difficult to ensure that messages in the written form are correctly decoded, or interpreted.

Sales manuals can be useful **reference documents** for the sales team, providing detailed information of products and procedures. However, these should be used to support other forms of staff briefing and training. Written documentation provides a formal record of communication, but it does little to guarantee either that it has been read or understood.

6.3 Sales bulletins

Sales bulletins can be seen as more immediate communication, useful when staff are not in regular contact with managers. They provide a means of keeping staff up to date on relevant issues between sales meetings. Information on product availability, promotional activity or price changes can all be communicated quickly in this way.

When presented as a **newsletter**, inclusion of positive success stories and achievement can build up team spirit and contribute towards positive motivation. Stories and pictures of themselves and friends increase the chance of a bulletin being read and other information being absorbed.

6.4 Sales meetings

Using face to face communication, these approaches have the advantage of offering two way communication opportunities. Feedback allows managers to assess attitude and monitor responses from their teams.

Sales meetings can take many forms; on a one to one basis; with a team; formally or informally; in the field, the office or an outside venue. When they are formal and involve a large number of sales staff, they are likely to be classified as a sales conference.

Meetings take time, and so their cost, not only in terms of staff time, but also lost sales opportunities can and often are calculated. As with all aspects of business, it is management's task to make sure that sales meetings are worthwhile; in other words that the benefits they generate exceed the costs of holding them. Effective meetings are those which are called for a specific reason – they have a clear objective.

There can be many reasons or objectives for a sales meeting ranging from motivating, to informing, planning and training to discussing and reporting.

The important thing is to make sure sales meetings work. They need planning and later evaluating. Venues, time and frequency of meeting needs careful consideration to minimise disruption to other sales activities and to ensure maximum support.

Objectives need to be translated into a clear agenda, with plenty of opportunity for participation from all those attending.

Results and outcomes need to be reviewed and analysed. Training inputs may need to be repeated and messages reinforced in other ways. Managers should avoid the temptation of holding fewer meetings but cramming more in. Keeping to a single or simple theme, but repeating and reinforcing the messages is much more likely to have a positive impact.

6.5 Sales conference

Sales conferences are often much more elaborate affairs, and seen as more social than normal sales meetings. Venues are often external, even glamorous or exotic and partners may be invited. Participants are still expected to work, attending presentations on training activities. They are an important occasion for developing a sense of corporate belonging and loyalty, networking with colleagues and being motivated by the latest products or plans proposed by the company.

As with any sales meeting the conference must not turn into an anti-sales event. A positive approach by management will become a positive view by the sales teams and positive results for the company. This positive push is a sales presentation to the sales force. They are being 'sold' on what they can achieve. The preparation for this pitch must be as thorough as for any other if it is to be effective.

Chapter roundup

- Sales objectives should be set in the context of the marketing strategy, which should also be set in the context of corporate objectives.
- The sales strategy varies dependant on the stage in the PLC of the product.
- If it is a new product the goal may be to get people to try the product, in growth to combat competitors, in maturity to maintain sales or look for new markets and in decline to analyse if it is still worthwhile to be in the market.
- Salesforces have to be organised in terms of salesforce size, nature and territory design.
- Territories are geographic groupings of sales areas. Advantages include:
  - low travel time and costs
  - close customer relationships
  - autonomy gives motivation to sales person
  - equality
  - simple to organise
- The salesforce may be organised instead by specialisation, for example by function, the nature of goods sold, the range of goods sold, the market, customers or outlets.
- Time and effort can be saved by careful journey planning.
- Communicating with the sales team is now much easier with e-mails, mobile phones and videoconferencing.
- Formal communications between the firm and the salesforce include sales manuals, sales bulletins, sales meetings and conferences.

Quick quiz

1. Marketing objectives should be set in the context of sales objectives. True or false?
2. What is usually the main aim for sales staff in the introductory phase of the PLC?
3. How might sales personnel selling in a mature market ensure customer loyalty?
4. A company in the mature stage for a product might decide to try to sell to new markets to extend the PLC. In what ways could it do this?
5. What input might the sales force have to management in the decline stage of the PLC?
6. Give some examples of specialised selling organisation structures by market segments.
7. How can time and effort be wasted if sales journeys are not adequately planned?
8. Are there any rules on how often a customer should be visited?
9. In what ways can management communicate with the sales team?

Answers to quick quiz

1. False. Sales objectives should be set in line with overall marketing objectives.
2. To get customers to try the product.
3. Effort in terms of customer care, ease of reordering and relationship building.
4. (i) With product modifications (ii) To a new market eg overseas (iii) Modification to other aspects of the marketing mix.
5. As they are close to the customer they can advise management about decisions to withdraw the product and the impact in terms of switching products.
6. Could include, UK and overseas, industrial and non industrial, customer characteristics such as demographics (eg male/female hair salons).
7. Time wasted waiting to see prospects, travelling between appointments, poor potential prospects and visiting unnecessarily.
8. Not really but management have to consider the importance of the customer, stock levels of the customer and what the buyer's requirements are.
9. Telephone (mobile), e-mail, sales manuals, bulletins, meetings and conferences.

Answers to activities

1 The objective was to alleviate to some extent the adverse reputation of the tobacco industry, and attempt to narrow the perceived area of risk from smoking.

The firm's wider strategy is to maintain levels of cigarette sales and minimise negative publicity.

2 Price concessions
Free salon equipment
Mention specific salons in advertising
Free samples
Samples inside magazines
Television advertising

3 Examples could include:

(a) 'New improved' washing powders, additional features on a personal computer, additional features on a mobile phone.

(b) Expanding overseas, such as financial services institutions, selling to a new segment or group of customers eg satellite TV selling.

(c) Selling at a cheaper price eg an offer on double-glazing to gain new customers. Advertising to gain a 'new' group eg children for a fruit drink such as SunnyD.

4 There is no specific answer to this.

5 By enabling them to concentrate on communicating with customers, rather than engaging in administration.

Chapter 8 :
MANAGING THE SALES TEAM

Introduction

This chapter will look at the skills that a good sales person requires. It will then concentrate on the recruitment process and how candidates for sales positions can be recruited and selected and fit into an existing sales team. Aspects of employee motivation are then discussed along with how job satisfaction – and increased customer service levels – can go hand in hand.

Your objectives

In this chapter you will learn about the following.

(a) The key personal skills a good salesperson needs

(b) How sales employees can be recruited

(c) What might motivate sales staff

(d) How customer service can be a key to job satisfaction

1 SALES SKILLS

1.1 The characteristics of a salesperson

The qualities and characteristics which make up a good salesperson are many and varied.

The role of a salesperson is not a particularly easy one. Often working alone, it is easy to become isolated and the need to be a **self-motivator** is essential. Contact with clients requires patience and tenacity and a sense of humour is likely to be a valuable commodity too. Although it is possible to develop some of the skills with training, and good management: support can reduce the impact of working alone, provide motivations.

- Enthusiasm (and an ability to be a 'self-starter')
- Intelligence
- Reliability
- Commitment
- Initiative and creativity
- Self-confidence
- Courtesy
- Sensitivity

Characteristic	Comment
Enthusiasm	For the **product and company** is likely to mean the person will be a good ambassador. Enthusiasm for the **job** will help provide the energy necessary for the self motivator.
Intelligence	The salesperson is to be a credible troubleshooter for the company and problem solver for the client. This intelligence does not necessarily need to be certificated by academic qualifications. It is more a natural wit and common sense which enables the individual to assess new people and situations, and react positively. Being able to communicate at different levels of seniority and modify the message according to its audience is also a reflection of a level of intelligence.
Reliability	Salespeople often work alone and are unsupervised. They have to be relied on to undertake their functions thoroughly and as briefed. Equally important is the client's perception of the company – late arrival for meetings and agreements which are broken, generate the image of an unreliable company as well as an unreliable salesperson.
Commitment	Commitment ensures that sales targets are pursued with determination, while commitment to the customer ensures their needs and problems are dealt with diligently. Commitment also encompasses a sense of loyalty to the firm. It is easy for a salesperson to fall into the trap of 'blaming head office'. A sense of loyalty and commitment to the rest of the team is an important anchor for the salesperson working alone.

Characteristic	Comment
Initiative and creativity	A salesperson will seldom be in the same situation twice. As the needs of the customer and market place vary, so there are new opportunities which need to be recognised and developed. This required both initiative and creativity. Developing new contacts and new avenues for business will be unlikely if the sales approach is routine and narrow.
Self-confidence	Constantly meeting new people and travelling to new places requires a confidence in oneself and also in the company and the products being represented. Not all potential buyers are pleasant and morale can take a considerable hammering if the individual is not of a resilient and confident nature.
Courtesy	'The customer is always right', is an easier philosophy to preach than it is to always follow. As sales staff are likely to be at the front line of dealing with customer complaints, their tact, integrity and customer care training will determine whether or not the customer remains loyal to the company, despite the lapse in product or service quality.
Sensitivity	In order to pick up the behavioural signals and messages and interpret them effectively, the sales person needs a degree of sensitivity.

Activity 1 **(20 minutes)**

Using the above table, assess yourself against these characteristics – be honest!

2 EXPANDING THE SALES TEAM

It will often be necessary to bring new people into the team.

- To fill an identified skills gap
- To replace staff who have been promoted or who have left
- Because the work of the team has expanded

The process of recruitment is very important. Getting the wrong person can cause problems within the existing group, and the person will require either extensive training and development, or will require replacing, with all the attendant disruption this involves.

The overall aim of the recruitment and selection process is to obtain the employees required by the human resource plan. This process can be broken down into three main stages.

(a) **Definition of requirements**, including the preparation of job descriptions and specifications.

(b) **Recruitment.** The identification and attraction of potential applicants, inside and outside the organisation.

(c) **Selection**. Selection is the part of the employee resourcing process which involves choosing between applicants for jobs: it is largely a 'negative' process, eliminating unsuitable applicants.

A sales manager may have the help and support of **human resources (HR) specialists** during the process but in smaller organisations, he or she will be responsible for all aspects of the search and selection process. Many firms outsource the early stages of the process to consultants or agencies.

2.1 An approach to recruitment and selection

If not approached systematically, the process of recruitment and selection can become costly and time-consuming. A methodical approach will probably involve the following stages:

(a) Detailed **human resource planning,** defining what resources the organisation needs to meet its objectives. At sales team level, this activity would require an analysis of the future sales skills needed.

(b) **Job analysis,** so that for any given job there are three things.

- (i) **A job description** giving a broad statement of the nature of the job
- (ii) **A job specification** giving detail of the job's responsibilities
- (iii) **A person specification** describing the ideal candidate for the job

(c) An identification of **vacancies,** from the requirements of the human resources plan or by a **job requisition** from the section needing a new post holder.

(d) Evaluation of the **sources of labour,** which should be in the HR plan. Internal and external sources, and media for reaching both, will be considered.

(e) **Advertising** has three functions.

- (i) To attract the attention and interest of potentially suitable candidates
- (ii) To give a favourable (but accurate) impression of the job and the organisation
- (iii) To tell candidates how to apply

(f) **Processing applications** and assessing candidates.

(g) **Notifying applicants** of the results of the selection process.

Activity 2 **(30 minutes)**

Find out what the recruitment and selection procedures are in your organisation and who is responsible for each stage. A procedures manual might set this out, or you may need to ask someone – perhaps in the Personnel or Human Resources department. In your own experience, what part does the manager play in these procedures? Get hold of some of the documentation your company uses.

- The job description for your job
- The personnel specification (if any) for your job
- If your firm is currently recruiting, a full set of the paperwork including the job ad

Before the search process can begin managers have a great deal to do. When the need for a new member of the team is recognised, a careful review should be undertaken to ensure that an extra full time post is justified by the contribution the person is expected to make.

Particular care is needed when the **vacancy is due to a team member leaving**. Simple replacement is not always appropriate. During the sales person's time in the job, he or she may have developed particular relationships with clients or expertise. These clients may feel concerned at the loss of their 'champion' within the organisation.

2.2 Job analysis and job specification

Job analysis is 'the determination of the essential characteristics of a job' (British Standards Institute) – that is, the process of examining a job to identify its component parts and the circumstances in which it is performed.

Information elicited from a job analysis includes both task-oriented and worker-oriented details.

(a) **Initial requirements** of the employee include aptitudes, qualifications, experience and training required.

(b) **Duties and responsibilities** include physical aspects, mental effort, routine or requiring initiative, difficult or disagreeable features, consequences of failure, responsibilities for staff, materials, equipment or cash and so on.

(c) **Environment and conditions** include physical surroundings, with particular features (eg temperature, noise, hazards), remuneration, other conditions such as hours, shifts, travel, benefits, holidays, career prospects, provision of employee services (eg canteens, protective clothing).

(d) **Social factors** include size of the department, teamwork or isolation. The sort of people dealt with (eg senior management, the public), the amount of supervision and job status.

A job analysis may cause some concern among employees from fear of standards being raised, rates cut or redundancy imposed. The job analyst will need to gain confidence; this can be done in a variety of ways.

- Communicating (explaining the process, methods and purpose of the analysis)
- Being thorough and competent in carrying out the analysis
- Respecting the work flow of the department, which should not be disrupted
- Giving feedback on the results of the appraisal, and the achievement of its objectives

2.3 Recruitment process

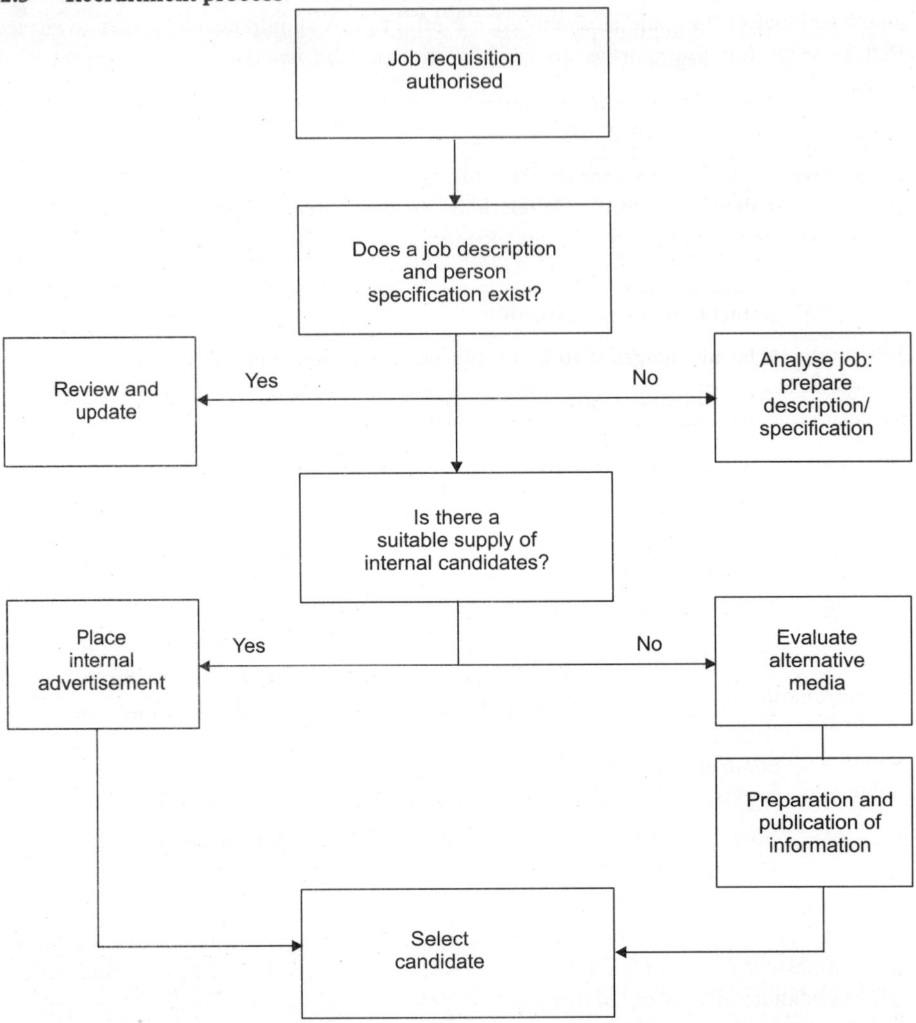

Figure 8.1: Recruitment process

The product of the job analysis is usually a **job specification**. This is defined as a statement of the activities involved in a job and a description of the environment in which work is undertaken. Job specifications are usually expressed in terms of **what the worker has to do.**

EXAMPLE: PROCTER AND GAMBLE

P&G, maker of everything from Pampers nappies to Old Spice deodorant to Pringles crisps, has a huge variety of customers and wants its workforce to reflect that.

'Our success depends entirely on our ability to understand these diverse consumers' needs,' Alan Lafley, the CEO told his company. A diverse organisation will out-think, out-innovate and out-perform a homogenous organisation every single time. I am putting particular importance on increasing the representation of women and minorities in leadership positions at all levels.'

P&G UK has a fairly good record already. Ethnic minority employees make up 6 per cent of P&G's UK workforce, compared with 5.4 per cent of the British population. 'But that is not a reason to be happy with ourselves. We primarily recruit graduates and 17 per cent of the students in this country are from ethnic minorities,' says Neil Harvey-Smith, UK Diversity Manager.

Why is PG not recruiting more of those students? 'It's not the case that people applying aren't getting in. It's that they're not applying.' Why not? 'It's probably fair to say that people perceive that we are a white company or an American company.'

Provided it fits in with their jobs, P&G staff of either sex can share jobs and change their hours. New parents can take up to a year's unpaid leave beyond their statutory maternity or paternity leave entitlements. The result is that the number of women appointed director or associate director in P&G Europe rose to eight last year from its previous rate of one or two a year.

Mr Harvey-Smith says the UK organisation has also made progress in attracting disabled recruits. It designed a computer program that could read out the questions on a problem-solving test so that a blind applicant could complete it. The technology is now being used by P&G in the US.

Financial Times

2.4 Job description

A **job description** is prepared from the job analysis. It is a broad statement of the purpose, scope, duties and responsibilities of a job. It describes the content of a job; and its relative importance in comparison with other jobs.

The job description states the principal details of the job.

- Job title/summary
- Location of the job (department, place)
- The relationship of the job to other positions such as who the job holder is responsible to and who are the job-holder's subordinates
- The main duties and responsibilities of the job
- The limits to the job holder's authority
- Any equipment for which the job holder is responsible

2.5 Person specification

Once the job has been clearly defined, the organisation can decide what kind of person is needed to fill it effectively. A **person specification** identifies the **type of person** the organisation should be trying to recruit – his or her character, aptitudes, qualifications, career aspirations, special abilities and experience.

Activity 3 **(30 minutes)**

Do you have a job description? (If you don't, draw one up.) Determine a person specification for the job. How far do you match the ideal requirements of your job?

EXAMPLE

	JOB DESCRIPTION
1 **Job title**	Area sales representative
2 **Location**	Northern sales office
3 **Job summary**	To develop the sales and customer base within this area
4 **Job content**	Typical duties will include: (a) prospecting for new customer contracts; (b) presenting new products to existing customers; (c) providing merchandising support to customers; (d) taking orders and dealing with customer queries.
5 **Reporting structure**	Marketing manager Northern area Sales manager (North) Area sales representatives
6 **Experience/ education**	Two 'A' levels, experienced negotiator, clean driving licence; experience of retail sales
7 **Training to be provided**	Induction and initial product knowledge training
8 **Hours**	40 per week, or as required
9 **Personal characteristics required**	Well motivated, good communicator, reliable and 'honest', prepared to travel
10 **Objectives and appraisal**	Sales targets set monthly in conjunction with sales manager. Annual appraisal
11 **Salary**	£25,000 plus car and commission *Job description prepared by:* Head office HR department Date: March 20X2

3 THE SEARCH PROCESS

The objective at this stage of the process is to identify candidates who are likely to be most suited to the vacancy. It is an exercise in segmentation and promotional targeting which marketers are well trained to manage.

3.1 Tapping unused labour resources

Older workers are a possible labour market. Some companies in the retail sector have targeted older workers (over-45s) for customer service positions. They bring important qualities.

- Skills and experience
- High regard for customer service
- Stabilising influence on younger staff
- Contribution to better staff retention rates

Women returners. There are a number of factors determining a woman's return to work.

(a) **Child care facilities.** If these are easily obtainable, a mother is likely to use them. Employers can provide them. Private child care is expensive. Some organisations, which do not wish to provide child care facilities themselves, might offer **child care vouchers.**

(b) **Career break schemes** have been introduced in particular in the financial services sector. Women are allowed to take time off for a few years to have children and return to the same job. Some organisations require a 'satisfactory performance record'. Other factors affecting retention include equal opportunity training schemes and assertiveness courses.

Activity 4 **(10 minutes)**

What would be the benefits of attracting an internal candidate? What would be the possible problems?

3.2 Internal recruitment

Internal candidates can be considered before advertising outside or they can be included in the process as candidates. It is worth remembering, though, that an internal candidate who fails to be offered a post requires much more sensitive handling, as there will be a strong sense of rejection and this can sour an otherwise happy team. The individual may resent the successful candidate and be unco-operative. In the worst case you might even lose what is otherwise a key member of the team, thereby creating a new search and selection problem.

3.3 Job advertisements

Despite these options, in the end many posts will be advertised. The advertisement is, in a way, already part of the selection process, because it will be placed where suitable people are likely to see it, and will be worded in a way that further weeds out people who would not be suitable for the job (or for whom the job would not be suitable). Obviously, for marketing posts, the advertisement is the recruit's first sight of the firm's marketing communications.

FOR DISCUSSION

In specialist markets salespeople from competitors will know each other. What are the advantages and disadvantages in recruiting in such markets?

In order for pre-selection to be effective, the advertisement must contain key details of the organisation and the job.

- Employer's **location** and **business**
- **Rewards**: the salary or wage benefits, training
- **The job**: title, main duties and responsibility, special factors
- **Career prospects**
- **Qualifications and experience required**/preferred, other aptitudes
- **How to apply**

It must present an attractive image, but also be honest, so as not to disillusion successful applicants.

Preparation of the job information documentation requires skill and attention if it is to meet its objectives of attraction and pre-selection. It should be:

(a) **Concise**, but comprehensive enough to be an accurate description of the job, its rewards and requirements.

(b) **Targeted** to attract the attention of the maximum number of the right sort of people.

(c) **Attractive**, conveying a favourable impression of the organisation, but not falsely so.

(d) **Relevant** and appropriate to the job and the applicant. Skills, qualifications and special aptitudes required should be prominently set out, along with special features of the job that might attract or deter applicants, such as shiftwork or extensive travel.

The way in which a job is advertised will depend on the type of organisation and the type of job. A factory is likely to advertise a vacancy for an unskilled worker in a different way from a company advertising vacancies for clerical staff. Managerial jobs may merit national advertisements, whereas semi– or unskilled jobs may only warrant local coverage, depending on the supply of suitable candidates in the local area. Specific skills may be most appropriately reached through trade, technical or professional journals, like *Marketing Week*.

The choice of **advertising medium** will depend upon three considerations.

(a) The **cost** of advertising. It is more expensive to advertise in a national newspaper than on local radio, and more expensive to advertise on local radio than in a local newspaper.

(b) The **type and number of readers** of the medium, and its suitability for the number and type of people the organisation wants to reach.

(c) The **frequency** with which the organisation wants to advertise the job vacancy. A monthly magazine or weekly newspaper are probably only useful for advertising a vacancy once. This is probably sufficient for a specialist or professional, or for a senior management position, since those who are interested will be on the look-out for vacancies advertised in certain magazines or newspapers.

Activity 5 **(10 minutes)**

What is the most usual type of medium used to advertise job vacancies in your field (or the field you would like to work in)? Assess the medium in terms of the above criteria.

Methods and media for advertising jobs.

(a) In-house magazines and notice-boards

(b) Professional and specialist newspapers or magazines, such as *Personnel Management, Marketing* or *Computing*

(c) National newspapers, especially for senior management jobs or vacancies for skilled workers, where potential applicants will not necessarily be found through local advertising. Local newspapers would be suitable for jobs where applicants are sought from the local area

(d) Local radio, television and cinema. These are becoming increasingly popular, especially for large-scale campaigns, for large numbers of vacancies

(e) Job centres. On the whole, vacancies for unskilled work (rather than skilled work or management jobs) are advertised through local job centres, although in theory any type of job can be advertised here

(f) School and university careers offices

(g) The Internet, especially for IT professionals and to attract candidates internationally

(h) Employment agencies and recruitment consultants for unusual or specialist posts

4 SELECTION

4.1 Application forms

Applicants who reply to job advertisements are usually asked to fill in a job application form, or to send a letter giving details about themselves and their previous job experience and explaining why they think they are qualified to do the job. An application form should elicit sufficient information to screen candidates into two groups.

- Those obviously unsuitable for the job
- Those who might be of the right calibre, and worth inviting to an interview

Application forms have two important aspects.

(a) An open-ended element, which will enable a candidate to give information about his or her abilities and achievements, including academic qualifications, work experience, activities and interests, career expectations and why the candidate thinks he or she is suitable.

(b) The closed element is much more structured. In this case the candidate is required to answer detailed questions (eg basic biographical information) which are posed in a restricted format (eg tick boxes). This element of an application form enables easier comparison between candidates.

4.2 The selection interview

The selection interview is the next stage of the selection process. Interviewing is a crucial part of the selection process.

The interview has a three-fold purpose.

(a) To find the best person for the job.

(b) To ensure that applicants understand what the job is and what the career prospects are. They must be allowed a fair opportunity to decide whether or not they want the job.

(c) To make applicants feel that they have been given fair treatment in the interview, whether they get the job or not. Current applicants may still be future employees or customers.

The interview must be prepared carefully, to make sure that the right questions are asked, and relevant information obtained to give the interviewers what they need to make their selection.

(a) The **job description should be studied** to review the major demands of the job.

(b) The **person specification should be studied and questions should be planned** which might help the interviewer make relevant assessments of the applicant's character and qualifications. The interview may concentrate on the following aspects:

- Confirming and expanding factual knowledge about the candidate. This means, for example, asking about the major problems the candidate faced in previous jobs
- Gauging the candidate's level of knowledge
- Judging how quick the candidate is to respond to questions
- Finding out likes and dislikes
- Establishing a trend in his or her thinking

(c) Each application form should be carefully studied, in order to decide on questions or question areas for the individual applicant.

The interview should be conducted in such a way that the information required is successfully obtained during the interview.

(a) The **layout of the room** and the number of interviewers should be planned carefully. Most interviewers wish to put candidates at their ease, and so it would be inadvisable to put the candidate in a 'hot seat' across a table from a large number of hostile-looking interviewers. However, some interviewers might want to observe the candidate's reaction under severe pressure, and deliberately make the layout of the room uncomfortable and off-putting.

(b) The **manner of the interviewers**, the tone of their voice, and the way their early questions are phrased can all be significant in establishing the tone of the interview.

(c) **Questions should be put carefully**. The interviewers should not be trying to confuse the candidate, but should be trying to obtain the information that they need.

(d) It is necessary to ask relevant questions, but the time of **the interview should be taken up mostly with the candidate talking,** and not with the interviewers asking questions. The more a candidate talks, the easier it should be to assess their suitability for the job. As a rule of thumb, the candidate should be talking for 70% of the time.

(e) **The candidate should be given the opportunity to ask questions**. Indeed well-prepared candidates should go into an interview knowing what questions they may want to ask. The choice of questions might well have some influence on how the interviewers finally assess them.

(f) Similarly the interviewer should be aware of the questions candidates are likely to ask. Candidates may well try to probe behind the statements made about the business, by asking for example why the interviewer chose or has remained with the organisation. Some candidate questioning may be a sign that the interviewer has failed to impart key information – for example the candidate's likely role within the organisation or the opportunities for advancement.

Activity 6 **(5 minutes)**

Role play with a friend or colleague an interview situation for a job you are relatively familiar with.

After each interview has been completed, notes should be made and, if more than one interviewer was present, impressions compared. Each candidate should be evaluated against the criteria for appointment. There are then three possible outcomes for each candidate.

(a) A job offer, possibly subject to conditions.

- Taking up references
- Obtaining evidence of educational and professional qualifications
- Medical examination

(b) An invitation to a **second interview**. Some organisations have a two-stage interview process, whereby first stage interview candidates are reduced to a short-list for a second stage interview. The second stage of the interview might well be based on a group selection method (see below). In many instances, the recruitment consultant might carry out the first stage interview.

(c) Rejection.

Interviews have often been criticised because they **fail to select suitable people** for job vacancies.

(a) **Assessment may be unclear**. The opinion of one interviewer may differ from the opinion of another. They cannot both be right, but because of their different opinions, a suitable candidate might be rejected or an unsuitable candidate offered a job.

(b) **Interviews fail to provide accurate predictions** of how a person will perform in the job.

(c) **The interviewers are likely to make errors of judgement** even when they agree about a candidate. There are several reasons for this.

(d) The candidate may be adept at being interviewed. Many will have received training, including video debriefs, in presenting themselves.

FOR DISCUSSION

What assumptions might an interviewer make about **you**, based on your:

(a) accent, or regional/national variations in your spoken English
(b) school
(c) clothes and hair-style
(d) stated hobbies, interests, 'philosophies'
(e) taste in books and TV programmes.

To what extent would any of these assumptions be fair?

For objectivity, you might like to conduct this exercise in class. What assumptions do you make about the person sitting next to you?

It might be apparent from the list of limitations above that a major problem with interviews is the **skill and experience of the interviewers themselves**. Any interviewer is prone to bias, but a person can learn to reduce this problem through training and experience. Inexperienced interviewers have other problems as well.

- **Inability to evaluate** properly information about a candidate
- **Inability to compare** a candidate against the requirements for a job or a personnel specification
- Bad interview planning
- A **tendency to talk too much** in interviews, and to ask questions which call for a short answer
- A tendency to act as an inquisitor and make candidates feel uneasy.

To some extent the problems can be overcome with training.

4.3 Selection testing

In some job selection procedures, an interview is supplemented by some form of selection test. The interviewers must be certain that the results of such tests are reliable, and that a candidate who scores well in a test will be more likely to succeed in the job.

There are four types of test commonly used in practice.

(a) **Intelligence tests** aim to measure the applicant's general intellectual ability.

(b) **Aptitude tests** are designed to predict an individual's potential for performing a job or learning new skills.

(c) **Proficiency tests** are perhaps the most closely related to an assessor's objectives, because they measure ability to do the work involved. An applicant for an audio typist's job, for example, might be given a dictation tape and asked to type it.

(d) **Psychological tests** may measure a variety of characteristics, such as an applicant's skill in dealing with other people, ambition and motivation or emotional stability.

Sometimes applicants are required to attempt several tests (a **test battery**) aimed at giving a more rounded picture than would be available from a single test.

This kind of testing must be used with care as it suffers from several limitations.

(a) It was mentioned above **that there must be a direct relationship between ability in the test and ability in the job.** One way of assessing a test is to try it on existing employees whose capabilities are already known. It is very unlikely that tests alone will be sufficient to assess an applicant's suitability. They should be supplemented by other information, such as that derived from interview.

(b) **The interpretation of test results is a skilled task,** for which training and experience is essential. It is not something a marketing manager would undertake.

(c) Particular difficulties are experienced with particular kinds of test.

(d) It is difficult to exclude **bias against racial and ethnic minorities** from these tests.

4.4 References

References provide further confidential information about the prospective employee. This may be of varying value, **as the reliability of all but the most factual information must be in question.** A reference should contain:

(a) straightforward factual information confirming the nature of the applicant's previous job(s), period of employment, pay, and circumstances of leaving

(b) opinions about the applicant's personality and other attributes, which should obviously be treated with some caution.

4.5 The offer

Once a selection is made the candidate should be approached with a formal offer. It is best not to notify a suitable second choice until the candidate has accepted. Unsuccessful candidates should be notified as quickly as possible.

The organisation should be prepared for its offer to be rejected at this stage. Applicants may have received and accepted other offers. They may not have been attracted by their first-hand view of the organisation, and may have changed their mind about applying; they may only have been testing the water in applying in the first place, gauging the market for their skills and experience for future reference, or seeking a position of strength from which to bargain with their present employers. **A small number of eligible applicants should therefore be kept in reserve.**

FOR DISCUSSION

Some companies have run into trouble from disgruntled employees because the companies have given them poor references. Certain companies have therefore tried to deal with this situation by giving references along the following lines: 'You will be lucky to have this person working for you.'

What are the potential problems with that reference?

EXAMPLE

Instead of using their own sales representatives, many companies are recruiting field marketing agencies to work for them, finding it cheaper and more efficient. When Mars launched 'Celebrations' an agency was used to persuade wholesalers to stock the new product.

5 INTEGRATING NEW MEMBERS INTO THE TEAM

Giving someone the job does not magically convert that person from an acceptable or good fit for the post to an ideal one. Action to fill the gaps with training or even to modify the job is needed.

The manager should be sensitive to potential problems and take action to help new team members settle in quickly and make a positive contribution. They might need new skills or knowledge and experience for the job, or their existing skills might need developing.

Once an applicant for a job is offered the job and accepts it, he or she has to be introduced to the job. This is **the process of induction**. If you are examined about the induction process, you should be able to draw on your own experience on first starting work. From the first day in a job, a new recruit must be helped to find his or her bearings. There are limits to what any person can pick up in a short time.

Good induction should set out performance targets and encourage quality work. It should also maintain the motivation of starters and develop a commitment to the company.

Induction starts before the first day with **joining instructions**. These should tell the joiner where, when and to whom to report, and also the documentation they need to bring in with them.

On the first day, a senior person should welcome the new recruit. The seniority of this manager is likely to vary according to the size of the organisation, and the size of the section where the recruit will be working. In smaller organisations a recruit is more likely to see a manager in a more senior position than in larger organisations. The manager might discuss in broad terms what is required from people at work, working conditions, pay and benefits, training opportunities and career opportunities and should then introduce the new recruit to the person who will be the recruit's immediate manager.

The immediate line manager should then take over the **continuing process of induction and development**. This involves a number of tasks.

(a) Pinpoint the **areas that the new staff member will have to learn** about **in order to start** his or her job. Some things (such as detailed technical knowledge) may be identified as areas for later study or training. A list of learning priorities should be drawn up so that the recruit and the manager are clear about the rate and direction of progress required.

(b) Explain first of all the **nature** of the job, and its **goals, in the context of the department as a whole**. This will help the recruit to work to specific targets and to understand how his or her tasks relate to the organisation as a whole.

(c) Explain the **structure** of the department – and introduce those who will be working with or for the new team member. He or she should meet all the members of the immediate work team. One colleague may be assigned to a recruit as a **mentor** for his or her first few days, to keep an eye on him or her, answer routine queries and 'show the ropes'.

(d) Plan and implement an appropriate **training programme** for whatever technical or practical knowledge is required. The programme should have a **clear schedule and set of goals** so that the recruit has a sense of purpose, and so that the programme can be efficiently organised to fit in with the activities of the department. Training should cover general information about the business and also the specific skills that the employee will need to perform properly.

(e) **Coach and train** the recruit; check regularly on progress. **Feedback** information on how he or she is doing will be essential to the learning process, correcting any faults at an early stage and building the confidence of the recruit.

(f) **Integrate** the recruit into the **culture** of the organisation. Much of this may be done informally to reinforce commitment by rewarding evidence of loyalty, hard work and desired behaviour.

6 MOTIVATION AND REWARD

Definition

> **Motivation** is simply reasons for behaviour. People at work display varying degrees of motivation to achieve the goals set by management. It is an important task of managers at all levels to enhance the individual's motivation to work effectively.

Managers can provide the team with the opportunity and resources to work, but without motivation, little effective work will result. Motivation is the magic ingredient or catalyst which the manager has to add to the work situation to generate results.

6.1 Why is motivation important?

It could be argued that a person is employed to do a job, and so will do that job and no question of motivation arises. A person who does not want to do the work can resign. The point at issue, however, is the **efficiency** with which the job is done. It is suggested that if individuals can be motivated, by one means or another, they will produce a better quality of work. Sales personnel, in particular, need to be motivated.

6.2 Motivators and motivation

In the most basic terms, an individual has **needs** which he or she wishes to satisfy. The means of satisfying the needs are **wants**. For example, an individual might feel the need for power, and to fulfil this need, might want money and a position of authority. Depending on the strength of these needs and wants, she/he may take action to achieve them. If successful in achieving them, she/he will be satisfied. This can be shown in a simple diagram.

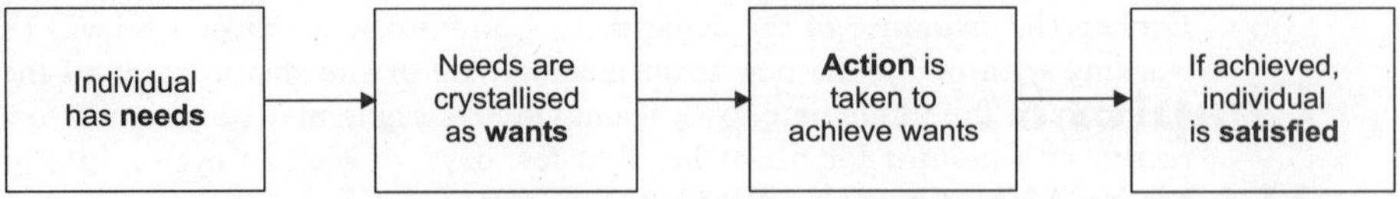

Motivators can be established which act as the wants of the individual. For example, the position of sales director might serve as a want to satisfy an individual's need for power, or access to the senior executive's dining room might serve as a want to satisfy a need for status. **Motivators may exist which are not directly controllable by management;** for example, an individual might want to be accepted by work mates, to satisfy a need for friendship and affiliation with others, and might therefore choose to conform to the norms and adopt the attitudes of the work group, which are not necessarily shared by the organisation as a whole.

Management has the problem of creating or manipulating motivators which will actually motivate employees to perform in a desired way.

6.3 Motivation theories

What we believe motivation is and what can be done with it will influence all our attitudes to individuals in organisations and to our management style.

(a) Some suggest that a **satisfied** worker will work harder, although there is little evidence to support the assumption. Satisfaction may reduce labour turnover and absenteeism, but will not necessarily increase individual productivity. Some hold that people work best within a compatible work group, or under a well-liked leader.

(b) There is a common assumption that individuals will work harder in order to obtain a desired reward. **Incentives** can work if certain conditions are satisfied.

  (i) The individual perceives the increased reward to be worth the extra effort

  (ii) The performance can be measured and clearly attributed to that individual

  (iii) The individual wants that particular kind of reward

  (iv) The increased performance will not become the new minimum standard

6.4 Maslow's hierarchy of needs

In his motivation theory, Maslow put forward certain propositions about the motivating power of people's **needs**.

(a) Every person's needs can be arranged in **a hierarchy of relative strength.**

(b) Each **level of need is dominant until satisfied;** only then does the next higher level of need become a motivating factor.

(c) **A need which has been satisfied no longer motivates** an individual's behaviour. The need for self-actualisation can never be satisfied.

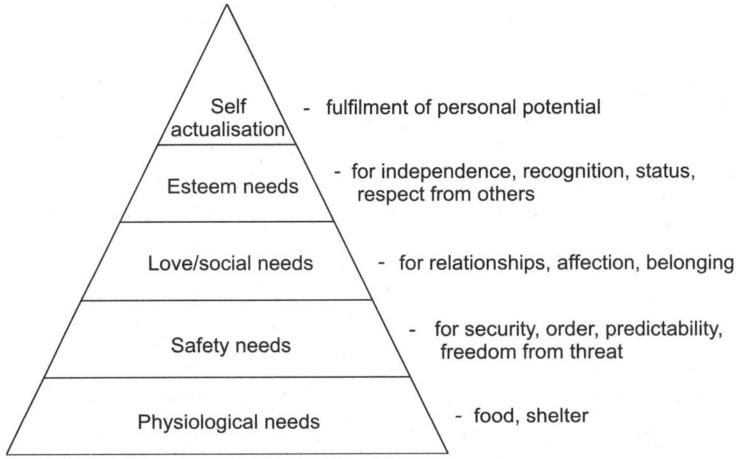

Figure 8.3: Maslow's hierarchy of needs

FOR DISCUSSION

What aspects of the sales job do you think relates to Maslow's need hierarchy?

6.5 Vroom's expectancy theory

Victor Vroom suggested that the strength of an individual's motivation to do something will depend on the extent to which he **expects** the results of his efforts to contribute towards his personal needs or goals, to reward him or to punish him. Put another way, expectancy theory states that people will effectively decide how much they are going to put into their work as a result of two considerations.

(a) The **value** that they place on the expected outcome, whether the positive value of a reward, or the negative value of a punishment. Vroom called this '**valence**'.

(b) The strength of their **expectation** that behaving in a certain way will in fact bring out the desired outcome. *Vroom* called this **expectancy**.

> **E**xpectancy x **V**alence = **F**orce of motivation.

This may be relevant to selling staff, if money is typically a reward.

6.6 Methods of improving motivation and job satisfaction

There are various ways in which managers can attempt to increase the motivation of their subordinates.

(a) Herzberg and others recommended better **job design**, in terms of content, and extent methods

(b) Various writers have suggested that subordinates' **participation in decision-making** will improve motivation through self-realisation and **empowerment**.

(c) **Pay and incentive schemes** are frequently regarded as powerful motivators.

We shall discuss each of these ways in turn.

The objectives of the job design process are to improve productivity, efficiency and quality and to satisfy the individual's needs for interest, challenge and accomplishment. The process begins with job design.

Job enrichment is planned, deliberate action to build greater responsibility, breadth and challenge of work into a job. A job may be enriched in a variety of ways.

(a) Giving it greater variety (although this could also be described as job enlargement)

(b) Allowing the employee in the job greater freedom to decide how the job should be done

(c) Encouraging employees to participate in the planning decisions of their superiors

(d) Ensuring that the employee receives regular feedback on his/her performance, comparing actual results against personal targets

---

EXAMPLE

At first, a **market researcher's** responsibilities for producing quarterly management reports ended at the stage of producing the figures. These duties were then extended so that she prepared the actual reports and submitted them, under her own name, to the senior management. This alteration in responsibilities not only enriched the job but also increased the workload. This in turn led to delegation of certain responsibilities to clerks within the department. These duties were in themselves job enrichment to the clerks and so a cascading effect was obtained. This highlights one of the basic elements of job enrichment – that what is tedious, mundane detail at a high level can represent significant job interest and challenge at a lower level in the organisation where a person's experience and scope is much less.

Job enrichment alone will not automatically make employees more productive. If jobs are enriched, employees will expect to be paid fairly for what they are doing. It might be more correct therefore to say that **job enrichment might improve productivity through greater motivation, but only if it is rewarded fairly**. 'Even those who want their jobs enriched will expect to be rewarded with more than job satisfaction. Job enrichment is not a cheaper way to greater productivity. Its pay-off will come in the less visible costs of morale, climate and working relationships'.

Job enlargement is frequently confused with job enrichment. **Job enlargement is the attempt to widen jobs by increasing the number of operations in which a job holder is involved.**

This has the effect of lengthening the cycle time of repeated operations; by reducing the number of repetitions of the same work, the dullness of the job should also be reduced. Job enlargement is therefore a horizontal extension of an individual's work, whereas job enrichment is a vertical extension. For most knowledge workers, like marketing staff, this may be less useful than job enrichment.

Aspects of well-designed jobs

(a) Scope for the individual to set work standards and targets

(b) Individual control over the pace and methods of working

(c) Provision of variety by allowing for inter-locking tasks to be done by the same person

(d) Opportunity to comment about the design of the product, or job

(e) Feedback to the individual about performance.

Job rotation

Job rotation may take two forms:

(a) An employee might be transferred to another job after a period of, say, two to four years in an existing job in order to give him or her a new interest and challenge, and to bring a fresh person to the job being vacated.

(b) Job rotation might be regarded as a form of training. Trainees might be expected to learn a bit about a number of different jobs, by spending six months or one year in each job before being moved on. The employee is regarded as a 'trainee' rather than as an experienced person holding down a demanding job.

No doubt you will have your own views about the value of job rotation as a method of training or career development. It is interesting to note Drucker's view: 'The whole idea of training jobs is contrary to all rules and experience. A person should never be given a job that is not a real job, that does not require performance from him'.

FOR DISCUSSION

Good sales people do not necessarily go on to managerial positions. How would **you** go about motivating a sales person through job enrichment or enlargement? Is it realistic?

6.7 Pay and incentive schemes

Pay as a motivator

Employees need income to live. The size of that income will affect the standard of living, and although they would obviously like to earn more, they are probably more concerned about two other aspects of pay.

(a) That they should earn **enough**.

(b) That pay should be **fair in comparison** with the pay of others both inside and outside the organisation.

Limitations to the use of money as a form of motivation

Rates of pay are perhaps more useful as a means of **keeping an organisation adequately staffed** by competent, qualified people, rather than as a means of getting them to work harder.

In most large companies, salary levels and pay levels are usually structured carefully so as to be 'equitable' or fair. Managers and workers will compare each other's pay and will be dissatisfied if the comparison is unfavourable. Pay is therefore more likely to be a hygiene factor than a motivator.

When employees expect a regular annual review of salary, increases in pay will not motivate them to work harder. Indeed, if the increase is not high enough, it may be a source of dissatisfaction.

6.8 Incentive schemes

Pay as a motivator is commonly associated with commission or incentive schemes, where a salesperson's pay depend on sales targets. If pay increases do not immediately follow improved performance, or completed tasks, they lose their 'connection' with results.

All incentive schemes are based on the principle that people are willing to work harder to obtain more money. However, the work of *Mayo* has shown that there are several constraints which can nullify this basic principle.

(a) The average employee is generally capable of influencing the timings and control systems used by management.

(b) Employees remain suspicious that if they achieved high levels of output and earnings then management would alter the basis of the incentive rates to reduce future earnings.

(c) Often, employees conform to a group output norm. The need to have the approval of their fellow workers by conforming is more important than the money urge.

(d) High taxation rates would mean that workers do not believe that extra effort produces an adequate increase in pay.

A short-term incentive scheme involves a direct observable link between personal or team efforts and the reward gained. However a long-term scheme such as a profit sharing scheme, has a less personal relevance and a slower pay-back.

Common types of short-term incentive schemes

Individual payment by results, such as a sales bonus over and above a basic wage ('day rate') for achieving set standards of sales over a prescribed period. There is thus a direct link between performance and earnings for each individual so the motivating effect is strong. However, it has its disadvantages.

(a) The system is complex and expensive to administer.

(b) If quantity of sales is the relevant index, margins may suffer as sales staff negotiate lower prices to make sales.

(c) Employees may manipulate sales, because of fears that high sales will become a new 'norm', with a reduction in the pay incentive.

(d) Employees outside the scheme may resent the wages levels of those inside: pay differentials may be eroded. It has been known for top sales people to earn more than the Managing Director.

(e) Employees may worry about losing pay because of illness, holidays and so on.

EXAMPLE

Brassington and Pettitt (2006) note different schemes for remuneration.

(a) Rentokil Initial offers a package of financial and non-financial benefits to attract and retain staff. These include mobile phone, pension scheme, car, regular training and promotion prospects. The culture of the firm values the salesforce, and strongly equates motivated sales representatives with additional sales.

(b) For an Avon representative, remuneration is based largely on commission, with commission rates increasing with larger customer orders. (www.avon.co.uk).

---

7 JOB SATISFACTION AND CUSTOMER SERVICE

7.1 Accountability

Many organisations now use **competency frameworks** in preference to person specifications, and **accountability profiles** in preference to job descriptions.

Whereas job descriptions conventionally consist of a comprehensive list of the various **tasks** and **activities** to be performed by the job-holder, accountability profiles focus on **results** and **outcomes**. The performance of tasks and activities is meant to contribute to the achievement of some desired result or other, so tasks and activities are not ends in themselves.

EXAMPLE

The significant difference between **doing** and **achieving** can be illustrated in the following (imaginary) conversation between a supermarket manager and one of his customer checkout staff.

Manager: What are you paid for?

Checkout operator: I'm a checkout operator

Manager:	That's your title. What are you paid for?
Checkout operator:	I'm paid to pass customer purchases in front of the barcode scanner, and then take the customer's money.
Manager:	Those are activities – the things you do. I still want to know what you're paid for.
Checkout operator:	Now that you mention it, I haven't a clue

It would be relatively straightforward to say to the checkout operator (as one UK supermarket company has already done) that her **principal accountability**, her key role is:

To make the customer want to come back

Against this principal accountability, everything the checkout operator does has a meaningful purpose.

All jobs can be outlined in this way, with a principal accountability defined as an **added-value output**, not simply as a summary of some key activities. It is important, too, that the principal accountability is kept simple, brief and straightforward.

Once the principal purpose (or 'mission') for any given role has been determined, it then becomes possible to identify up to six **Key Performance Areas** some companies call them Key Accountabilities or Key Performance Indicators, which represent the principal ways in which the role occupant will be measured. Note that KPAs are not the same as competencies: KPAs refer to the results which should be achieved within the occupational role, whereas competencies describe the attributes of the individual job-holder. When discussing recruitment and selection, we often talk of finding the right 'peg' (person) for the 'hole' (the job): KPAs are part of the 'hole', and competencies represent a way of describing the 'peg'.

EXAMPLE

The following are Key Performance Areas used within front-line customer service roles for a major UK water utility. Note the combination of KPAs which are concerned with day-to-day performance plus others which focus on 'added-value' outcomes like change and continuous improvement.

The effective performer will:

(1) Provide immediate, positive and constructive responses to all customer contact.
(2) Provide excellent customer service to all our customers.
(3) Demonstrate a flexible attitude to the requirements of a changing business.
(4) Achieve required performance levels (quality and quantity).
(5) Supply a multi-functional service.
(6) Highlight customer service opportunities.

7.2 The position of customer service

If, strictly speaking, people in organisations are not employed to **do** anything, but are employed in order to **achieve** something, then what is customer service meant to achieve?

Customer service used to be something done by reactive people who waited for complaints, were shouted at, then put things right and organised compensation. Now it is more widely believed that customer service will be a powerful ingredient for

competitive advantage and **corporate survival** in the years ahead. In some organisations the people at the top may not have encountered customers for more than ten years. Their ideas about customers may not have kept up to date, and they may be out of touch with customer aspirations.

7.3 Developments in customer care

A major development in terms of customer care is Total Quality Management (TQM). This is the fulfilment of corporate objectives alongside the satisfaction of customer needs. TQM looks into the following areas to develop an effective customer care strategy.

- Quality
- Availability
- Service
- Support
- Reliability
- Value for money

Relationships need to be managed between the organisation and customers. Relationship marketing occurs where a long term view of the customer's value to the organisation is developed. The main aim is to build customer loyalty. This approach can be used in both consumer and business markets, but is perhaps more well developed in business markets. Sometimes this is combined with specific delivery requirements such as Just in Time (JIT) systems, where stock is not held by the manufacturer in bulk. Purchasing agreements involve stock being ordered and supplied at short notice.

7.4 Customer-related competency models

Increasingly popular in organisations – not always connected to the requirement for improved customer service – are **competency frameworks** which list the standard of behaviour required in any given job.

Competency frameworks can be used for **many purposes:** human resource planning, recruitment, selection, induction, training, development, performance appraisal, and promotion. They may consist simply of a collection of **defined and classified behaviours**, or they may be prioritised between the 'Essential' and the 'Desirable'.

It cannot be expected that the precise behaviours associated with any given competency will be the same at all levels of the organisation and within all functions. Look at the following example, which can be visualised as part of the competency framework for people working in a retail or financial services operation.

Key result areas are the following.

- Creating value through customers
- Creating value for the business
- Working with others
- Working smarter
- Managing change

We expand upon the result area of 'creating value through customers' in the example box below.

EXAMPLE

Competences linked to creating value through customers

- Providing excellent customer service
- Managing the customer relationship

Core behaviours linked to providing excellent customer service

- Always keeps promises
- Develops excellent understanding of customer needs and concerns
- Takes personal responsibility for resolving all customer issues
- Strives to exceed customer expectations
- Consults regularly with customers to secure performance feedback
- Tries to anticipate customer needs and act accordingly

Role-specific behaviours linked to providing excellent customer service

Directors and senior executives

- Establishes clear criteria to measure customer satisfaction
- Identifies new opportunities to create competitive advantage through customer service
- Reinforces a commitment to customer service excellence in self and others
- Seeks to understand trends and developments elsewhere, with a view to adopting them for the company's use
- Takes 'best practice' ideas/solutions and makes them work for the company

People managers and team leaders

- Reinforces key messages about customer service to all staff and team members
- Assists staff and team members to meet/exceed customer service standards by creating the right working environment
- Encourages, motivates, trains and coaches others in the assimilation of a customer-focused culture

Front-line customer service

- Treats each contact with customers as an opportunity to impress them with the service offered by the business
- Acts as the key ambassadorial interface between the business and its customers

Core behaviours linked to managing the customer relationship

- Builds rapport by taking a real interest in customers
- Builds customer trust by meeting their needs and fulfilling all promises
- Regularly seeks customer feedback and takes action accordingly
- Presents a positive image of the company to customers
- Listens sensitively to customer communications
- Remains polite, tactful, courteous and friendly towards customers

Role-specific behaviours linked to managing the customer relationship

Directors and senior executives

- Defines policies which enable all staff to understand the value of individual customer relationships

- Differentiates the services and products offered by the business from those of competitors
- Influences the external perception of the organisation and its brand(s) by raising the profile of the company

People managers and team leaders

- Makes the management of customer relationships a regular agenda item for team meetings, coaching session, and performance reviews
- Focuses attention on those customer relationships which are especially crucial in terms of their commercial significance
- Personally makes periodic contact with selected customers in order to retain expertise in the management of customer relationships
- Seeks out customers' views to establish realistic service level agreements (principally so far as internal customers are concerned)

Front-line customer service

- Collects and disseminates relevant information about customers
- Sensitively reacts to customer concerns and responds accordingly, with restitution if necessary
- Takes the heat out of what might otherwise be confrontational scenarios involving customers

---

7.5 Competency frameworks for personal learning and development

We have already discussed the benefits of competency profiling for recruitment, selection and appraisal. Several organisations majoring on customer service as a source of competitive advantage have begun to use competencies for purposes of **self-appraisal, self-learning** and **self-development.**

Once a competency framework has been developed, individual employees may score themselves against each element within the system; they can also assess the relative importance of each competency.

(a) The competences which deserve attention will be those where

  (i) Current achievement is unsatisfactory.

  (ii) Improvement is essential if the individual is likely to achieve career progression.

(b) The questions to be asked in the self-evaluation process should include:

  (i) Which competencies within the competency framework do I already display, and in what measure?

  (ii) Which of the components do I really need in order to do my present job satisfactorily?

  (iii) Which of the competencies do I need to concentrate on in order to prepare myself for predicted changes to my current role?

  (iv) Which of the competencies do I need to concentrate on in order to prepare myself for a career move?

  (v) Which of the competencies do I need to address in relation to my current performance?

Here is an example of some learning activities linked to a customer focus competency.

(a) Select up to five named individuals as customers for your services.

(b) Consciously initiate a customer feedback programme in which you seek assessments from each of these five customers about their perceptions of what you supply for them, which areas could be improved, and which aspects are perceived to be either particularly important or relatively insignificant.

(c) Produce an action plan for personal customer-service improvement, with a timetable for measuring progress.

(d) Identify a '**benchmark**' customer-service performance comparison, and seek to apply the lessons to be learned.

Chapter roundup

- Characteristics of a good sales person include enthusiasm, intelligence, reliability, commitment, initiative, creativity, self-confidence, courtesy and sensitivity.
- Recruiting new people into the sales function may be necessary if there is a gap in the skills of the existing sales force, to replace staff or to increase the sales force because the work has expanded.
- The recruitment and selection process starts with a definition of requirements.
- Job analysis involves the examination of the essential characteristics of the job. The product of a job analysis is usually a job specification followed by a job description and person specification.
- In searching for new sales personnel, companies may use internal recruitment (recruiting perhaps from other departments) and/or job advertisements.
- Selection is usually based on the written application, interview and in some cases tests.
- The induction process should help new staff become effective members of the sales team. It should involve welcoming the staff, explaining about the organisation and pinpointing additional training requirements.
- Sales personnel will respond to different aspect of motivation.
- Incentives are often used in sales force management.
- Job enrichment can be used as a motivator where a job is changed to have greater responsibility, interest and challenge.
- Job enlargement occurs where jobs are widened by increasing the number of operations in which a job holder is involved.
- Incentive schemes can include pay or monetary rewards such as commission and bonuses.
- Reward can also be expressed in terms of job satisfaction and personal responsibility for good customer service.

Quick quiz

1 List three characteristics of a good sales person.

2 Give an outline of the recruitment and selection process.

3 What information should be gathered in job analysis?

4 What basic elements should be on a job description?

5 What important qualities might recruiting older employees bring?

6 Are there any problems in internal recruitment?

7 What considerations should a company take into account when deciding on an advertising medium for job vacancies?

8 What are aptitude tests used for?

9 Is pay a good motivator?

10 Salespeople are often at the front line of customer service. This puts them in a unique position – why?

Answers to quick quiz

1 Could include three of enthusiasm, intelligence, reliability, commitment, initiative, creativity, self confidence, courtesy or sensitivity.

2 Human resource planning – job analysis – vacancies – sources of labour – advertising – process applications – notifying applicants.

3 Initial requirements, duties and responsibilities, environmental conditions and social factors.

4 Job title, location, accountability (who reports to who), and main duties.

5 Skills and experience, regard for customer service, stabilising influence and better staff retention.

6 Yes, if an internal candidate does not get the job there could be resentment towards the successful candidate and a sense of rejection on the part of the unsuccessful internal candidate.

7 The cost, type and number of readers or users of the medium, frequency.

8 To try to predict an individual's potential for performing a job or learning new skills.

9 It can be, but there are some problems.

10 They can react to customer concerns, give and receive information about service and can handle problems and manage the client – organisational relationship.

Answers to activities

1 There is no specific answer to this activity.

2 There is no specific answer to this activity.

3 There is no specific answer to this activity.

4 *Benefits*

- Existing knowledge of the business
- Existing contracts
- No learning curve
- Continuity

Problems

- Lack of a refreshing approach
- Resentment among other employees
- Loss of an opportunity to bring in new talent

5 There is no specific answer to this activity.

6 There is no specific answer to this activity.

Chapter 9 : SALES OUTPUT

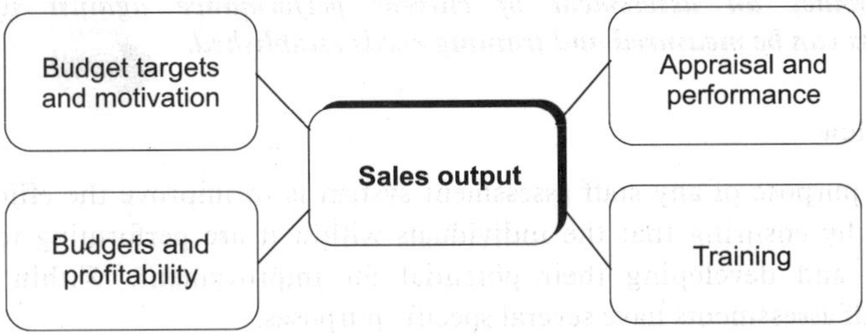

Introduction

This chapter will look at some of the outputs of the sales function. It will explore how appraisal systems can be put into place and made effective and aspects of staff training. Finally this chapter will concentrate on the role of budgets in terms of both profits and as an employee motivator.

Your objectives

In this chapter you will learn about the following.

(a) Different types of appraisal systems

(b) The need for up to date relevant training

(c) The link between budgets and profitability

(d) How the budget process can affect sales force motivation by the use of targets

1 APPRAISAL AND PERFORMANCE

Motivation is concerned with attempts to improve the performance of groups and individuals. Appraisal is a systematic approach to providing that feedback and for putting praise and criticism in context.

It also provides an assessment of current performance against which future improvements can be measured and training needs established.

1.1 Overview

The general purpose of any staff assessment system is to improve the efficiency of the organisation by ensuring that the individuals within it are performing to the best of their ability and developing their potential for improvement. Within this overall objective, staff assessments have several specific purposes.

(a) To review **performance,** to plan and follow up training and development programmes; and to set targets for future performance

(b) To review **potential,** as an aid to planning career development by predicting the level and type of work the individual will be capable of in the future

(c) To increase **motivation by providing feedback**

(d) To review **salaries**: measuring the extent to which an employee is deserving of a salary increase as compared with peers

Features of a typical system

(a) **Identification of criteria for assessment,** perhaps based on job analysis, performance standards and person specifications

(b) The preparation by the subordinate's manager of an **assessment report**

(c) An **appraisal interview,** for an exchange of views about the results of the assessment and targets for improvement

(d) **Review of the assessment by the assessor's own superior,** so that the appraisee does not feel subject to one person's prejudices. Formal appeals may be allowed, if necessary to establish the fairness of the procedure

(e) The preparation and implementation of **action plans** to achieve improvements and changes agreed

(f) **Follow-up**: monitoring the progress of the action plan

There may not need to be standard forms for appraisal (and elaborate form-filling procedures should be avoided) as long as managers understand the nature and extent of what is required, and are motivated to take it seriously. Most systems, however, provide for assessments to be recorded, and report forms of various lengths and complexity may be designed for standard use, A written record of some form is essential to prevent doubts and uncertainties at a later date.

1.2 The assessment report

The basis of assessment must first be determined. Assessments must be related to a **common standard**, in order for comparisons to be made between individuals, and of a particular individual's progress over time. They should also be related to meaningful performance criteria, which take account of the critical variables in each different job.

1.3 Techniques of appraisal

(a) **Overall assessment** is the simplest method, simply requiring the manager to write in narrative form judgements about the appraisee, possibly with a checklist of personality characteristics and performance targets to work from. There will be no guaranteed consistency of the criteria and areas of assessment, however, and managers may not be able to convey clear, effective judgements in writing.

(b) **Guided assessment** requires assessors to comment on a number of specified characteristics and performance elements, with guidelines as to how the terms (eg 'application', 'integrity', 'adaptability') are to be interpreted in the work context. This is a more precise, but still rather vague method.

(c) **Grading** adds a comparative frame of reference to the general guidelines, whereby managers are asked to select one of a number of levels or degrees to which the individual in question displays the given characteristic. These are also known as **rating scales**, and are much used in standard appraisal forms. Their effectiveness depends to a large extent on the **relevance** of the factors chosen for assessment and the definition of the agreed standards of assessment.

(i) Numerical values may be added to ratings to give rating 'scores'. Alternatively a less precise **graphic scale** may be used to indicate general position on a plus/minus scale, for example:

Factor: job knowledge

High		Average	✓	Low

(ii) The principal drawback of such schemes is that the subordinate may not agree with the precise ratings given. This may lead to the subordinate questioning the judgement of the appraiser. The appraisal may degenerate into an argument about the appraiser's use of the grading system rather than what the assessment tells the subordinate about his or her performance.

(d) **Results-oriented schemes.** The above techniques will be concerned with results but are commonly based on behavioural appraisal. A wholly results-oriented approach (eg Management by Objectives) sets out to review performance against specific targets and standards of performance agreed in advance by manager and subordinate together. This scheme has a number of advantages.

- The subordinate is more involved in appraisal because success or progress is measured against specific, jointly agreed targets.
- The manager is relieved, to some extent, of the role of **critic**, and becomes a **counsellor**.
- Learning and motivation theories suggest that clear and known targets are important in modifying and determining behaviour.

(e) **Self-appraisals,** where the individuals carry out their own self-evaluation, can be an alternative to management/subordinate appraisals. They have the advantage that the system is evidently aimed at the needs of the individual. Self-appraisal schemes can also be combined with training schemes where the individuals decide on the training they require.

Activity 1 **(20 minutes)**

What type of appraisal scheme does your organisation have? How effective do you think it is? If you are not employed, which appraisal scheme would you prefer to be appraised by?

The effectiveness of any scheme will depend on the realistic and clear statement of targets; and the commitment of both parties to make it work. The **measurement of success or failure is only part of the picture: reasons** for failure and opportunities arising from success must be evaluated.

Managers will need guidance, or perhaps training to help them make a relevant, objective and helpful report. Most large organisations with standard review forms also issue detailed guidance notes to aid assessors with the written and discussion elements.

Assessing sales performance

Much sales performance is easily assessed against targets: such targets might relate to activity, such as call rate, but are more likely to be set for achievement, using such measures as those below.

- Value of orders secured
- Number of units sold
- Gross profit margin achieved
- Number of leads converted into orders

Sales people generally are accustomed to having their performance assessed against performance-related targets and many will actively seek employment in firms that not only assess them in such terms but reward them according to quantified performance measures, using commission or bonus systems.

1.4 Appraisal interview

The report may be shown to the appraisee and thus form a basis for discussion. Some organisations, however, do not show the report to the employee; this is likely to lead to resentment and anxiety about the correctness or otherwise of its contents.

Approaches to appraisal interviews

Approach	Comments
The **tell and sell** method	The manager gives details of the assessment to the subordinate and then tries to **gain acceptance** of the evaluation and the improvement plan. This requires unusual human relations skills in order to convey constructive criticism in an acceptable manner, and to motivate appraisees to alter their behaviour.
The **tell and listen** method	The manager gives the assessment and then **invites response**. The manager no longer dominates the interview, and there is greater opportunity for **counselling**. The employee is encouraged to participate in the assessment and the working out of improvement targets and methods. Managers using this method will need to have good listening skills.

The **problem solving** approach	The manager abandons the role of critic altogether, and becomes a counsellor and helper. The discussion is centred not on the assessment, but on the employee's work problems. The employee is encouraged to think solutions through, and to commit to the recognised need for personal improvement.

Many organisations waste the opportunities for **upward communication** embedded in the appraisal process. In order to get a positive contribution from employees, the appraisal interviewer should ask positive and thought-provoking questions.

Here are some examples.

- What parts of your job do you do best?
- Could any changes be made in your job which might result in improved performance?
- Have you any skills, knowledge, or aptitudes which could be made better use of in the organisation?

Follow-up procedures

- Having the report agreed and counter-signed by a more senior manager.
- Informing appraisees of the final results of the appraisal, if this has been contentious in the review interview.
- Carrying out agreed actions on training, promotions and so on.
- Monitoring the appraisee's progress with agreed actions.
- Taking necessary steps to help the appraisee for example by guidance, providing feedback or upgrading equipment.

1.5 The effectiveness of appraisal

In practice, the system often goes wrong.

(a) There may be a divergence between the subordinate's and interviewer's perceived and actual needs. The subordinates may **want** praise, they may, however, **need** constructive criticism. The interviewer may wish to concentrate on criticising, whereas the appraisal could be used to give feedback on management practice.

(b) Appraisal interviews are often **defensive on the part of the subordinate,** who believes that any criticism will bring sanctions. There may also be some mistrust of the validity of the scheme itself.

(c) Interviews are also often **defensive on the part of the superior,** who cannot reconcile the role of judge and critic with the 'human relations' aspect of the interview. As a result there may be many unresolved issues left at the end.

(d) The superior might show **conscious or unconscious bias** in the report. Systems without clearly defined standard criteria will be particularly prone to the subjectivity of the assessor's judgements.

(e) The general **level of ratings** may vary widely from manager to manager.

(f) There may be **bias** resulting from the personal interaction between appraiser and appraisee.

(g) Appraisals may deal with specific problems which should have been dealt with at the time they arose by counselling. Appraisals ought to concentrate on ongoing matters that are important to career development.

(h) Appraisals may be seen merely as a bureaucratic form-filling exercise or as no more than an annual formality.

FOR DISCUSSION

An appraisal process that is simply a once a year bureaucratic exercise is a wasted opportunity for both sales staff and management.

1.6 Upward appraisal

A notable modern trend, adopted in the UK by companies such as BP, British Airways TV and others, is upward appraisal, whereby **employees are not only rated by their superiors but also (or instead) by their subordinates.** The followers appraise the leader.

- Subordinates tend to know their superior better than superiors know their subordinates.
- As all subordinates rate their managers statistically, these ratings tend to be more reliable – the more subordinates the better.
- Subordinates' ratings have more impact because it is more unusual to receive ratings from subordinates.

Problems with the method include fear of reprisals, vindictiveness, and extra form processing. Some bosses in strong positions might refuse to act, even if a consensus of staff suggested that they should change their ways.

1.7 Peer rating

An alternative approach to individual appraisal (which also removes the link between past performance and reward) is **peer rating** in which an individual is judged and counselled by workmates or colleagues. It has been argued that peer rating will be devoid of mistrust and fear of missing promotion and will therefore be more honest and constructive, thus aiding the individual to develop in his job. It may be a useful strategy amongst professionally qualified staff.

1.8 360-degree appraisal

A final variant on appraisal schemes is the 360-degree appraisal. In this case, effectiveness is appraised by all the people with whom the subject has dealings – superiors, subordinates, customers and suppliers, internal and external.

Advantages of 360-degree feedback

(a) It **highlights every aspect** of the individual's performance, and allows comparison of the individual's self-assessment with the views of others.

(b) Feedback tends, overall, to be **balanced**, covering strengths in some areas with weaknesses in others, so it is less discouraging.

(c) The assessment is based on the normal work environment and circumstances. The feedback is thus felt to **be fairer and more relevant**, making it easier for employees to accept.

Potential pitfalls of 360-degree feedback

(a) **Negative emphasis**. Feedback on weaknesses should be balanced by positive feedback on strengths and potential, to encourage the employee to develop.

(b) '**Flavour of the month approach**'. The technique and its results are seen as interesting but no thought has been given to follow-up action.

(c) **Lack of confidentiality**. Respondents must be anonymous, or they may fear to tell the truth in an assessment.

(d) **Poor communication about the purpose of the exercise**. It can be daunting, and employees need to understand that it is not a political exercise, or a rod to beat anyone.

(e) **Lack of action and support**. The organisation must support the employee in the development suggested by the feedback.

2 TRAINING

Procuring the most appropriate human resources for the task and environment is an on-going process. It involves not only recruitment and selection, but the training and development of employees prior to employment, or at any time during their employment, in order to help them meet the requirements of their current, and potential future job.

2.1 The contribution of training

The increasingly dynamic nature of modern business (changes in technology, products, processes and control techniques) and the need for planned growth mean that a working organisation's competitiveness depends more and more on the continuous reassessment of training needs and the provision of planned training to meet those needs.

Training can certainly contribute, given the following provisos:

(a) It must be the correct tool for the need: it cannot solve problems caused by faulty organisation, equipment or employee selection.

(b) Reasons for neglecting training must be overcome: these include cost, inconvenience, apathy and an unrealistic expectation of training in the past.

(c) Limitations imposed by intelligence, motivation and the psychological restrictions of the learning process must be understood.

Activity 2 **(10 minutes)**

Make a list of the training you have received (if any) in your current post. Do you still have some training needs?

Sales training

Training the sales team recruit was discussed in the previous chapter. Such training cannot be regarded as fulfilling the sales person's training. There will be a continuing need for training in order to maintain and improve performance. This will deal with a range of topics.

(a) Sales techniques develop as time passes and individuals develop habits that may lead to under-performance. Training in selling is required to refresh staff and make sure they are using the best methods.

(b) Company systems and procedures must be followed, even by star sales people. Matters such as customer credit worthiness checks, completion of sales reports and submission of expenses claims do not help with the task of selling, but they are prescribed for good reason. Managers must ensure that their sales staff know how to carry out necessary administrative tasks and understand why they are required.

(c) New products usually create a training requirement. Sales staff must understand features, advantages and benefits and learn how to present them most effectively.

Continuing professional development

Generally, professional membership bodies require that their members undertake a minimum amount of training each year. This is known as continuing professional development (CPD). Some of this training will be left to the individual to choose and undertake, but some may have specified requirements, such as updates on relevant law and regulation. Both the Chartered Institute of Marketing and the Institute of sales and Marketing Management have CPD programmes.

2.2 On-the-job training (OJT)

OJT is very common, especially when the work involved is not complex. For example a new recruit can accompany a senior sale executive to the customer.

Coaching

Coaching is a common method of OJT; the trainee is put under the guidance of an experienced employee who demonstrates how to do the job and helps refine the trainee's technique.

All forms of training require the commitment of the organisation to the learning programme. It must believe in training and developing employees, and be prepared to devote both the money and the time. The manager will largely dictate the department's attitude to these things.

FOR DISCUSSION

What are the problems of relying on 'on the job' training?

A training programme

Training is often concerned with teaching a person how to do a particular job, or how to do it better. Many firms have structured training programmes.

A systematic approach to training

(a) **Identify areas** where training will be beneficial.

(b) **Establish learning targets**. The areas where learning is needed should be identified and specific, realistic goals stated, including standards of performance.

(c) Decide on the **training methods to be used.**

(d) **Plan a systematic learning and development programme**. This should allow for practice and consolidation.

(e) **Identify opportunities for broadening the trainee's knowledge and experience** such as involvement in new projects, extending the job or greater responsibility.

(f) **Take into account the strengths and limitations of the trainee.** A trainee from an academic background may learn best through research-based learning like fact-finding for a committee; whilst those who learn best by doing may profit from project work.

(g) **Implement** the scheme in full.

(h) **Exchange feedback**. The manager will want performance information in order to monitor the progress, adjust the learning programme, identify further needs and plan future development.

(i) **Validate the results** to check that the training works and benefits exceed costs.

2.3 Analysis of training needs

Training needs can be identified by considering the **gap** between **job requirements,** as determined by job analysis, job description and so on, and the **ability of the job holder,** as determined by testing or observation and appraisal.

The training department's management should make an initial investigation of the problem. Even if work is not done as well as it could be, training is not necessarily the right answer. We have seen that poor working standards might also be caused by other factors.

Objectives

If the training department concludes that the provision of training could improve work performance, it must analyse the work in detail in order to decide what the requirements of a training programme should be. In particular, there should be a training objective or objectives. These are tangible, observable targets which trainees should be capable of reaching at the end of the course.

The training objectives should be clear, specific and measurable, for example: 'at the end of a course a trainee must be able to describe ..., or identify ..., or list ..., or state ..., or distinguish x from y ...'. It is insufficient to state as an objective of a course 'to give trainees a grounding in ...' or 'to give trainees a better appreciation of ...'. These objectives are too woolly, and actual achievements cannot be measured against them.

EXAMPLE

In addition to in-house training, there are a number of independent training companies that specialise in sales courses.

2.4 Training methods

Having decided what must be learned and to what standard of achievement, the next stage is to decide what method of training should be used.

2.5 Course training methods

(a) **Lectures.** Lectures are suitable for large audiences and can be an efficient way of putting across information. However lack of participation may lead to lack of interest and/or failure to understand by most of the audience.

(b) **Discussions.** Discussions aim to impart information but allow much greater opportunities for audience participation. They are often suitable for groups up to twenty and can be a good means of maintaining interest.

(c) **Exercises.** An exercise involves a particular task being undertaken with pre-set results following guidance laid down. They are a very active form of learning and are a good means of checking whether trainees have assimilated information.

(d) **Role plays.** Trainees act out roles in a typical work situation. They are useful practice for face-to-face situations. However, they may embarrass some participants and may not be taken seriously.

(e) **Case studies.** Case studies identify causes and/or suggest solutions. They are a good means of exchanging ideas and thinking out solutions. However trainees may see the case study as divorced from their real work experience.

(f) **Programmed learning** can be provided on a computer terminal, but it is still associated with printed booklets which provide information in easy-to-learn steps. The booklet asks simple questions which the trainee must answer. If they are answered correctly, the trainee is instructed to carry on with more learning. If the questions are answered wrongly, the booklet gives an alternative set of instructions to go back and learn again. Programmed learning has a number of advantages.

   (i) Trainees can work through the course in simple stages and continually checks their progress. Misunderstandings are quickly put right.

   (ii) Trainees are kept actively involved in the learning process because they must keep answering questions put to them in the booklet.

   (iii) Giving correct answers immediately reinforces the learning process.

   (iv) Trainees can work at their own pace.

FOR DISCUSSION

Have you used any computer aided learning packages? What did you think of them? Would you (or did you) find it easier than more traditional methods?

Teambuilding

Selling is often a team activity and even where sales representatives travel and work in isolation, they must interact with other staff members to deal with leads, customer complaints, credit ratings, sales reports and so on. Team effectiveness is therefore an important aspect of sales management and much attention is directed to enhancing it.

Definition

> **Teambuilding** is defined by Mullins (2007) as
>
> '. . . the process of diagnosing task procedures and patterns of human interaction within a work group. The basic objective is to improve the overall performance of the organisation through improvements in the effectiveness of teams. Attention is focused on work procedures and interpersonal relationships

Teambuilding training generally takes the form of group exercises designed to enhance one or more aspects of team performance. A basic exercise may focus on simple team bonding; more complex exercises may explore individual relationships and group dynamics, perhaps in an entirely synthetic setting or possibly simulating aspects of the work environment.

2.6 Cost/benefit analysis of training

The training course should only go ahead if the **likely benefits are expected to exceed the costs** of designing and then running the course. **Costs** include training materials, the salaries of the staff attending training courses, their travelling expenses, the salaries of training staff and training overheads. **Benefits** might be measured in a variety of ways.

- Quicker working and therefore reductions in overtime or staff numbers
- Greater accuracy of work
- More extensive skills
- Improved motivation

As you will appreciate, the **benefits are more easily stated in general terms than quantified in money terms**. Indeed, it is often difficult to measure benefits such as increased identification with business objectives and increased cohesion as a team, but these benefits may nevertheless be significant.

2.7 Implementation and evaluation of training

When the training course has been designed, **a pilot course may be run**. The purpose of the test would be to find out whether the training scheme appears to achieve what it has set out to do, or whether some revisions are necessary. After the pilot test, the scheme can be implemented in full.

Implementation of the training scheme is not the end of the story. The scheme should be validated and evaluated.

(a) **Validation** means observing the results of the course, and measuring whether the training objective has been achieved.

(b) **Evaluation** means comparing the actual costs of the scheme against the assessed benefits which are being obtained. If the costs exceed the benefits, the scheme will need to be re-designed or withdrawn.

Validation methods

(a) **Asking the trainees** whether they thought the training programme was relevant to their work, and whether they found it useful. This is rather inexact and does not measure results for comparison against the training objective.

(b) **Measuring what the trainees have learned** on the course, perhaps by means of a test at the end of the course.

(c) Studying the **subsequent behaviour of the trainees** in their jobs to measure how the training scheme has altered the way they do their work. This is possible where the purpose of the course was to learn a particular skill.

(d) Finding out whether the training has affected **the work or behaviour of other employees not on the course**. This form of monitoring would probably be reserved for senior managers in the training department.

(e) Seeing whether training in general has contributed to the **overall objectives of the organisation**. This too is a form of monitoring reserved for senior managers and would perhaps be discussed at board level in the organisation.

DISCUSSION

Training is one of the aspects organisations cut back on in hard times.

EXAMPLE

It is useful to consider recent trends in marketing training, particularly its interaction with the rest of the organisation. This reflects a change in emphasis in the role of marketing in many companies, away from product management and towards anticipating and supplying customer needs.

Companies are supplying increased marketing training to operating departments in topics such as brand awareness and are giving marketing departments training which consists of two parts. The first part focuses on normal technicalities such as research and promotional techniques. The second gives marketers a wider perspective on the rest of the company, focusing on issues such as systems, distribution, customer service and financial management. Motivating operating departments to become more innovative and centred on the customer is seen as being very important.

2.8 Personal development plans

Definition

> **Personal development plans (PDPs)** are essentially action plans for people's career development. It is the individuals responsibility to seek and organise training.

The most popular PDP schemes take account of people's wider needs and aspirations, rather than focusing simply on skills required to do their current job better. Such schemes are undoubtedly popular because of the changes in the employment market. Most people believe they need to obtain skills and experiences which will be of benefit should they move jobs. **As a result people are better able than companies to assess their training requirements.** They will choose courses, where the form and content assist their personal development, and will avoid courses which are of no value to their personal development.

This trend is also reflected in employee development programmes (EDPs), company-run schemes which offer employees a wide range of development opportunities, not necessarily related to the job. The effect of such schemes is to develop a culture in which learning and adaptability are valued as well as to enhance employee satisfaction and morale. Expense has hitherto confined EDPs to large companies such as Ford and Unipart.

The importance of personal development plans

Managers have to take responsibility for their own learning. Personal development needs to be considered and managed by the individual, working, where possible, in partnership with the employer.

(a) The habit of setting personal development targets should be a long-term commitment for the successful manager.

(b) As a manager, you are likely to be faced with helping others with their personal development. Your personal experience of the process will be of some help then.

(c) The plans can be part of a **learning contract,** whereby targets are agreed with the employer, and their attainment is monitored.

2.9 Learning contracts

Definition

> A **learning contract** is an agreement between:
>
> (a) the person undergoing the training or education or experience; and
>
> (b) the provider or the sponsor of the training, education or experience.

The learning contract will normally detail three things.

- The type of **learning process** involved
- The expected **achievement** (in terms of the increase in skills)
- The **timescale** required

> **Activity 3** **(30 minutes)**
>
> Look back at Activity 2. Did you identify any training needs? Develop these into a learning contract.

The learning contract is a way for the individual to get a commitment out of the firm.

3 BUDGETS AND PROFITABILITY

Aspects of budgeting are also covered in Chapter 4, part of Unit 18 Advertising and Promotion.

Definition

> A **budget** is a quantitative statement for a defined period of time which may include planned revenues, expenses, assets, liabilities and cash-flows.

3.1 The purpose of budgets

Communication, co-ordination and control are general objectives of budgetary control systems: more information is provided by an inspection of specific objectives.

(a) **To ensure the achievement of the organisation's objectives**

Objectives for the organisation as a whole, and for individual departments and operations within the organisation, are set. Quantified expressions of these objectives are then drawn up as targets to be achieved.

(b) **To compel planning**

This is probably the most important feature of a budgetary planning and control system. Planning forces management to look ahead, to set out detailed plans for achieving the targets for each department, operation and each manager and to anticipate problems.

(c) **To communicate ideas and plans**

A formal system is necessary to ensure that each person affected by the plans is aware of what he or she is supposed to be doing.

(d) **To co-ordinate activities**

The activities of different departments of the organisation need to be co-ordinated. This concept of co-ordination implies, for example, that the production budget should be based on sales expectations. Although straightforward in concept, co-ordination is remarkably difficult to achieve, and there is often conflict between departmental plans in the budget.

(e) **To provide a framework for responsibility accounting**

Budgetary planning and control systems require that managers of budget centres are made responsible for the achievement of budget targets for the operations under their control.

(f) **To establish a system of control**

Control over actual performance is provided by the comparisons of actual results against the budget. Departures from budget can then be investigated and the reasons divided into controllable and uncontrollable factors.

(g) **To motivate employees to improve their performance**

The interest and commitment of employees can be retained via a system of feedback of actual results, which lets them know how well or badly they are performing against their budgeted targets.

In order to achieve these various objectives, budgets should be broken down into relevant business segments. These should naturally fit both the products and the markets in which the company operates. This will be set in the context of the **overall marketing plan.**

3.2 The budgeting process

In overall terms the budget tries to put into a **financial framework** the predicted result of all the activities that will achieve the overall corporate objectives.

Data for the budgeting process

Internal information available

(a) **Marketing and sales information** on, for example, performance, revenues, market share and distribution channels

(b) **Production and operational information** on, for example, manufacturing capacities and capabilities and lead times

(c) **Financial information** on, for example, how much cash it has in the bank, how much it could borrow, profits, costs, cash-flows and investments

(d) **Research and development information** on, for example, new products and developments

(e) **Personnel information** on, for example, labour skills, labour availability and expected wage increases

External information available

(a) **Market and competitors**. The organisation must assess its competitors. It should analyse its market (and any other markets that it is intending to enter) to identify possible **new opportunities**.

(b) **Economic conditions**. The state of the world must be considered. Is it in recession or is it booming? The organisation should gather information on forecasts for growth, inflation, GDP and so on and the effect of developments such as the European Community single market.

(c) **Industrial structure**. The organisation should determine whether a process of rationalisation or concentration is taking place within the industry, whether there are any privatisation issues to take into consideration and whether many new firms are entering the industry.

(d) **Political factors**. Any political instability, especially in overseas markets, and any significant political decisions, should be assessed.

(e) **Technological change**. Information on any new technology of which the organisation might be able to take advantage should be collected.

(f) **Demographic trends and social factors**. The organisation should assess the effects of any changes in the population structure, the age profile of customers, family patterns, and attitudes to consumption and savings.

Activity 4 **(30 minutes)**

You work for a company within the mobile 'phone industry. Conduct an analysis of the above external information needs.

The master budget

An overall **master budget** consists of the following.

(a) A **budgeted profit and loss account**. The total profit and loss account budget will often be sub-divided into departmental budgets (a budgeted profit and loss account for each department, division or other profit centre in the organisation).

(b) A **cash budget**. A business needs to make sure that it will have enough cash to continue operating, or that an overdraft facility is available with a bank to cover the expected need.

(c) An end-of-period **budgeted balance sheet**.

Preparing the sales budget

Since the sales budget is usually the budget from which cost budgets and the budgeted profit and loss account are developed, it is obviously very important that sales in the budget should be **reasonable and realistic**.

It is not easy to assess potential sales with any degree of accuracy. All that a business can do is put as much care as possible into preparing the sales budget.

(a) An organisation might produce a large number of products or services, and sell them in a wide geographical area. In such cases, sales budgets should be prepared for each **product or product group** and for each region.

(b) For many organisations, sales have seasonal peaks and troughs. **Seasonal variations** in sales should be recognised in the budgets.

FOR DISCUSSION

What is meant by 'reasonable' and 'realistic' in terms of sales budgets?

Preparing other resource budgets

Budgets for **marketing and administration costs** must be prepared. Many cost items will be fixed, although there may be some variable costs (for example sales commission). Some of the marketing budget will have to be prepared in conjunction with the sales budget since the level of sales anticipated will rely on marketing support. The balance of the budget may well be determined by the activity anticipated from new products which may be launched during the year.

3.3 The nature of selling costs

Management's job is to ensure that:

(a) the sales effort is used efficiently and effectively; and
(b) its cost are controlled.

Selling costs can be considered in terms of their fixed and variable elements.

(a) **Fixed sales costs** are those which would have to be paid even in a week when the salesperson was inactive. Salary, employer's contributions to pension schemes and National Insurance, cost of leasing and maintaining a car and the person's share of sales administration, support and management costs are all likely to be considered as fixed costs.

(b) **Variable sales costs** are those which change with the volume of sales. They would include commission payments and sales expenses.

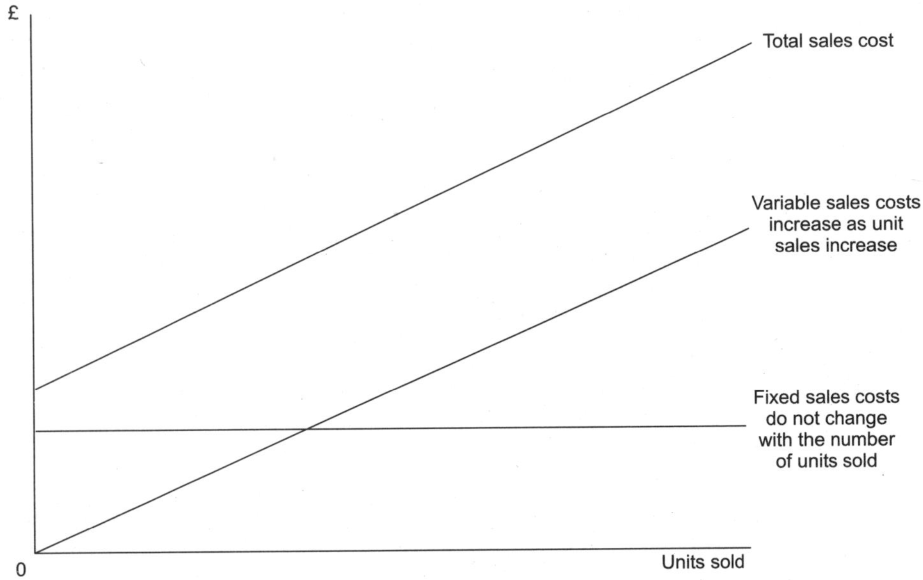

Figure 9.1: Nature of selling costs

Total sales costs are the sum of the variable and fixed costs elements.

The proportion of fixed to variable costs varies according to the nature of the business and the terms and conditions under which the salesperson is employed. In some sales activities, for example in door to door selling of products like cosmetics, the sales personnel are self-employed agents, earning commission only and paying their own sales expenses. In this case the variable cost element would be very high, with sales costs directly linked to sales success. In other sectors, particularly where the sales activity emphasises the non sales elements of the sales task, staff may be salaried with no commission. In this case the fixed cost element of sales is very high.

Management decisions can have a significant impact on sales costs. In particular, territory design and the organisation of the sales force can alter both the expenses incurred in selling and the travelling time between sales calls eg when the sales force is organised by product rather than geography, it is possible to have two sales people, both travelling the length and breadth of the country to visit customers. A different basis for territory design may increase the call rate and reduce the sales expenses.

3.4 Allocation of resources in sales budgets

Budgets can be analysed in a variety of ways. The sales budget reflects the estimated sales costs and forecast sales revenues for the department as a whole. But in turn these need to be further split by:

(a) Product/(to help operations planning)
(b) Market/customer group
(c) Sales area

Budgets need to be allocated in a manner which is **both meaningful to the way the department is organised** and **easy to administer**.

(a) If the sales force is organised on a geographic basis, then that is how the sales budget should be sub-divided. If the sales force is organised on a product basis the system of budget allocation should be based by product, too.

(b) The budget's allocation of resources also needs to take into account **variations in the potential of sales areas,** products or customer groups. Simply dividing the forecast sales by the number of products in the company portfolio takes no account of differences in their sales potential, the stage of the product life cycle or the sales objectives for each product. Likewise, each sales area may have a different sales forecast because of economic or cultural variations influencing demand.

(c) Once analysed, it should then be broken down further so that it becomes possible to generate **sales targets** for the individual members of the sales team. If everyone achieves their targets, within cost, the overall sales budget will also be met.

(d) Sales *targets* are supposed not just to be reached but perhaps exceeded. The sales *budget* is not like this; it is used to coordinate the resources of the organisation. An excess of sales orders might put a strain on operations and possibly the organisation's cash flow.

The administration of the budget must be up-to-date if it is to be of value. The ability to know about the current position to assess the variance between planned and actual activity levels, is necessary to give managers the maximum opportunity to take corrective action. The contribution of management accountants to this process is very important.

3.5 Sales activities and their impact on profitability

Every salesperson should be interested in the profitability of the organisation and should fully appreciate the impact of their performance and actions on that **profitability**. Sales personnel sometimes naturally look to revenue – but profitability is as significant.

Revenue impact. The success of the sales team is influenced by:

(a) The number of customers they contact
(b) The sales:call conversion rate
(c) The average order value.

Effectiveness of effort

Equally the sales team can improve **profitability** by selling more without increasing selling costs or by selling the same volume but at a lower cost. The individual sales person needs to appreciate the impact of their expenses on profitability and take responsibility for controlling these costs.

Many sales staff will have the flexibility and authority to negotiate with customers. It is very easy to give profit away with generous discounts. If the organisation's costs are 80% of revenue, a case of products with a selling price of £100 represents £20 profit. A discount of £5 reduces the profits earned by 25%.

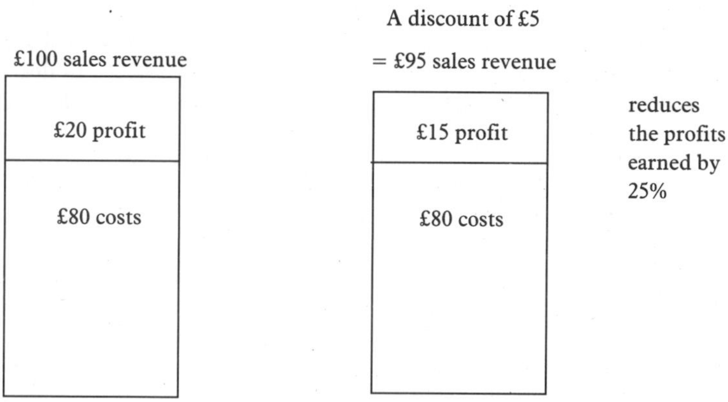

The salesperson has to sell another £25 worth of product at the original profit margin to make up the difference.

It is also possible to see that the value of discount to the customer is just £5. Providing £5 additional product instead would give the customer the same perceived value, but would only cost the firm £4.

4 BUDGET TARGETS AND MOTIVATION

The purpose of a budgetary control system is to assist management in planning and controlling the resources of their organisation by providing appropriate control information. The information will only be valuable, however, if it is interpreted correctly and used purposefully by managers *and* employees.

The correct use of control information therefore depends not only on the content of the information itself, but also on the behaviour of its recipients. This is because control in business is exercised by people. Their attitude to control information will colour their views on what they should do with it and a number of behavioural problems can arise.

(a) The **managers who set the budget** or standards are **often not the managers** who are then **made responsible for achieving budget targets.**

(b) The **goals of the organisation as a whole**, as expressed in a budget, **may not coincide with the personal aspirations of individual managers.**

(c) **Control is applied at different stages by different people.** A supervisor might get weekly control reports, and act on them; his superior might get monthly control reports, and decide to take different control action.

Different managers can get in each others' way, and resent the interference from others.

4.1 Motivation and budgets

Motivation is what makes people behave in the way that they do. It comes from individual attitudes, or group attitudes. Individuals will be motivated by personal desires and interests. These may be in line with the objectives of the organisation, and some people 'live for their jobs'. Other individuals see their job as a chore, and their motivations will be unrelated to the objectives of the organisation they work for.

It is therefore vital that the goals of management and the employees harmonise with the goals of the organisation as a whole. This is known as **goal congruence**. Although obtaining goal congruence is essentially a behavioural problem, **it is possible to design and run a budgetary control system which will go some way towards ensuring that goal congruence is achieved.**

Management should therefore try to ensure that employees have positive attitudes towards **setting budgets, implementing budgets** (that is, putting the organisation's plans into practice) and feedback of results (**control information**).

Poor attitudes when setting budgets

If managers are involved in preparing a budget, poor attitudes or hostile behaviour towards the budgetary control system can begin at the **planning stage.**

(a) Managers may **complain that they are too busy** to spend much time on budgeting.

(b) They may **build 'slack' into their expenditure estimates** or be too conservative in their sales estimates.

(c) They may argue that **formalising a budget plan on paper is too restricting** and that managers should be allowed flexibility in the decisions they take.

(d) They may set budgets for their budget centre and **not coordinate** their own plans with those of other budget centres.

(e) They may **base future plans on past results,** instead of using the opportunity for formalised planning to look at alternative options and new ideas.

Poor attitudes when putting plans into action

Poor attitudes also arise **when a budget is implemented.**

(a) Managers might **put in only just enough effort** to achieve budget targets, without trying to beat targets.

(b) A formal budget might **encourage rigidity and discourage flexibility.**

(c) **Short-term planning** in a budget **can draw attention away from the longer-term consequences** of decisions.

(d) There might be **minimal cooperation and communication** between managers.

(e) Managers will often try to make sure that they **spend up to their full budget allowance, and do not overspend,** so that they will not be accused of having asked for too much spending allowance in the first place.

It has been argued that participation in the budgeting process will improve motivation and so will improve the quality of budget decisions and the efforts of individuals to achieve their budget targets (although obviously this will depend on the personality of the individual, the nature of the task (narrowly defined or flexible) and the organisational culture).

There are basically two ways in which a budget can be set: from the top-down (imposed budget) or from the bottom-up (participatory budget).

4.2 Top-down budgeting

In this approach to budgeting, **top management prepare a budget with little or no input from operating personnel** which is then imposed upon the employees who have to work to the budgeted figures.

Times when imposed budgets are effective

- In newly-formed organisations
- In very small businesses
- During periods of economic hardship
- When operational managers lack budgeting skills
- When the organisation's different units require precise coordination

There are, of course, advantages and disadvantages to this style of setting budgets.

(a) **Advantages**

- Strategic plans are likely to be incorporated into planned activities.
- They enhance the coordination between the plans and objectives of divisions.
- They use senior management's awareness of total resource availability.
- They decrease the input from inexperienced or uninformed lower-level employees.
- They decrease the period of time taken to draw up the budgets.

(b) **Disadvantages**

- Dissatisfaction, defensiveness and low morale amongst employees. It is hard for people to be motivated to achieve targets set by somebody else.
- The feeling of team spirit may disappear.
- The acceptance of organisational goals and objectives could be limited
- The feeling of the budget as a punitive device could arise.
- Managers who are performing operations on a day to day basis are likely to have a better understanding of what is achievable.
- Unachievable budgets could result if consideration is not given to local operating and political environments. This applies particularly to overseas divisions.
- Lower-level management initiative may be stifled.

4.3 Bottom-up budgeting

Definition

Participative/bottom-up budgeting is a budgeting system in which all budget holders are given the opportunity to participate in setting their own budgets.

In this approach to budgeting, **budgets are developed by lower-level managers who then submit the budgets to their superiors.** The budgets are based on the lower-level managers' perceptions of what is achievable and the associated necessary resources.

When participative budgets are effective

(a) In decentralised organisations
(b) In well-established organisations
(c) In very large businesses
(d) During periods of economic affluence
(e) When operational managers have strong budgeting skills
(f) When the organisation's different units act autonomously

Advantages of participative budgets

(a) They are based on information from employees most familiar with the department.

(b) Knowledge spread among several levels of management is pulled together.

(c) Morale and motivation is improved.

(d) They increase operational managers' commitment to organisational objectives.

(e) In general they are more realistic.

(f) Co-ordination between units is improved.

(g) Specific resource requirements are included.

(h) Senior managers' overview is mixed with operational level details.

(i) Individual managers' aspiration levels are more likely to be taken into account.

Disadvantages of participative budgets

(a) They consume more time.
(b) Changes implemented by senior management may cause dissatisfaction.
(c) Budgets may be unachievable if managers are not qualified to participate.
(d) They may cause managers to introduce budgetary slack.
(e) They can support 'empire building' by subordinates.
(f) An earlier start to the budgeting process could be required.
(g) Managers may set 'easy' budgets to ensure that they are achievable.

4.4 Negotiated style of budgeting

Definition

A **negotiated budget** is one in which allowances are set on the basis of negotiations between budget holders and those to whom they report.

At the two extremes, budgets can be dictated from above or simply emerge from below but, in practice, different levels of management often agree budgets by a process of negotiation. In the imposed budget approach, operational managers will try to negotiate with senior managers the budget targets which they consider to be unreasonable or unrealistic. Likewise senior management usually review and revise budgets presented to them under a participative approach through a process of negotiation with lower level managers. **Final budgets are therefore most likely to lie between what top management would really like and what junior managers believe is feasible**. The budgeting process is hence a **bargaining process** and it is this bargaining which is of vital importance, **determining whether the budget is an effective management tool or simply a clerical device.**

4.5 Budgetary slack

Definition

> **Budgetary slack** is the difference between the minimum necessary costs and the costs built into the budget or actually incurred.

In the process of preparing budgets, managers might deliberately overestimate costs and underestimate sales, so that they will not be blamed in the future for overspending and poor results. This is especially true if bonuses are based on meeting targets.

In controlling actual operations, managers must then **ensure that their spending rises to meet their budget**, otherwise they will be 'blamed' for careless budgeting.

After a run of mediocre results, some managers deliberately overstate revenues and understate cost estimates, no doubt feeling the need to make an immediate favourable impact by promising better performance in the future. They may merely delay problems, however, as the managers may well be censured when they fail to hit these optimistic targets.

4.6 The use of budgets as targets

Once decided, budgets become targets. As targets, they can motivate managers to achieve a high level of performance. But **how difficult should targets be**? And how might people react to targets of differing degrees of difficulty in achievement?

(a) There is likely to be a **demotivating** effect where an **ideal standard** of performance is set, because adverse efficiency variances will always be reported.

(b) A **low standard of efficiency** is also **demotivating**, because there is no sense of achievement in attaining the required standards, and there will be no impetus for employees to try harder to do better than this.

(c) A **budgeted level of attainment** could be 'normal': that is, the **same as the level that has been achieved in the past**. Arguably, this level will be **too low**. It might **encourage budgetary slack.**

It has been argued that **each individual has a personal 'aspiration level'**. This is a level of performance in a task with which the individual is familiar, which the individual undertakes for himself to reach. This aspiration level might be quite challenging and if individuals in a work group all have similar aspiration levels it should be possible to incorporate these levels within the official operating standards.

Some care should be taken, however, in applying this.

(a) A salesperson's tendency to achieve success is stronger than the tendency to avoid failure, budgets with targets of intermediate levels of difficulty are the most motivating, and stimulate a manager to better performance levels.

(b) A salesperson's **tendency to avoid failure might be stronger than the tendency to achieve success**. (This is likely in an organisation in which the budget is used as a pressure device on subordinates by senior managers). Managers might then be discouraged from trying to achieve budgets of intermediate difficulty and tend to avoid taking on such tasks, resulting in poor levels of performance, worse than if budget targets were either easy or very difficult to achieve.

It has therefore been suggested that in a situation where budget targets of an intermediate difficulty *are* motivating, such targets ought to be set if the purpose of budgets is to motivate; however, although budgets which are set for **motivational purposes** need to be stated in terms of **aspirations rather than expectations,** budgets for planning and decision purposes need to be stated in terms of the best available estimate of expected actual performance. The **solution** might therefore be to have **two budgets.**

(a) A **budget for planning and decision making based on reasonable expectations.**

(b) A second **budget for motivational purposes,** with **more difficult targets of performance** (that is, targets of an intermediate level of difficulty).

These two budgets might be called an '**expectations budget**' and an '**aspirations budget**' respectively.

FOR DISCUSSION

What do you think the impact of demanding targets are on:

(a) A field salesforce
(b) A customer service centre in a call-centre?

Chapter roundup

- An appraisal system is designed to be a systematic approach to provide feedback and to review performance and potential. Sometimes it is also designed to review salaries.
- Usually an appraisal system will have criteria for assessment, an assessment report, an appraisal interview, a review of the assessment, action plans and follow up.
- In practice, appraisal systems are often seen not to be working effectively.
- Training is very important for sales personnel; however it needs to be carefully planned and executed. Structured training programmes may be beneficial.
- Training methods can be on the job, or more formal such as lectures, discussions, exercises, role plays and case studies.
- Individual action plans can be called personal development plans. This approach gives an individual the responsibility for their own training needs.
- A learning contract can be formally drawn up between the sales person and the organisation and is often used to get commitment from the organisation.
- Budgetary control systems are used to ensure communication, coordination and control.
- Sales budgets should be reasonable and realistic.
- Allocations of sales budgets can be divided by product, market/customer group and/or sales area.
- Budgets can have a major impact on employees of an organisation and their motivation.
- Budget setting can either be top-down, bottom-up or negotiated.

Quick quiz

1 Why are appraisals linked to motivation?

2 What is a results-oriented appraisal scheme?

3 Give some examples of how the appraisal system can go wrong.

4 What types of appraisal system are there?

5 How can training needs be identified?

6 What advantages are there to programmed learning?

7 What should a learning contract include?

8 Give some examples of the use of budgets in the selling function.

9 Total sales costs is equal to ....costs plus .... costs.

10 What is meant by a 'negotiated budget'?

Answers to quick quiz

1 Appraisals are the systematic approach to providing feedback as a tool for motivation.

2 An approach that reviews performance against specific targets agreed in advance by the appraisee and appraisor.

3 Divergence of needs
Subordinate is defensive
Risk of bias
Different ratings from different managers
Perceived as a bureaucratic exercise

4 Downward, upward, peer rated, 360 degree.

5 By research by the training department, by individuals or by the appraisal system.

6 Trainees can monitor their progress, they can learn interactively and at their own pace.

7 The type of learning process, expected achievement and timescale.

8 To make sure objectives and plans are set and met, to communicate plans, to establish a system of control and to motivate sales staff.

9 Fixed and variable.

10 A budget that is set largely on the basis of negotiations between budget holders and those to whom they report.

Answers to activities

1 There is no specific answer to this activity.

2 There is no specific answer to this activity.

3 There is no specific answer to this activity.

4 Your answer should be structured around the headings in the Course Book.

Chapter 10 :

SELLING IN DIFFERENT ENVIRONMENTS

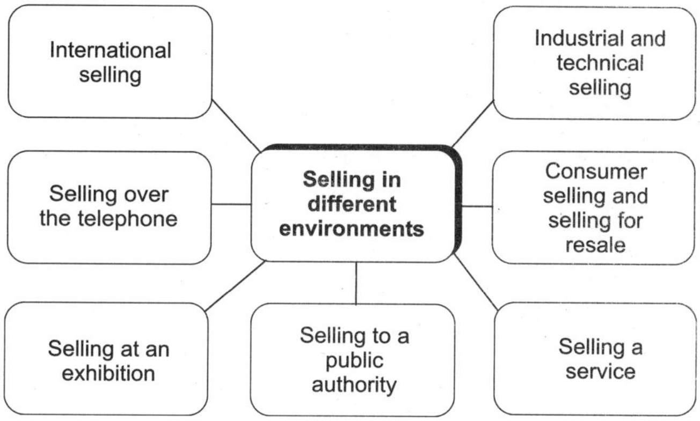

Introduction

As we have already seen, the many variables influencing a sale makes every purchase in its way unique. The situation in which the sale occurs plays an important part in influencing the process by which decisions are made and affects the moods and motives of the buyer.

The salesperson needs to appreciate these differences and be able and willing to vary the sales approach to the selling activity in different sectors.

The frequency, cost and risk involved in purchases in each of these categories varies and so the DMU (Decision-Making Unit) and DMP (Decision-Making Process) will also vary significantly. It is, however, possible to identify a number of characteristics likely to typify industrial markets and which provide important background for the salesperson.

Your objectives

In this chapter you will learn about the following.

(a) The differences between industrial and consumer selling

(b) The implications of selling a service

(c) The characteristics of public authorities

(d) Uses of telephone selling and attendance at exhibitions

(e) The selling decisions which organisations have to make when selling overseas

1 INDUSTRIAL AND TECHNICAL SELLING

Demand levels in business to business markets are directly influenced by the demand for the client's products. (The term, borrowed from economics, is **derived demand.**) Sales levels and potentials are directly tied to the business climate experienced by the customer. Business confidence is an important factor when forecasting sales in this section. It can be helpful for the salesperson to known about the client's industry, anticipated changes in demand, new competitive activity and emerging opportunities.

As demand is derived, the pattern of demand (for example for raw materials, parts or supplies), will reflect the pattern of demand for the client's products.

1.1 Characteristics

Industrial markets are made up of those sectors where the customer is buying products to be used in the process of producing more goods or services. Because customers are in fact firms, we often use the term 'business to business marketing', when working in these sectors.

Industrial goods are not all the same and in turn they can be classified into:

- Raw materials
- Fabricated materials
- Capital equipment
- Supplies

Distribution channels are typically short

This gives the industrial supplier control over the marketing of the product, but also increases the costs of providing the distribution services. As many industrial suppliers work directly with their clients, the salesperson can be critical in taking care of many of the distribution services from order processing, assistance with installation to collecting payment. The sales element in the industrial communication mix is usually particularly important.

The DMU in these sectors is often complex, difficult to identify and hard to access. At the same time the decision making process can be protracted. Even supplies like office stationery may be provided on a contract basis and so only negotiated and reviewed periodically. Therefore, once a client's custom has been won, there is a move towards **relationship marketing** where suppliers work in partnership with clients to help solve the client's problems. Client loyalty therefore develops in time.

As a result, repeat business is commonly automatic once the initial order is secured – providing that after sales service and all aspects of quality remain satisfactory. Industrial sectors are thus often characterised by inertia in the decision making unit. Making decisions is a time consuming, often very involved process. A manager's life is made easier if the manager chooses to stick with the known supplier, unless there are very positive reasons for change.

1.2 Large orders

Because of the size of contracts and orders the average value per purchase is substantially greater than in a consumer market, and for large capital purchases a single order can be worth millions of pounds. This has the following implications.

(a) The average marketing spend per enquiry or sale is likely to be high leading to a particular need for careful monitoring and control.

(b) Negotiations which lead to 1 or 2% off the price can have a large impact on a firm's profitability.

(c) Agreements to sell only a few per cent more to a large client can have major implications for increasing production capacity.

(d) Losing a client can be a serious business.

1.3 Price sensitivity

It is traditionally believed that buyers in industrial markets behave 'rationally': this does not necessarily equate with buying the cheapest. Industrial markets are not always particularly price sensitive. Quality, reliability and performance are much more likely to influence purchase decision than price. Management's overriding needs are equipment and materials which help their jobs run smoothly!

In industrial markets, the individuals who make up the DMU are likely to be specialists and expert in their particular areas. This places additional pressures on the salesperson who:

(a) Must have complete product knowledge; and

(b) Where necessary, be able to call on the support of in-house specialists within the company to assist in negotiations.

Industrial buyers will themselves be trained in the process of negotiation and so represent a further test of the salesperson's selling skills.

Although the background and experience necessary varies according to the particular category of industrial products being sold, increasingly in the component and capital goods sectors, sales teams are being drawn from the ranks of qualified engineers and technicians who have the necessary product knowledge. These staff need to be trained in a customer-oriented approach.

FOR DISCUSSION

Industrial buyers are more price sensitive and rational than consumer buyers.

1.4 Technical selling

When the sales staff are themselves technical experts, the sales activity may be referred to as **technical selling**. In these cases, the product's features and functions are usually complex; expert product knowledge is needed for the required sales function to be performed. Computer systems are an example of where the salesperson needs technical qualifications to recommend an appropriate system, and, possibly, to help the client during installation and staff training.

The salesperson may also need to understand the client's business effectively and may even be seconded to work with the customer for a period of time. The close working relationship between sales staff and client can become very strong. Maintaining a strong sense of loyalty to the employer, not the customer can become difficult in situations where these close working partnerships are established. Good management and communication is essential to ensure the sales team does not become estranged from each other and from management.

2 CONSUMER SELLING AND SELLING FOR RESALE

Owing to the greater number of potential customers and their geographic distribution, consumer goods are less likely to be supplied directly from manufacturer to customer. The channels of distribution which characterise this sector include retailers, wholesalers and other middlemen. As a result, in these industries, manufacturers have tended to develop the non-personal elements of the communication mix, such as advertising and sales promotion techniques to get their messages direct to the consumer.

Despite using predominantly **advertising pull** strategies to encourage the consumer to seek out brands and literally pull then through the distribution channels, **selling push** does still have an important role to play in these markets.

Personal selling features strongly in two possible areas of consumer product marketing:

- Ensure distribution for the products – selling for resale;
- The retail interface with the customer.

2.1 Selling for resale

The manufacturer's use of personal selling is likely to be limited to the sales effort necessary to ensure **distribution**, by selling the products to middlemen. Availability is an essential element in the marketing mix. Without access to the final customer the product is unlikely to be successful. So the manufacturer is likely to adopt two distinct communication strategies:

(a) An advertising based mix to attract customers to the brand;

(b) A sales push strategy designed to take the product to the distributors and encourage them to stock it.

The potential distributors are relatively few in number, and are easy to identify and access. This is particularly true in the fast moving consumer goods (fmcg's) markets selling convenience categories of products. However, even in the more fragmented markets for consumer durables, distribution is likely to be controlled by a fairly small number of key wholesale chains and distributors.

Distributor's positioning

There is however, an important difference in selling to these markets. The retail **customer** is not the **end** user. The retailer is acting as an indirect adviser in the DMU of the final consumer. Supermarkets select, on behalf of their customers, four or five brands of toothpaste, soap powder, coffee etc, which they believe will satisfy customer needs. By endorsing a brand, (ie by stocking it), the retailer is in effect recommending it. Ultimately therefore, distributors only stock products which they believe will be attractive to their customers. The **product's positioning** has to match the **distributor's positioning,** so Harrods would be unlikely to stock 'value for money' discount products and Aldi unlikely to offer premium priced ranges of speciality delicatessen products.

Opportunity cost

Sales staff must find out the type of customer shopping at a particular retailer, to ensure that the products being offered reflect the benefits likely to be attractive to that market segment. Products will only win and retain shelf space if it can be demonstrated that they are worth that space. That means achieving an earnings per square foot of shelf space which is acceptable to the distributor. The retailer is looking for the best use of his/her limited resource – space. Therefore the **opportunity cost** of stocking product A is the revenue which would have been generated by stocking product B, so product A must generate more than B to be acceptable.

Both manufacturer and distributor share the same goal, which is to encourage the customer to buy. Bad selling lines may never be re-ordered, but once placed, the distributor will normally take legal title to the goods and so will have a vested interest in helping to sell them. Stock turnover is essential to the financial health of a middleman.

Distribution needs

The manufacturer must consider the distributor's need throughout the development of the marketing mix.

(a) Products should be attractive to the end users, but they must also be easy to handle, stock and distribute (eg packaging has to be stable on the shelves).

(b) In any pricing strategy, the price to the end user will have to include the distributor's margin and this must be carefully assessed.

(c) Brands backed by strong promotional campaigns are likely to be more attractive to the retailer. While merchandising and sales promotion activities encourage sales, they should be designed to be easy to handle and implement on the shop floor.

With the increased sophistication of retail information systems provided by electronic point of sale devices, the distribution function has up to the minute information on stock turnover, sales value and fluctuations in demand for any product line stocked. In the past, the manufacturer would have had much more detailed sales information from delivery data etc. The big multiples which supermarket chain operate centralised distribution systems for themselves now tend to have a much fuller picture of sales patterns than the producer. This imbalance in information can disadvantage the sales person during negotiations.

The balance of power rests firmly with those who are the gatekeepers to the consumers. Negotiations over price levels and promotions support have, over recent years, tended to go in favour of the retailer. The manufacturer's sales staff have to be very skilled at developing long term relationships with clients, so that increasingly they can work together to develop new products for emerging market opportunities.

Activity 1 **(30 minutes)**

Interview someone from the purchasing department of an organisation you are familiar with (you could interview someone at college or a small retailer if you do not have other contacts). Ask them about who sells to them and find out if anyone acts as gatekeepers. Ask also about the purchasing process and who is involved in purchase decisions.

2.2 Selling in the retail environment

In the markets for convenience goods, the retail sales assistant has in the main been replaced by self service systems, but in many markets for shopping and specialist goods, the retail sales activity is an important element in the communication mix.

These purchases are less frequently made, cost more than convenience goods and the purchase entails more perceived risk for the customer. From shoes to lounge furniture, electrical goods to motor cars, product features and performance are likely to be the most important factors influencing consumer demand. The DMP will take longer and the DMU will typically involve more people.

The retail salesperson will most likely be employed by the distributor, not the manufacturer and so has no real brand loyalty.

(a) The role is to ensure the customer is satisfied with the retailer by:

   (i) helping the customer solve his or her problem;
   (ii) therefore ensure a sale.

(b) Retail sales staff often are important 'advisers' in the DMU.

The task of the retailer has not become any easier over recent years.

(a) Customers are more knowledgeable and demanding. The Internet has facilitated information search and information sharing among consumers. It has become much easier to find where the cheapest deals are, and to bypass traditional 'bricks and mortar' retailers altogether by making online purchases.

(b) Their behaviour is less easy to predict than in the traditional male dominated household of the past.

(c) Product choice has been extended.

(d) Products have become functionally more complex requiring considerable product knowledge on the part of the retailer.

FOR DISCUSSION

How have changes in retailing made consumers behave differently?

Activity 2 **(30 minutes)**

Consider a family holiday that is purchased with input from different members of the family. Gather some brochures and look at whether there are different messages for different members of the family. Consider what would appeal to different family members.

Manufacturers of these products need to ensure that retail staff fully understand features and benefits of the products they sell by providing training support and/or good sales support literature. Many will consider incentives which encourage the retailer to promote their brand, eg joint promotions, sales incentives to the staff etc.

3 SELLING A SERVICE

In marketing we often include services under the umbrella of products assuming both are treated similarly from the marketing standpoint. Certainly marketing a service is not fundamentally different from marketing a product. In essence services are simply products with no shelf life they are intangible and this characteristic makes working with services more difficult than working with products.

The dimensions of services which make them very different from products are given below.

(a) **Intangibility** means that services cannot be stockpiled to meet peaks in demand.

(b) Intangibility means that customers have to **buy on trust,** unable to try out a service before a purchase.

(c) **Services are frequently produced, distributed and consumed in one place.** The distribution staff are also often the producers of a service. They have all to be skilled in customer care and sales techniques, because they are often involved directly with customers.

FOR DISCUSSION 

Intangibility means that it is difficult to see, taste, smell, touch etc the product before purchase. Think of examples that are purely intangible and some that are attached in some way to physical products.

Customer services

As most of the staff involved in service provision have direct contact with customers, most of them need to have some sales training. Hotel receptionists, restaurant waiters, airline staff and service engineers all have the opportunity to increase company revenue by encouraging additional customer purchases and repeat business. However, service industries employ staff with a more exclusive sales brief and title, and so we would probably classify them as service sellers (eg insurance sales representatives and sales teams from commercial service providers).

Selling role

Because of the intangibility of a service, the sales staff are even more likely to be perceived to represent and personify the company. Those employed in the service sector are more likely to wear uniforms, in order to provide users with a sense of security. The quality and cut of those **uniforms** will be taken as indicative of the quality of the whole service.

Within the overall title of services it must be recognised that some sales activity will be focused in the industrial sectors, others in the public and consumer markets. In each of these, the basic characteristics of the DMU and DMP of the market will still be relevant and need to be taken into account when developing the sales and marketing strategy.

Activity 3 **(10 minutes)**

What implications will there be for an accounting firm selling its services both to organisations and members of the public (eg preparation of tax returns)?

4 SELLING TO A PUBLIC AUTHORITY

The public sector still represents almost half of the total spending undertaken in the UK economy, making the government to largest customer for many businesses. Suppliers for defence, health and education are amongst those who must be able to sell to the public sector.

Characteristics

(a) **Public sector organisations do not primarily exist to make a profit.** Their objectives are therefore more likely to involve providing satisfactory service levels and constrained by the available budget. However, they are likely to be cost conscious.

(b) **Decision making will be influenced by political considerations** and suppliers need to take these into account when presenting product benefits to public sector decision makers. More importantly changes in the political climate at local, regional, or national levels can occur quickly and these need to be considered when forecasting future demand and developing marketing strategy for these sectors.

(c) **Public sector employees are not usually the decision makers in the DMU.** These are normally some sort of elected representatives for example, school governors, local authority councillors, government ministers etc. These people are harder to identify and access than even industrial decision makers. Unravelling the DMU from the bureaucracy of public sector organisations is a particular challenge for the sales person.

The development of executive agencies may mean that there is less central control.

Contractors working in partnership for example providing cleaning and catering services for the health services, will be at the forefront of developing 'relationship marketing'. The role of the sales contract will increasingly be to monitor performance, negotiate standards of service delivery and tackle management problems jointly with the public sector clients.

5 SELLING AT AN EXHIBITION

Most sales representatives and managers are likely at some point, to find themselves in the situation of selling at an exhibition or trade show. These are unusual buying situations, artificially created to bring together buyers and sellers, with a shared area of interest. Some are aimed at consumers, others at industry insiders.

Exhibitions and trade fairs (for example, the Ideal Home Exhibition, the Boat Show or the London Book Fair) offer several opportunities.

(a) **Public relations** (both to visitors and via media coverage, taking advantage of the interest generated by the exhibition organisers).

(b) **Promoting and selling** products/services to a wide audience of pre-targeted potential customers, particularly where demonstrations (eg of technical innovations) or visual inspection (eg clothes or motor cars) are likely to influence buyers.

(c) **Networking** within the industry and with existing clients.

(d) **Testing the response** to new products.

(e) **Researching competitor products** and promotions.

(f) **Researching suppliers' products** and services and making contacts along the supply chain.

FOR DISCUSSION

The key to successful exhibitions is to know who will be attending – both visitors and other exhibitors.

5.1 Considering exhibiting

The wide range of activities that can be undertaken at exhibitions means that attendance must be carefully considered. The overall aim must be to ensure that the exhibition is carefully **integrated** into the overall **promotional mix**. Objectives must be derived from corporate strategy *via* the marketing strategy and activities must support and be supported by the wider marketing effort. A simple example would be the introduction of a new product: a major exhibition might be a very good occasion for a resounding product launch, but the implications of a launch would have to be carefully considered. Not only would the product itself have to be ready, sales staff would have to be trained on it, its price would have to be determined and delivery lead times would have to be known.

Most industries are catered for by at least one annual or bi-annual exhibition in the UK, as well as internationally. The events themselves are set up by **exhibition organisers** who are responsible for booking and preparing the venue, registering participants and organising seminars and events, issuing catalogues of stand-holders and events, providing stand construction services, organising lounges, amenities and catering facilities, access and parking, power and lighting, promotion and press coverage.

At the time of booking a stand or space, you will have to decide on several issues.

(a) The **size** of your site.

(b) The **location** of your site.

(c) The **design** and **construction** of your site.

(d) The **information** you will provide for the exhibition catalogue, press pack and signage.

5.2 Planning and preparation

Exhibitions can be a huge logistical exercise. They require planning well in advance – and then compress a lot of activity all at once into a very hectic period.

There are a number of areas in which **advance planning** will pay off.

(a) **Stand design, display and services.** As we mentioned above, specialist stand contractors can set up the structure, fixtures and fittings of a stand to your specifications, but you need to have considered what your needs for display and facilities will be.

(b) **Stand staffing**

Trade show networking and selling is hectic, intense and tiring. You will need to arrange for a **rotating roster** of stand staff, including a Stand Manager to organise the stand and liaise with exhibition organisers, reception staff, sales staff, technical staff (if the product requires expert demonstration or advice) and multilingual export staff.

(c) **Accommodation and transport for personnel**

A large exhibition can absorb available transport and accommodation even in a major city. If you are outside your home area, ensure that you have booked transport to the exhibition city, hotel or other accommodation and also any hire cars required, well in advance.

(d) **Pre-arranged meetings and visits**

In order to maximise your return on investment, ensure that you hit as many of your target audience as you can. Make a 'hit list' of key customers, suppliers and agents (from your database or from the pre-circulated list of exhibitors and attendees).

5.3 At the exhibition

During the **set-up** period before the exhibition, you will work with contractors and your own staff to check that all the structures, fixtures, fittings and services associated with the stand are in place and functioning correctly.

Day-to-day **administration** of the stand

- Appointment making, communications, offering refreshments
- Providing information, screening and routing 'serious' prospects
- Distributing leaflets or running competitions
- Recording all visits and sending visitors away with information

---

EXAMPLE

Websites have been said to be taking over from exhibitions. However evidence suggests that instead of posing a threat, IT is actually boosting exhibition efficiency and making it more rewarding. It can be used to extend the life of an exhibition. Stand displays can use IT to illustrate styles and colours.

5.4 After the exhibition

Once an exhibition is finished, the stand will need to be dismantled, and its various components sent back where they came from.

The most important stage of the exhibition is **follow-up**.

(a) The contact information gained needs to be input to the organisation **database** and immediately utilised, even if it is only an e-mail to thank the contact for the visit.

(b) All promises made during the show (to send out literature or make a sales call) must be fulfilled as soon as possible.

5.5 Exhibiting expenses

(a) Site fees, stand construction and display (estimated 66% by the Exhibition Industry Federation)

(b) Staff costs, including opportunity cost of staff being withdrawn from their normal sales work (22%)

(c) Promotion and entertainment of visitors (12%)

A **budget** should be drawn up to cover all costs associated with going to the show/exhibition. This should be compared with forecast revenue from the show in order to assess the show's viability. After the event, the show's **profitability** can be evaluated in the same way.

However, it should be recognised that your objectives for a particular show may not solely be sales revenue. You may want to find a **distributor** in a new international market, or to **raise awareness** of your brand with the trade press, or to **introduce your product** to a new market. Such achievements may take time to 'ripen' into confirmed sales. In the Exhibition Industry Federation survey, the average time to convert an exhibition lead to a sale was seven months, and in some cases, two years or more.

5.6 Exhibition checklist

- Book space and pay direct
- Draft and supply catalogue/signage information
- Design stand/lighting/fixture and fittings
- Order lighting, flooring, furniture, shelving, and storage
- Order water, power, heating, telecom, drainage
- Order fire extinguisher, check safety regulations
- Insure stand and exhibits
- Organise products/brochures/display materials for exhibit
- Arrange delivery/export of large items, and return
- Contract for stand cleaning, plant/flower supply and maintenance, security
- Plan staffing of stand
- Plan VIP appearances
- Arrange transport and accommodation of staff, VIP's
- Design and prepare promotional literature, signage, incentives to visitors
- Gather stationery and equipment for use on stand
- Invite customers/prospects, arrange meetings
- Arrange for photography, prepare press releases
- Order stand catering/refreshments
- Brief stand personnel; prepare task lists, rotas

5.7 The view of the sales team

The poorly motivated or badly trained sales team may take a fairly jaundiced view of an exhibition. They may well be seconded to staff a stand. A number of factors may reduce the sales person's enthusiasm of the event.

(a) It takes him or her away from normal weekly activities and duties, which may not be undertaken by anyone else. The members of sales team return to overflowing in-trays.

(b) Sales targets and quotas may not be modified to take account of time spent at an exhibition.

(c) They may resent lost selling days, which reduce commission opportunities and therefore average pay.

(d) Contacts made at an exhibition may have to be referred to a colleague because of the way the sales organisation is structured. It can lead to a 'what's in it for me?' feeling, if the colleague gets the commission.

(e) The sales situation at an exhibition is very enclosed, formal and public, very different to the normal sales environment of a representative. Some do not like the change.

(f) Following up exhibition leads may be seen as added work and so not undertaken effectively.

The attitude and motivation of the staff working on an exhibition stand is critical to the success of the event. Management's job is to recognise the problems of those involved and ensure they are overcome (eg with special incentive schemes for leads handed over to colleagues, bonus payments to ensure earnings are maintained etc).

Activity 4

If you have not been involved in exhibition selling make a point of attending an exhibition over the next few months. There are often smaller 'business to business' exhibitions run by the Chamber of Commerce or you could visit a work related event or a big consumer show like the Motor Show or Ideal Home. Take a note of the selling done at this event. Critically evaluate the stand management and try to identify the objectives. If staff are not too busy try and talk to them about the process of exhibition selling.

6 SELLING OVER THE TELEPHONE

6.1 Uses of telephone selling

The telephone is a very important tool in the salesperson's toolbox. Like any other tool the effective use of telephone selling depends on the appropriate situation, and the skill of individuals who have learned the techniques of selling by telephone.

The single biggest advantage of using the telephone is that it provides person to person contact at a much lower cost than a sales visit. It can therefore be used to:

(a) Maintain contact with existing customers, taking repeat orders and so on;

(b) Generate a list of interested contacts, to increase the sales conversion rates from sales visits;

(c) Create awareness of special offers, new products etc;

(d) Make the sale by telephone.

Definition

> **Telemarketing** can be defined as a marketing communication system using trained personnel to conduct planned, measurable marketing activities by phone which are directed at targeted groups of customers.

6.2 The benefits of using the telephone

The telephone provides the seller with a number of positive advantages.

(a) **Quick response**

- Prospects receive immediate information about your product/service.
- Sellers get immediate response (feedback) from consumers and *vice versa*.
- Selling is speeded up – no tea, no coffee, no telephone calls or indeed visitors to delay or interrupt discussions.

(b) **Interaction**

- Although both parties (buyer and seller) do not see each other, telephone provides the fastest person-to-person contact with two way traffic of information and instant personal reaction.
- A successful telephone conversation can result in an appointment to visit or even a sale.

(c) **Accessibility**

- It is often possible to gain access to individuals who would never agree to an appointment.
- Little preparation is needed to access your target audience.
- It enables access to large number of potential customers in a very short time period.

(d) **Easy assessment**

The telephone allows the seller the opportunity to assess the individuals willingness or readiness to buy. If out of every group of 50 people you could expect to sell to five, the telephone allows those prospects with the greatest potential to be assessed quickly and easily.

(e) **Cost**

- Although telephone contact is still labour intensive, it allows personal contact to be made without the expense of travel. This is particularly important in geographically diverse markets.
- Used in preparation of personal visits it can ensure the most effective use of sales time with appointments established prior to the visit etc.

6.3 Limitations and problems with the telephone

The telephone does have its limitations and it needs to be used with care to avoid problems.

(a) Unsolicited calls can cause annoyance, particularly amongst householders when calls can be intrusive or received at an inconvenient time. The proliferation of outsourced call centres has not helped to improve consumer perception of the 'cold caller', particularly when these call centres operate from foreign countries.

(b) Calls may be disguised as research or other information-generating activities, and so are therefore misleading.

(c) Sales calls leave an intangible record. Without support literature, the buyer or seller may misunderstand the communication and verbal contracts negotiated by phone are difficult to prove. In the business sectors, the increased availability of fax machines to be used in conjunction with or instead of direct telephone selling does offer the chance for instant tangibility of messages.

(d) Telephone selling provides no opportunity to judge body language, making negotiation by phone much more difficult than face to face contact.

(e) There is equally no chance to demonstrate or show samples thus increasing the buyer's risk unless the seller is already known.

(f) Many consumers are hostile to unsolicited 'cold' calls anyway, and might be less inclined to buy if they feel they are put under pressure.

EXAMPLE

Telephone selling: good practice. The Office of Fair Trading published guidelines for the use of telephones in selling.

(a) Callers should ask whether the timing of the call is convenient. If it is not they should offer to ring back at a more convenient time. Calls should not be made after 9.00pm

(b) The caller's name and that of the company responsible for the call should be given at the start of the call and repeated at any time if requested.

(c) The purpose of the call should be made clear at the start, and the content of the call should be restricted to matters directly relevant to its purpose. Calls should never be made under guise of market research, nor combined with the offer of unrelated goods and services.

(d) Callers should not mislead, be evasive, exaggerate or use partial truths and they should answer any questions honestly and fully. Companies should accept responsibility for statements made by their sales staff or agents and take appropriate disciplinary action if breaches of these guidelines occur.

(e) The caller should always recognise the right of the person called to terminate the telephone conversation at any stage and should accept such a termination promptly and courteously.

(f) The caller should provide the person called with a clear opportunity to refuse any appointment or offer.

(g) If the caller makes an appointment for someone to visit the consumer's home, he or she should provide a contact point in order to facilitate possible cancellation or alteration of the visit by the consumer.

(h) Unsolicited calls should not be made to people at their place of work.

(i) Callers should ensure that they do not obtain information or appointments or orders from minors and that they do not call unlisted telephone numbers.

(j) Consumers should be sent copies of all relevant documents, including agreements, contracts and statements of their legal rights if they place an order. A cooling-off period of at least seven days should apply following receipt of such papers during which the consumers could, if they wished, cancel their order and be entitled to a refund of any payment which they may have made.

Managers need to ensure that they establish clear policy when staff are engaged in telephone selling and they must be thoroughly trained to ensure the medium is not abused.

Taking on board these possible problem areas, it is still possible to make effective and positive use of the telephone as part of the sales process.

Activity 5 **(5 mins)**

Think about the last time someone called you at home or at work to try and sell you something. Did they abide by the code of conduct? Did you purchase anything? How happy were you with the call?

6.4 Incoming sales calls

When used in conjunction with advertising and direct mail, interested customers can be encouraged to phone enquires in. This allows queries to be handled, quotations to be given, appointments made or orders taken.

Using Freephone numbers

When encouraging incoming sales enquiries a Freephone number is highly recommended. It is your objective to make it as easy as possible for the enquirer to contact you. A Freephone number:

(a) Prevents individuals being put off by the cost of a call – which may affect the household sector.

(b) Means that customers do not have to remember a phone number. This is particularly helpful when using the radio or TV as an advertising medium, where individuals may not have a pen and paper with them.

FOR DISCUSSION

Call centres have expanded hugely over the past few years. Some are now both physically remote (even located in other countries, such as India) and service a number of suppliers. Some UK companies have more recently brought call centres back to the UK.

6.5 Outgoing sales calls

Outgoing sales calls are generally unsolicited from the customer's point of view. They are however, particularly valuable as a means of keeping in contact with existing customers and giving them information about special offers etc.

Used in conjunction with other marketing tools, it does provide a quick and easy method for identifying prospects which can increase the effectiveness of limited sales resources.

6.6 Sales research and the phone

The telephone can be used to gain information very rapidly, either in preparation of a sales strategy or a specific sales visit. Sales research in this context can help the sale team assess the viability of various target markets or identify the DMU in a particular organisation.

Activity 6 **(20 minutes)**

Find out how the telephone is used in the selling process of your company or one you are familiar with. Could it be used more effectively?

7 INTERNATIONAL SELLING

Exporting is the easiest, cheapest and most commonly used route into a new foreign market.

(a) The principal benefit is that exporters are able to concentrate production in a **single location**, giving economies of scale and consistency of product quality.

(b) Firms lacking the **know-how and experience** can try international marketing on a small scale.

(c) Exporting enables firms to **develop and test** their plans and strategies.

(d) Exporting enables firms to minimise their **operating costs,** administrative overheads and personnel requirements.

Although exporting requires a **low involvement** in the overseas market, this does not necessarily imply that only low investment is needed. Exporting requires investment in **market research, strategy** formulation and careful **implementation of the marketing mix**. The initial success of Japanese car firms in the USA and Europe was based on research and strategic planning that was both extensive and costly.

7.1 Indirect exports

Indirect exporting is where a firm's goods are sold abroad by other organisations. There are four ways of indirect export.

- Export houses
- Specialist export managers
- UK buying offices of foreign stores and governments
- Complementary exporting

Export houses

Export houses are firms which facilitate exporting on behalf of the producer. There are three main types of export house.

(a) **Export merchants** act as export principals. They buy goods from a producer and sell them abroad.

(b) **Confirming houses** also act as principals. Their main function is to provide credit to customers when the producer is unwilling to do so.

(c) **Manufacturers' export agents** are based at home, but sell abroad for the producer. An agent will usually cover a particular sector or industry, (eg pottery). Remuneration is by commission.

Advantages of export houses

(a) The producer gains the benefits of the export house's market knowledge and contacts.

(b) Except in the case of export agents the producer is relieved of the need to do the following.

- **Finance** the export transaction
- Suffer the **credit risk**
- Prepare **export documentation**

(c) The producer does not bear the **overhead costs** of export marketing.

(d) In some cases export merchants receive preferential treatment from foreign institutional and organisational customers.

(e) Where export agents are used, the producer retains considerable **control** over the market.

Disadvantages of export houses

(a) Ultimately, it is not the producer's but the merchant's decision to market a product, and so a producer is at the merchant's mercy.

(b) Any goodwill created in the market usually benefits the merchant and not the producer.

(c) As with all intermediaries, an export house or merchant might service a variety of producing organisations. An individual producer cannot rely on the merchant's exclusive loyalty.

(d) Export houses are not normally willing to enter into long-term arrangements with a producer.

Specialist export managers

Specialist **export management firms** (SEMs) offer a full export management service. In effect, they perform the same functions as an in-house export department but are normally remunerated by way of commission.

(a) Advantages of using a specialist export manager are the same as those for export houses. In addition, the manufacturer (or service provider) immediately gains its own export department without incurring overheads, retains full market control and can normally expect a long-term relationship with the export manager.

(b) Disadvantages do exist however.

(i) As the export manager is an independent organisation, it can leave the producer's service and the producer will have gained **no in-house exporting expertise.**

(ii) As the producer does not learn from the experience of exporting, this may adversely affect future options by restricting those available.

(iii) The SEM may not have sufficient knowledge of all the producer's markets.

UK buying offices of foreign stores and governments

Many foreign governments and foreign companies (eg department stores) have buying offices set up permanently in the UK. In addition, other foreign companies send representatives on buying expeditions to the UK.

Complementary exporting

Definitions

Complementary exporting ('**piggy back exporting**') occurs when one producing organisation (the **carrier**) uses its own established IM channels to market the products of another producer (the **rider**) as well as its own. The carrier may act as:

(a) A simple transporter, using spare capacity in its distribution network;
(b) An agent, selling the rider's goods for commission;
(c) A merchant, buying and selling the rider's goods.

Advantages of complementary exporting

(a) The carrier earns increased profit from a better use of distribution capacity and can sell a more attractive product range.

(b) The rider obtains entry to a market at low cost and low risk.

Turnkey contracts may also provide opportunities for complementary exporting. A single firm engaged on a particular project overseas (eg construction and civil engineering projects in the Middle East) will often acquire products and services from other firms in the home country for the project.

7.2 Direct exports

Direct exporting occurs where the producing organisation itself performs the export tasks rather than using an intermediary. Sales are made directly to customers overseas who may be the wholesalers, retailers or final users. Sales may increasingly be made via e-commerce on the Internet.

Sales to final user

In this case there are clearly no intermediaries. Typical customers include industrial users, governments or mail order customers. Marketing in this environment is similar to marketing in the domestic market, although there are the added problems of distance, product regulations, language and culture.

Overseas agencies

Strictly speaking an **overseas export agent** is an overseas firm hired to effect a sales contract between the principal (ie the exporter) and a customer. Agents do not take title to goods; they earn a commission. In practice, however, the phrase is often understood to include distributors (who do take title). Some agents merely arrange sales; others hold stocks and/or carry out servicing on the principal's behalf.

Advantages of overseas agents

(a) They have extensive knowledge and experience of the overseas market and the customers.

(b) Their existing product range is usually complementary to the exporter's. This may help the exporter penetrate the overseas market.

(c) The exporter does not have to make a large investment outlay.

(d) The political risk is low.

Disadvantages

(a) An intermediary's commitment and motivation may be weaker than the producer's.

(b) Agents usually want steady turnover. Using an agent may not be the most appropriate way of selling low volume, high value goods with unsteady patterns of demand, or where sales are infrequent.

(c) Many agents are too small to exploit a major market to its full extent. Many serve only limited geographical segments.

(d) As a market grows large it becomes less efficient to use an agent. A branch office or subsidiary company will achieve economies of scale.

As with all intermediaries, the use of an agent requires careful planning, selection, motivation and control.

7.3 Distributors/stockists

Distributors are customers with preferential rights to buy and sell a range of a firm's goods in a specific geographical area. Distributors earn profit, not commission. They differ from wholesalers only in that their selling and marketing activities on behalf of a producer are restricted geographically.

Stockists are distributors who receive more favourable financial rewards than distributors as they normally undertake to carry at least a certain minimum level of stock. The advantages and disadvantages of distributors and stockists are similar to those associated with overseas agents.

EXAMPLE

In some markets, such as Japan which has a complicated distribution system of retailers, a knowledgeable local distributor is essential. Tie-ups with Japanese partners and expensive marketing are necessary before discussions can start.

7.4 Company branch offices abroad

A firm can establish its own office in a foreign market for the purpose of marketing and distribution.

Advantages

(a) When sales have reached a certain level, branch offices become more effective than agencies.

(b) Sales performance will improve, as the commitment and motivation of a producer's own staff should be more effective than those of an agent.

(c) The producer retains complete marketing control.

(d) The producer should be able to acquire more accurate and timely market information.

(e) Customer service should improve. Intermediaries are notorious for poor performance in this respect.

Disadvantages

(a) Higher investment, overhead and running costs are entailed.

(b) There can be a political risk, particularly expropriation of assets.

(c) The firm will be subject to local employee legislation (eg minimum number of local staff, dismissal, trade union membership) which it may not welcome.

7.5 The export sales team

Export selling is an opportunistic, toe in the water approach, frequently as a reaction to an overseas enquiry. In this instance the same product as the home market is provided, often with little modification to the domestic marketing mix. In these scenarios, the sales team is often expected to handle negotiations with little specific training or background understanding of the market place, with probably minimal knowledge of the buyer's language, customs and culture.

This sort of 'hit and miss' introduction to overseas markets, places the sales team at a considerable disadvantage. They will be working away from home, will be very isolated in cultural terms and will not receive adequate marketing support. Sales opportunities are unlikely to be maximised in such situations and the cost of winning and servicing customers can be high when compared with the domestic market. Companies with twenty representatives working in the UK will appoint one person for Southern Europe, say, and this unsophisticated targeting is unlikely to deliver realistic marketing objectives in terms of market share, turnover, profit or awareness.

To summarise, international selling would appear to be poorly supported, poorly managed and is really the 'poor relation' of its domestic base. Where management are not fully committed to developing overseas markets they would be better off remaining in their domestic market only and developing it further.

Some companies, having identified a market opportunity abroad, set about developing it in a proactive customer-orientated way. This requires evaluating the potential markets available and deciding on priorities.

EXAMPLE

When Marks & Spencer twice sent a two-man team to have a look at Japan, they twice came back to its Baker Street headquarters shaking their heads. Japan may be another country, but Japanese retail is on another planet. The Boots mission to 'planet Japan' has as its prize a £17 billion-a-year healthcare market four times larger than that of Britain.

The more you browse around Japanese health and beauty stores, the more you see the difficulties. They sell medieval-style devices for stretching your neck or widening your smile. The best selling drug is a medicinal-tasting caffeine and vitamin drink gulped down by exhausted businessmen. The next bestseller is a cream that makes skin look whiter. Boots itself sells condoms according to blood group (the Japanese believe this denotes spiritual compatibility), and even sells multi-packs covering blood types A, B and C.

Then come the health regulations. Of the 2,000 Boots lines sold in Japan, almost every one had to be reformulated at great expense, to get around the country's strict rules banning substances common in everyday British medicine.

Distribution is often the key factor in international markets and decisions here will determine the extent of the **selling** role. Joint ventures or agents often represent the quickest route into a market. In this way the overseas partner provides local knowledge, contacts and sales effort and the domestic sales role may be limited to management and co-ordination of the process.

Where selling is direct to the customer, for example in industrial markets, a sales organisation may need to be established.

(a) This may take the form of **regional sales office**, or include warehousing and finishing processes close to the internal customer base.

(b) It is likely that both the product and its marketing mix are likely to have been modified to meet the needs of this new target market (for example sales literature provided in the user's language, advertising approaches modified to be culturally effective and perhaps to meet legal requirements of the market).

(c) Eventually the sales team may be drawn from the export market, as they might be more effective at selling than expatriates. However, it should be noted that as many customers are also becoming more global or at least European in their operations, so it is less acceptable to organise the sales force on a geographic basis.

7.6 Organising sales teams for export marketing

Sales teams organised by country are likely to remain isolated units with little communication across the teams.

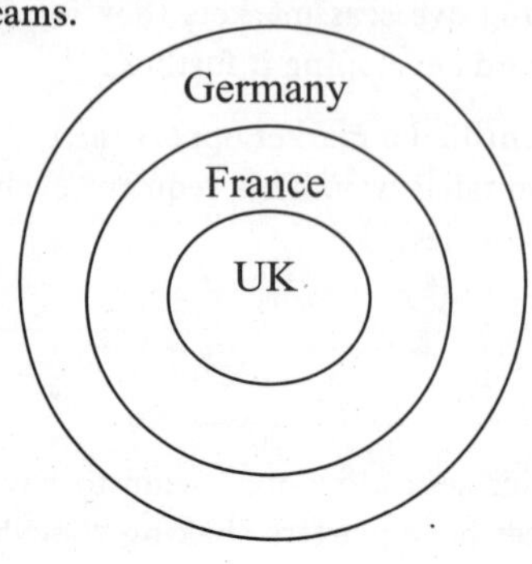

As the needs of for example European firms becomes more similar so specialisation by sector across country, as a matrix organisation structure becomes more attractive.

Over time the cultural difference and barriers between European countries will begin to diminish and selling across Europe will be no different than selling across America. Of course each region will have its particular characteristics, but these will be recognised and accommodated. Until then, or while operating in countries outside Europe, the sales team has to recognise the cultural differences and their implications on negotiating and the selling process.

7.7 Expatriates or locals?

For an international company, which has to 'think globally' as well as act 'locally', there are a number of problems.

- Do you employ mainly **expatriate staff** to control local operations?
- Do you employ **local sales personnel**, with the possible loss of central control?
- Is there such a thing as the **global manager**, equally at home in different cultures?

Expatriate staff are sometimes favoured over local staff.

(a) Poor **educational opportunities** in the market may require the 'import' of skilled technicians and managers. For example, expatriates have been needed in many western firms' operations in Russia and Eastern Europe, simply because they are familiar with the meaning of 'profit'.

(b) Some senior managers believe that a business run by expatriates is easier to **control** than one run by local staff.

(c) Expatriates might be better able than locals to **communicate** with the corporate centre.

(d) The expatriate may **know more about the firm** overall, which is especially important if he or she is fronting a sales office.

The use of expatriates in overseas markets has certain disadvantages.

(a) They **cost** more (eg subsidised housing, school fees).

(b) **Culture shock**. The expatriate may fail to adjust to the culture (eg by associating only with other expatriates). This is likely to lead to poor management effectiveness, especially if the business requires personal contact.

(c) A substantial training programme might be needed.

  (i) **Basic facts** about the country will be given with basic language training, and some briefings about cultural differences.

  (ii) **Immersion training** involves detailed language training, simulation of field experiences etc. This is necessary to obtain an intellectual understanding and practical awareness of the culture.

Employing local managers raises the following issues.

(a) A '**glass ceiling**' might exist in some companies. Talented local managers may not make it to board levels if, as in many Japanese firms, most members of the board are drawn from one country.

(b) In some cases, it may be hard for locals to assimilate into the corporate culture, and this might led to communication problems.

(c) They will have greater local knowledge – but the difficulty of course is to get them to understand the wider corporate picture, but this is true of management at operational level generally.

Those firms which export sporadically might employ a home-based sales force. Their travel expenses will of course be high, and it might not always be easy to recruit people willing to cope with the pace.

7.8 Management effectiveness

A problem is that there are often severe cultural differences as to what constitutes 'management' in the first place. Are **management** principles universally applicable? The marketing function needs awareness of effective management approaches in different cultures.

7.9 Human resources management

Definition

Human resources management involves recruitment and selection, training, appraisal systems and such like, in other words the organisation's relationship with its employees. From management's point of view, HRM is designed to get the best possible performance from employees.

Relevant issues to keep in mind are these.

(a) **Recruitment and training.** In countries with low levels of literacy, more effort might need to be spent on basic training.

(b) **Career management**. Can overseas staff realistically expect promotion to the firm's highest levels if they do well?

(c) **Appraisal schemes**. These can be a minefield at the best of times, and the possibilities for communications failure are endless. For example, in some cultures, an appraisal is a two-way discussion whereas in others arguing back might be considered a sign of insubordination.

(d) **Communications**. HRM tries to mobilise employees' commitment to the goals of the organisation. In far-flung global firms, the normal panoply of staff newsletters and team briefings may be hard to institute but are vital. Time differences also make communication difficult.

  (i) **E-mail** and satellite linkages between branch offices can be used for routine messages: e-mail is especially useful, as it allows swift access to a person's electronic mailbox.

  (ii) Major conferences are also necessary.

  (iii) Firms with many subsidiaries face additional problems of **language.** What language should be used for business communications? Some multinational firms have decreed English the language of official internal communications, even if they are not headquartered in the English speaking world.

ICT in export management

ICT will, potentially, have the same applications in an export market as in the home market. Depending on the extent of local Internet and mobile phone access, emails, text messages, banner advertising and website selling can be used effectively. The employment of these techniques is best left to the local staff, mentored and assisted by central staffs as required to achieve efficiency and the desired degree of standardisation.

ICT also has important applications in the management of export activities. Just as in the home market, sales staff are likely to be geographically remote from their national base, while the national management are themselves remote from the global base. Traditionally, a programme of secondments and visits has been used to manage and motivate national managements under these circumstances. However, modern communications techniques can reduce the need for these expensive expedients.

Intranets are private networks using Web technology. Their pages and hyperlinks can be set up to provide world-wide communication of managerial messages; budgets; results; and product, customer and administrative information.

Email and **instant messaging** provide rapid communication.

Video conferencing can replace many visits, though its cost will probably restrict its use to fairly senior people.

Mobile phones make individual staff members in foreign countries as accessible as those in the home country: however, global time differences have to be considered.

Chapter roundup

- There are characteristics of industrial or business markets that make buying processes and decision making different from consumer markets.
- Essentially these characteristics can be listed as short distribution channels, large orders, price sensitivity and technical selling.
- In consumer markets although advertising pull strategies are predominant, selling does have an important role – mainly in terms of selling products to distributors and the retail-customer interface.
- Services can also be marketed and 'sold'. There are particular characteristics that make it different and sometimes more difficult to sell in these markets.
- Selling to the public sector (whether it is services or goods) has additional special characteristics especially in terms of the decision-making process and who is involved in the decision-making unit.
- Exhibitions are unique selling situations for salespersons and require specific skills and planning.
- Telephone selling and call centres are used increasingly but have pros and cons.
- There are specific implications and decisions to make in terms of selling in international markets. This is both in general strategic terms and in recruitment terms.

Quick quiz

1 How can industrial goods be classified?

2 What implications are there for sales people in industrial markets selling technical products?

3 What two types of strategies do sellers to a retailer market use to communicate their products?

4 How should the manufacturer consider the distributor in packaging design?

5 What are the implications of intangibility of a service to the sales person?

6 What characteristics of public authorities make them different to sell to?

7 What opportunities do exhibitions and trade fairs present to organisations?

8 What benefits are there to telephone selling?

9 What is the difference between indirect and direct exporting?

Answers to quick quiz

1 Into raw materials, fabricated materials, capital equipment, supplies.

2 They have to have specialist product knowledge and be as technically aware as the customer.

3 (i) Advertising to attract end customers and/or (ii) sales push to encourage distributors to stock the product.

4 Packaging should be attractive to end users but also has to be stable on shelves, easy to handle, stock and distribute.

5 They represent the company so their appearance is of importance. They also have to appear to be trustworthy and professional to customers.

6 They (i) do not exist primarily to make profits. (ii) Decision-making may be political (iii) Employees may not have much influence/involvement in the DMU.

7 Opportunities in public relations, promoting and selling, networking, testing new products, researching competitors and researching suppliers' products.

8 A quick response, interaction, accessibility, easy assessment and cost.

9 Indirect exporting occurs where a firm's goods are sold abroad by other organisations; direct exporting occurs where an intermediary is not used.

Answers to activities

1 There is no specific answer to this activity.

2 There is no specific answer to this activity.

3 *Costs:* organisations will be willing to bear a higher cost than an individual.

Work: will be of a different nature, eg corporation tax vs personal tax.

Staff: need staff to be able to cope with both.

Different *advertising* media will be needed

4 There is no specific answer to this activity.

5 There is no specific answer to this activity.

6 There is no specific answer to this activity.

Bibliography

Allen, C. (2002) 'Presentation to Lehman Brothers media conference, London, 17 September'

Ansoff, I. (1987), *Corporate Strategy* revised ed, London: Penguin

Arnold, M. (2001), Can Railtrack Ever Win Back The Public's Trust?, *Marketing*, 28 June, p.1

Beard, M. (2002) Sainsbury Signs Jamie Oliver in £2M Deal, *The Independent*, 17 January, p.11

Belbin, M. (1993) *Team Roles at Work*, Oxford: Butterworth: Heinemann

Bickerton, P. Bickerton, M. and Simpson-Holley, K. (1998) *Cyberstrategy*, Butterworth-Heinemann

Bowen, D. (2002), Handling the Bad News, *Financial Times*, 25 January, p.11

Brassington, F. and Pettitt, S. (2006), *Principles of Marketing* (4th edition), FT Prentice Hall

Burt, T. (2002) He's Bond, James Bond, the man who's licensed to sell, *Financial Times*, 5 October, p.22

Carter, H. C. (1986) *Effective Advertising*, The Daily Telegraph Guide for Small Businesses, Kogan Page

Chaffey, D. (2002) *E-business and E-commerce Management; Strategy; Implementation and Practice*, FT – Prentice Hall, Pearson Education

Chisnall, O.M. (1997), *Marketing Research*, McGraw-Hill

Colley, R. (1961) Defining Advertising Goals for Measured Advertising Results, *Association of National Advertisers*

Cowell, D. (1995), *The Marketing of Services*, Heinemann

Cowlett, M. (2001), Research Can Be Child's Play, *Marketing*, 10 May p. 35

Crosby, P.B. (1978), *Quality is free*, McGraw-Hill Education

CyberAtlas, (2002), *B2B E-Commerce Headed for Trillions*, http:/cyberatlas.internet.com

Daffy, C. (2000), *Once a Customer, Always a Customer*, Oak Tree Press

Dow, B. (2001), Tanks a Lot, Boss, *Daily Record*, 3 December, p.7

Doyle, P (2000), Value-Based Marketing , John Willey & Sons Ltd, Chicester

Drucker, P (1955), The Practice of Management, William Hememann Ltd, London

Drummond, J. , Ensor, G. & Ashford, R. (2008), *Strategic Marketing: Planning and Control*, 3rd edition, Butterworth-Heinemann

Ehrenberg, A. S. C. (1992), Comments on How Advertising Works, *Marketing and Research Today*, August, pp.167–9

Engel, J. F., Warshaw, M.R. and Kinnear, T. C. (1994), *Promotional Strategy*, Irwin

Engel, J. F., Blackwell, R. D. and Miniard, P. W. (1990), *Consumer Behaviour*, Dryden

Festinger, L. (1957), *A Theory of Cognitive Dissonance*, Stanford University Press

Fill, C. (2002), *Marketing Communications: Contexts, Strategies and Applications*, (3rd edition), FT Prentice Hall

Flack, J. (1999), Child Minding, *Marketing Week*, 8 July, pp 41–4

Folkard, C. (eds), (2003) *Guinness World Records*, Gullane Education

Francis, R. (2000), Leaders of the Pack, *Brandweek*, 26 June, pp.28–38

Grunig, J. E. and Hunt, T. (1984), *Managing Public Relations*, Thompson Learning

Gummesson, E. (1987), *The New Marketing: Developing Long-Term Interactive Relationships*, Long Range Planning, 20: pp.10–20

Hall, M. (1992) Using Advertising Frameworks: Different Research Models for Different Campaigns, *Admap*, March, pp.17–21

Hamel, G. (1996) Strategy as Revolution. *Harvard Business Review* July/August

Hamel, G. and Prahalad, C. K. (1996), *Competing for the Future*, Harvard Business School Press

Heider, F. (1958), *The Psychology of Interpersonal Relations*, Wiley

Herzberg, F. (1968) *Work and the Nature of Man*, Cleveland: World

Hill, L. and O'Sullivan, T. (1999), *Marketing*, (2nd edition), Longman, Essex

Hill, L. and O'Sullivan, T. (2004), *Foundation Marketing* (3rd edition), FT Prentice Hall, London

Hooley, G. Saunders, J. and Piercy, N. (2003), *Marketing Strategy and Competitive Positioning*, FT Prentice Hall

Jobber, D. 2007) *Principles and Practice of Marketing* (5th edition), McGraw Hill, Maidenhead

Johns, T. (2003), *Perfect Customer Care*, Random House Business Books

Johnson, G., Scholes, K., & Whittington, R. (2007), *Exploring Corporate Strategy* (8th edition), Harlow: FT Prentice Hall

Keating, M. (2001) Milk in a Bag Knocks Old-time Bottles off the Doorstep, *The Guardian*, 14 August, p.15

Kent, R. (1993), *Marketing Research in Action*, Routledge, London

Kotler, P. 2008), *Marketing Management*, 13th edition, Prentice Hall

Kotler, P & Lee, N. (2008), *Social Marketing: Influencing Behaviors for Good*, 3rd edition, Sage Publications

Kotler, P., Armstrong, G., Saunders, J. and Wong, V. (2008) *Principles of Marketing*, 5th edition, FT Prentice Hall

Lannon, J. (1991), Developing Brand Strategies Across Borders, *Marketing and Research Today*, August, pp.160–7

Marketing, (2001) 'Outstanding Marketing Achievement' The Marketing Society Awards 2001 supplement to *Marketing*, 14 June pp. 6–7

Maslow, A. (1954) *Motivation and Personality* New York: Harper and Row

McDaniel, C. and Gates, R. (1996), *Contemporary Marketing Research* (3rd edition), West Group

McDonald, M. and Christopher, M. (2003), *Marketing: A Complete Guide*, Palgrave Macmillan, Hampshire

McDonald, M. 2007), *Marketing Plans: How to Prepare Them, How to Use Them*, Butterworth-Heinemann

McLuhan, R. (2002), Brands Put Service Under the Spotlight, *Marketing*, 21 February, p 33

Morgan, R. M. and Hunt, S. D. (1994), The Commitment – Trust Theory Of Relationship Marketing, *Journal of Marketing*, pp.58 : 20–38

Mullins, LJ (2007), Management and Organisational Behaviour (8th edition) FT Prentice Hall, Harlow

Museums Journal, (2002), *Free Entry means traditional audience keep coming back*, October, p.13

Oakland, J. S. (2003), *Total Quality Management Text with Cases*, Butterworth-Heinemann

Ohmae, K. (1983), *The Mind of the Strategist*, Penguin

Osgood, C. E. Suci, G. J. and Tannenbaum, P. H. (1957), *The Measurement of Meaning*, University of Illinois Press

Pastore, M. (2001) *Global Companies Lead B2B Charge*, 14 August, http:/cyberatlas.internet.com

Peattie, K. and Peattie, S. (1993), Sales Promotion: Playing to Win?, *Journal of Marketing Management.* 9, pp 255–69

Phillips, K. (2001), *Marketing Quality*, Research, June, pp.30–1

Piercy, N. and Evans , M. (1983) *Managing Marketing Information*, CroomHelm

Piercy, N. 2008), *Market-Led Strategic Change – Transforming the Process of Going to Market*, 4th edition, Butterworth Heinemann

Piercy, N. (1987), The Marketing Budgeting Process: Marketing Management Implications, *Journal of Marketing*, pp.51 (4), 45–59

Porter, M. (2004), *Competitive Advantage*, New edition, Free Press

Rogers, E. M. (1962) *Diffusion of Innovation*, The Free Press

Saunders, M. Lewis, P. and Thornhill, A. (2003), *Research Methods for Business Students* (2nd edition), Financial Times Pitman Publishing

Schiffman, L.G. and Kanuk, L.L. (2004) *Consumer Behaviour* (8th edition), Pearson Prentice Hall

Schultz, D. , Tannenbaum, S. & Lauterborn, R. (2000) *Integrated Marketing Communications: Putting It Together & Making It Work*, illustrated edition, McGraw-Hill Contemporary

Sclater, I. (2002) Wish you were here, *Marketing Business*, July/August, pp 26–27

Simms, J. (2001), The Value of Disclosure, *Marketing*, 2 August, pp 26–7

Smith P.R. and Taylor, J. (2004) *Marketing Communications: An Integrated Approach* (4th edition), Kogan Page

Snodly, J. (2001), Fallen for an old flame? Just Log on for Counselling, *The Independent*, 9 September, p 8

Solomon, M. Bamossya, G. and Askegaard, S. (1999), *Consumer Behaviour*, Prentice Hall

Sunderland, P. (2002), Wish you were here, *Marketing Business*, July/August, pp 26–27.

Vroom, V. (1964) *Some Personality Determinants of the Effects of Participation*, Englewood Cliffs, New Jersey: Prentice Hall

Williams, K. C. (1981), *Behavioural Aspects of Marketing*, Heinemann Professional Publishing

Woods, R. (2002) Pop Idol or Puppet, *Sunday Times*, 10 February, p 12

www.marketingpower.com (American Marketing Association)

Zikmund, W. G. (1997), *Exploring Marketing Research* (Sixth edition), Dryden

Index

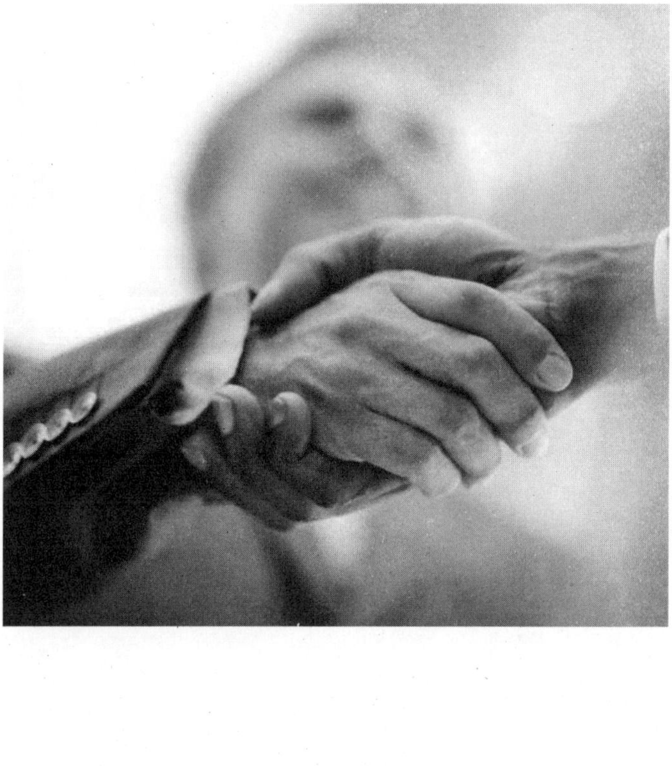